Seychelles

PUBLISHER'S FOREWORD

The first Bradt travel guide was written in 1974 by George and Hilary Bradt on a river barge floating down a tributary of the Amazon. In the 1980s and '90s the focus shifted away from hiking to broader-based guides covering new destinations – usually the first to be published about these places. In the 21st century Bradt continues to publish such ground-breaking guides, as well as others to established holiday destinations, incorporating in-depth information on culture and natural history with the nuts and bolts of where to stay and what to see.

Bradt authors support responsible travel, and provide advice not only on minimum impact but also on how to give something back through local charities. In this way a true synergy is achieved between the traveller and local communities.

*

I first met Lyn Mair in the Seychelles when we were fellow lecturers on the *Caledonian Star*, an expedition ship that cruised the Indian Ocean, so I shared her excitement when the tide-borne Zodiacs swept through the narrow gap in the rim of Aldabra's atoll into the lagoon and another world. Together we climbed the highest point in Mahé, marvelled at the *coco de mer* in Praslin, and sought the black paradise flycatcher in La Digue. Although we were both first-timers, Lyn could identify every bird and most of the other animals. Word soon got around among the passengers and they almost fought to get a place in the queue to join her for land excursions (those who were slow off the mark reluctantly came with me). Since then she has made many return visits, and the qualities that make her such a good tour leader spill over into the pages of this book: enthusiasm, knowledge of the natural world, and an instinctive understanding of what tourists want. Her friend and co-author, Lynnath Beckley, brings her extensive experience of marine life to ensure that this is the most comprehensive guide to the Seychelles in print.

Hilary Bradt

23 High Street, Chalfont St Peter, Bucks SL9 9QE, England
Tel: 01753 893444; Fax: 01753 892333
info@bradtguides.com www.bradtguides.com

Seychelles

THE BRADT TRAVEL GUIDE

Lyn Mair
Lynnath Beckley

Bradt Travel Guides, UK
The Globe Pequot Press Inc, USA

Second edition July 2005
First published 2001

Bradt Travel Guides Ltd
23 High Street, Chalfont St Peter, Bucks SL9 9QE, England
www.bradtguides.com
Published in the USA by The Globe Pequot Press Inc,
246 Goose Lane, PO Box 480, Guilford, Connecticut 06437-0480

British Library Cataloguing in Publication Data
A catalogue record for this book is available from the British Library

ISBN-10: 1 84162 125 0
ISBN-13: 978 1 84162 125 8

Photographs
Front cover Anse Lazio, Praslin (Johnathan Smith/Sylvia Cordaiy Picture Library)
Text Lynnath Beckley (LB), Lyn Mair (LM), Johnathan Smith (JS), Seychelles Tourist
Offfice (STO)

Illustrations Carole Vincer
Maps Alan Whitaker, Terence Crump
390090003419 70
Typeset from the authors' disc by Wakewing
Printed and bound in Italy by Legoprint SpA, Trento

Authors/Acknowledgements

AUTHORS

Lyn Mair is a naturalist and travel guide who specialises in the islands of the western Indian Ocean and Antarctica. Passionate about birdwatching, she regularly leads tours to exotic places, and lectures on board ships plying the southern oceans and tropical waters off Africa. When not gadding round the world she is resident in Cape Town, South Africa.

Lynnath Beckley is a marine scientist who has worked, travelled and sailed extensively in the western Indian Ocean. She has been writing for magazines, journals and books for several years and currently lives in Perth, Australia.

ACKNOWLEDGEMENTS

It is always a pleasure to visit the Seychelles and doing the research for this second edition was no exception. After an absence of 18 months, it was good to note all the changes but, even better, to see that the islands are still lovely and the infrastructure for tourism is in good working order. The most outstanding feature was the genuine kindness from so many helpful people in the tourism industry who were keen to show off all the improvements, new accommodation and special features.

The Seychelles Tourism Marketing Authority in Mahé went out of their way to assist us; it is hard to mention all the names but Althea Hall and Verena Joseph were particularly helpful, as was Jenny Kearney from the Seychelles Tourist Office in Johannesburg. Jane from Seyunique and Deon Fremantle from Air Seychelles assisted with travel and accommodation arrangements. Guillaume Albert and Vesna Rakic from Creole Holidays facilitated our travel between Mahé and Praslin. Paul and Karen from Le Petit Village patiently answered all my questions as well as dealing with many emails and long-distance phone calls. It was a marvellous experience for us to stay on Frégate Island and be subjected to the bubbly enthusiasm of Beate Sachse, the resident ecologist. Jon Duncan shared a wealth of information on the rehabilitation and development of North Island and Matt and Bart La Buschagne of Coco de Mer on Praslin were charming and knowledgeable hosts. Raymond Duvergé of the Sainte Anne Resort and Spa and Mrs Chung Faye from Sunrise Small Hotel were also most helpful. Sandra and John Fowkes and Tony Rogers helped out with office support.

Now we would just like to go there on holiday!

Contents

LIST OF MAPS

For key to map symbols, see page VIII

KEY TO STANDARD SYMBOLS

— · — ·	International boundary		▲	Summit
— — — —	National park boundary			Glacis
	National park			Cave
✈	Airport (international)		❋	Scenic viewpoint
✈	Airport (other)		↑	Coconut palm
✚	Airstrip			Coco de mer palm
	Helicopter service			Bamboo
	Cruise-ship berth			Pisonia woodland
	Passenger ferry			Screw pines
	Bus station etc			Mangrove
· · · · · ·	Footpath			Botanical garden
	Petrol station, garage			Waterfall
⚲	Cycle hire			Marsh
	Hotel, inn with restaurant or café			Bird nesting site
	Hotel, inn guesthouse etc			Turtle nesting site
	Visitor shelter			Coral reef
♀	Bar			Beach
✕	Restaurant, café etc			Scuba diving
⊠	Post office			Fishing sites
(	Telephone			Lighthouse
e	Internet café			Wreck
✚	Hospital, clinic etc			
	Museum			
i	Tourist information			
$	Bank			
	Statue, monument			
∴	Archaeological or historic site			
	Historic building			
✝	Church, cathedral			
▲	Hindu temple			
(	Mosque			

Other map symbols may be shown in separate key boxes with individual explanations for their meanings.

Introduction

In the deep blue of the western Indian Ocean, 115 unique and exquisitely beautiful islands lie randomly scattered like emeralds and sapphires from a jeweller's purse.

Palm-fringed, silvery sands, secluded coves bounded by granite boulders, misty mountain peaks cloaked in verdant forest and coral reefs extending into the warm ocean are all vivid images of the romantic Seychelles. Coupled with idyllic days in the tropical sun, velvet nights under starry southern skies, delightful Seychellois people and charming Creole culture, they beckon discerning travellers to their shores.

The main, populated islands of the Seychelles lie a few degrees south of the Equator and rise from shallow banks as huge granite rocks, reflecting their ancient continental origin. Other remote, coralline islands, inhabited by millions of seabirds, arc out towards the shores of Africa and Madagascar. One of these is Aldabra – a wilderness atoll where time flows with the tides and nature rules supreme.

Aldabra was the first Seychelles land I set foot on, but before going ashore a quick dive into the perfectly clear water assaulted my senses with an array of corals teeming with colourful reef fishes. When I took a break from the underwater scenery, I found that I was being scrutinised by a couple of inquisitive fairy terns while other seabirds – frigates, boobies and noddies – circled overhead. Traversing the mangrove-fringed lagoon, I watched turtles and rays lazing in the clear turquoise water. I was able to explore a small part of the rugged, limestone interior where giant tortoises slept in the shade of salt-resistant bushes shaped by the persistent trade winds. I was completely captivated by the wild, remote and near pristine atoll. My love affair with the Seychelles began right there and then. After visiting the Seychelles on numerous subsequent occasions and getting to know many of the other islands, I had the good fortune actually to stay on Aldabra as the assistant to the warden. The two months that I spent there rank high on my list of life's best experiences.

The Seychelles has a short, but fascinating, history of explorers, pirates and settlers. The Creole people, a harmonious mélange of African, European and Asian descent, have a happy-go-lucky lifestyle and, although global travel has come to them, they maintain their traditions of language, music, dance and food. The Seychellois are almost nonchalant about the beauty that surrounds them.

The Seychelles has an ambience of remoteness far from the rush of everyday life back home. It is a modern country with accommodation ranging from exclusive island lodges to small family-run guesthouses. Island hopping can be accomplished with ease using fast ferries, aeroplanes and helicopters, and what better way to explore than in your very own (or chartered) yacht? However, there is more to the Seychelles than basking in the sun and going home with a golden tan. The Seychelles has many secrets, discovered only as you explore the islands – *coco de mer* palm forests, the busy little capital of Victoria, picturesque La Digue, island bird sanctuaries, weather-beaten *glacis*, the local market, Creole cuisine. . . After a day's exploring, savour the Seychelles evening. Sip a Seybrew on a beach coloured by a fiery sunset, wait for the southern constellations to grace the enveloping night, and plan another perfect day in paradise.

Lyn Mair

Fruit bat

Part One

General Information

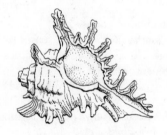

SEYCHELLES AT A GLANCE

Location Indian Ocean

Islands 115 islands

Size 455km^2 across 1.3 million km^2 of ocean

Climate Equatorial; temperatures 24–30°C.

Status Republic

Population 81,755 (2002)

Main islands Mahé (71,420), Praslin (7,103), La Digue and inner islands (2,104)

Capital Victoria (on Mahé) (population 24,994 including surrounding districts)

Life expectancy 70.9 (2003)

Economy Fishing, tourism

GDP SR3867 million (2004)

Languages English, French, Creole

Religion Predominantly Roman Catholic

Currency Seychelles rupee (SR)

Exchange rate £1 = SR9.55, US$1 = SR5.08, €1 = SR5.56 (April 2005)

International telephone code +248

Time GMT +4. Sunrise 06.15 approx, sunset 18.30 approx

Electrical voltage 240 volts; three-point, square-pin plugs

Weights and measures Metric

Flag Five colours (green, white, red, yellow and blue) radiating out from bottom left

National anthem Koste Seselwa ('Come together Seychellois')

National flower Tropicbird orchid

National bird Black parrot

Public holidays January 1 and 2, Easter, May 1, June 5. June 18. June 29, August 15, November 1, December 8, December 25

Background Information

The magnificent Seychelles islands are spread out over a vast swathe of tropical Indian Ocean between Madagascar and India. They extend over a straight-line distance of some 1,500km from Aldabra (located at 9° south 46° east) in the southwest to Denis and Bird (both at 3° south 55° east) to the northeast. The ecology of the islands and surrounding waters reflects the complex geology, oceanography and climate of the region.

GEOGRAPHY
Location
The 115 islands of the Seychelles, with a collective landmass of only 455km², are surrounded by a vast oceanic Exclusive Economic Zone (EEZ) of 1.3 million km². The islands are located in the western Indian Ocean, between latitudes 4° south and 10° south and longitudes 46° east and 56° east. The nearest neighbours are Madagascar and the great continent of Africa. Geologically, the islands of the Seychelles have two distinct origins. The inner islands are continental, granitic remnants and the outer islands are coralline in nature. About 30 of the islands are inhabited while the others exist as sandy cays, atolls, coral reefs and great clumps of rock, uninhabited except for noisy seabird colonies.

Large granitic islands
Mahé is the largest granitic island (152km²). It is spectacular with grey, granite boulders dotting the verdant slopes that rise steeply out of the blue ocean to form a range of mist-enshrouded peaks, the highest being 905m above sea level. The town of Victoria, the busy commercial and administrative capital of the Seychelles, nestles below the mountains on the east coast.

Praslin, the second largest island (37km²), lies 37km northeast of Mahé. The central hills, which reach a height of 367m, rise up from the soft, white, sandy beaches and are covered in palm forests. The voluptuous *coco de mer* palm is protected in the Vallée de Mai, a World Heritage Site.

Silhouette is the third largest island, covering 20km² and reaching a height of 740m. It lies 19km to the northwest of Mahé but it has only a small population and very little development.

La Digue, with its majestic, sculptured boulders creating sheltered and secluded beaches, is 5km from Praslin and 50km from Mahé. It covers an area of 10km² and rises to a height of 333m.

ISLANDS OF THE SEYCHELLES
Granitic islands

Mahé	L'Islette	**Cousin**
Ste Anne	Ile Chauve Souris	**Cousine**
Cerf	Ile aux Vaches	**La Digue**
Long	L'Ilot	Zave
Round	Mamelles	**Félicité**
Moyenne	**Silhouette**	Marianne
Ile Cachée	**North**	Grande Soeur
Beacon	**Praslin**	Petite Soeur
Anonyme	Round	Ile Cocos
Hodoul	Chauve Souris	Ile la Fouche
Rat	Ile St Pierre	Ile aux Récifs
Ile Souris	**Curieuse**	**Frégate**
Thérèse	**Aride**	L'Ilot Frégate
Conception	Booby	

Coralline islands

Bird	**Plat**
Denis	**Coëtivy**

Amirantes group

African Banks	St Joseph	Vars
Rémire	Fouquet	Ile Paul
D'Arros	Ressource	Banc de Sable
Desroches	Petit Carcassaye	Banc Cocos
Etoile	Grand Carcassaye	**Poivre Atoll**
Boudeuse	Benjamin	Poivre
Marie-Louise	Banc Ferrari	Florentin
Desnoeufs	Chien	Ile du Sud
St Joseph's Atoll	Pélican	

There are about three dozen smaller, satellite, granitic islands in close proximity to the main islands. **Bird** and **Denis** are different in that they are volcanic in origin and lie to the far north, on the edge of the Seychelles Bank.

Outer coralline islands

The outlying coralline islands trickle away to the south and west of the granitic islands:

The Amirantes, which straddle 6° south, stretch from the African Banks to Desnoeufs. Other islands in this group are Rémire, Desroches, St Joseph's Atoll, D'Arros, Poivre and Marie-Louise.

The Alphonse group, at 7° south, comprises Alphonse with its own satellite islands of Bijoutier and St François.

Alphonse group

Alphonse	Bijoutier	St François

Farquhar group

Providence Atoll	**Farquhar Atoll**	Goëlette
Providence	Ile du Nord	Lapin
Banc Providence	Ile du Sud	Ile du Milieu
St Pierre	Manaha Nord	Déposé
Ile Cerf	Manaha Milieu	Banc de Sable
	Manaha Sud	

Aldabra group

Astove	Pagode	Ile Michel
Assumption	Ile Sud Ouest	Ile Esprit
Cosmoledo Atoll	Ile Moustiques	Ile Moustiques
Menai	Ile Baleine	Ilot Parc
Ile du Nord	Ile Chauve Souris	Ilot Emile
Ile Nord Est	**Aldabra Atoll**	Ilot Yangue
Ile du Trou	Grande Terre	Ilot Dubois
Goëlette	Picard	Ilot Magnan
Grand Polyte	Polymnie	Ilot Lanier
Petit Polyte	Malabar	
Grand Ile (Wizard)	Ile aux Cèdres	

*Names in **bold** indicate major islands.*

The Farquhar group, at 10° south, consists of the atolls of Providence and Farquhar, each composed of small islands.

The Aldabra group, with the island of Assumption and the atolls of Aldabra, Astove and Cosmoledo, is the most southwesterly part of the Seychelles land territory. Aldabra, a World Heritage Site, is the largest raised coral atoll in the world and is situated near 9° south.

GEOLOGY

The geological origins of the Seychelles can be traced to the disintegration of the Gondwanaland super-continent over a hundred million years ago. The drifting apart of the tectonic plates in various directions gave rise to the continents of South America, Africa, Australia and Antarctica. At the end of

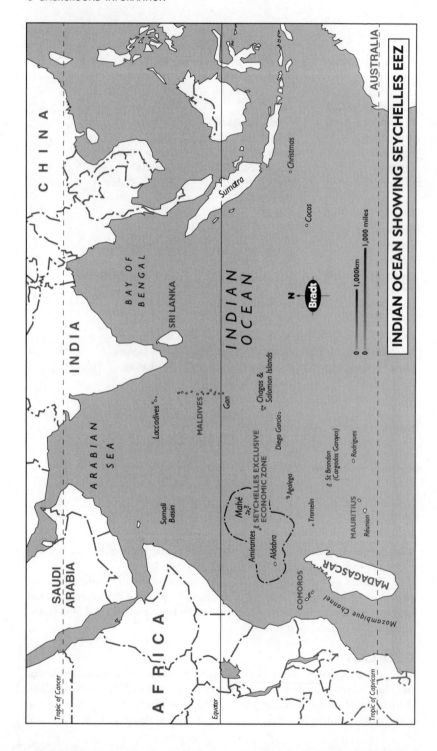

INDIAN OCEAN SHOWING SEYCHELLES EEZ

the Cretaceous period, Madagascar and India, to which the Seychelles Bank was attached, drifted northeastwards. Before India crashed into Asia (producing the Himalayas) the Seychelles Bank separated off and lodged in its current position. The Seychelles Bank and its islands thus constitute a 'microcontinent' isolated by the slow process of sea floor spreading in the Indian Ocean.

The Seychelles Bank, surrounded by deep ocean, is a shoal area of some 31,000km² with water depths less than 60m. Rising from the Seychelles Bank are about 40 granitic islands and islets, located from 4° to 5° south, 55° to 56° east. The largest island, Mahé, with an area of 152km², rises to 905m in Morne Seychellois, the highest point in the group. Praslin, which has an area of 37km², rises to 367m and Silhouette, with an area of 20km², rises to 740m. These islands consist of rugged granitic mountains – often with smooth, bare rock slopes known as *glacis*, surrounded by narrow coastal plains and marsh. The granitic rocks of Mahé are reputed to be over 500 million years old.

The other islands in the Seychelles comprise low sand cays on sea-level platform reefs, atolls or raised atolls. The sand cays are usually less than 5m above sea level, while the raised reef islands are about 8m above sea level, though some may have sand dunes up to 32m high. Low sand cays include Bird and Denis on the Seychelles Bank, Plat and Coëtivy, some of the Amirantes islands and Providence. Farquhar is the largest true atoll. Raised coral atolls include Aldabra, Cosmoledo and Astove, which all enclose central lagoons. On Aldabra there are two distinct terraces at 8m and 4m above sea level which formed as the sea level fell.

Most of the atolls also reflect a history of recent erosion by sea water with characteristic mushroom-shaped undercut limestone platforms known as *champignon*.

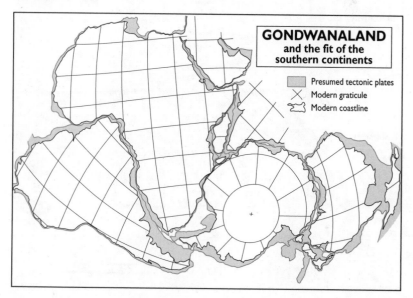

GONDWANALAND
and the fit of the
southern continents

Presumed tectonic plates
× Modern graticule
Modern coastline

OCEANOGRAPHY

Ocean depths around the Seychelles are generally about 3,000–4,000m but in the Somali Basin, located between the Seychelles and Africa, the inky depths exceed 5,000m. In addition to the Seychelles Bank, there are several other shallow banks in the Seychelles EEZ, and the large granitic Saya de Malha Bank extends southeastwards in a gentle arc towards Mauritius.

Ocean currents are an important feature of the Indian Ocean and they vary seasonally with the monsoons. The main stream of the South Equatorial Current flows westwards across the Indian Ocean at about 10° south. When it reaches the western Indian Ocean it splits into the southward-flowing East Madagascar and Mozambique currents and the northward-flowing East African coastal current. However, during the northwest monsoon (November to March), the northerly flow of this current is reduced and its course changes, becoming the equatorial counter current which flows eastwards through the Seychelles.

Tides in the Seychelles are semi-diurnal, with two high tides and two low tides daily. Tidal amplitude is generally small but, at those islands located in the southwest nearer the Mozambique Channel, amplitude increases. So,

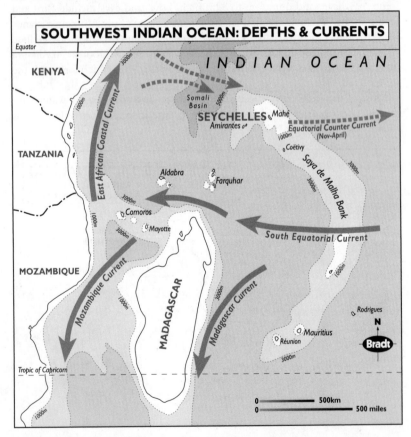

RESHAPING THE SEYCHELLES

Seventy million years ago, after the breakup of the super-continent of Gondwanaland, the granitic Seychelles islands separated from Madagascar and India and lodged in their current position just south of the Equator in the western Indian Ocean. Rising from the shallow Seychelles Bank, the granitic islands have, over eons of time, developed substantial fringing coral reefs. These reefs protect the islands from coastal erosion, support valuable fisheries and attract thousands of tourists, the mainstay of the Seychelles economy.

In the 1960s, a considerable amount of reef was reclaimed on the east coast of Mahé to provide sufficient land for the construction of the Seychelles international airport. Recently, in an ambitious, even larger scheme, the Seychelles government has gone ahead with the reclamation of enormous amounts of fringing reef around the capital, Victoria, to provide land for industrial development and housing.

Large tracts of fringing reef extending over about 10km, from the southeast near Ile Anonyme, along the Mahé side of Cerf Passage, past the port of Victoria, and up to North East Point, were encircled by vast enclosures of granite boulders quarried from the island. Simultaneously, a huge dredging operation to deepen access to the port took place, with the dredging spoil pumped into the enclosures, thereby filling them with sand and reef rubble and destroying the reefs.

On nearby Praslin, the horseshoe-shaped embayment of Baie Ste Anne has also succumbed to the reclamation process. The dredger deepened the approaches to the jetty and the spoil was dumped into yet another enclosure over the reefs along the western side of the bay.

It is well nigh impossible to mitigate against such an environmental onslaught and rather difficult to believe that such enormous amounts of reclaimed land are necessary for a country with such a small total population.

for example, at Mahé spring tidal range is only about 1.2m, while at Aldabra it is about 2.6m. Mean local time of low spring tide is 11.00, so during full- and new-moon periods one can expect beaches and the tops of fringing reefs to be exposed around this time. In islands with lagoons, tidal currents can be quite considerable, particularly around mid-tide as water enters or leaves the lagoon through narrow channels or passes. The water is warm all year round with temperatures of 27–8°C during the summer and 23–4°C in the winter.

CLIMATE AND WEATHER

The humid, tropical climate of the Seychelles and the western Indian Ocean is controlled by a host of interrelated factors. These include the monsoonal

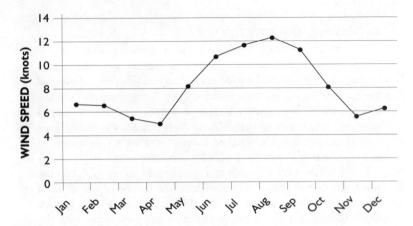

Average daily wind speed at Mahé airport

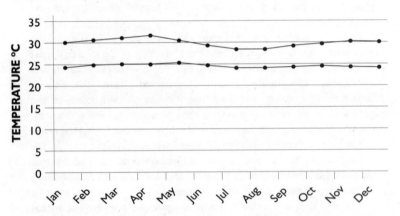

Average daily maximum and minimum temperatures at Mahé airport

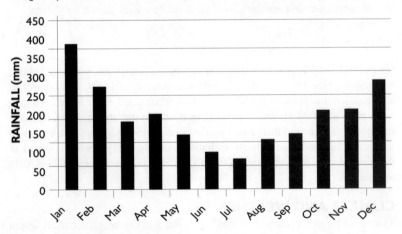

Average monthly rainfall at Mahé airport

wind shifts induced by seasonal barometric pressure changes over the Indian Ocean, Africa and India; changes in the position and intensity of the South Indian Ocean high pressure zone; seasonal migration of the complex inter-tropical lows; and ocean currents and sea surface temperature patterns in the equatorial Indian Ocean.

Wind direction and speed in the Seychelles display clear seasonal patterns. In the southern hemisphere winter (May to October), southeast trade winds (*vent swet*) extend over the western Indian Ocean south of the Equator and, in the Seychelles, there is dry weather with low rainfall. In the southern hemisphere summer (December to March), on the other hand, the south Indian Ocean high pressure system shifts southwards, and the rainy northwest monsoon (*vent nord*) sets in over the islands. In the transitional months of April and November winds tend to be light and variable. In general, mean wind speed is higher in Aldabra than Mahé. Tropical cyclones do not occur in the granitic Seychelles as they lie too close to the Equator but they do occur infrequently at Aldabra and Assumption.

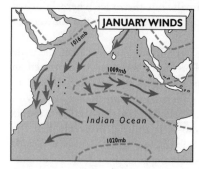
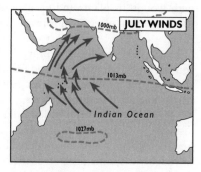

The Seychelles experiences a humid, tropical climate, with annual rainfall exceeding 800mm and temperatures that are always above 20°C. There are, however, important climatic variations between the islands which arise primarily because of the wide expanse of ocean covered by the islands, and altitudinal differences between the high granitic islands and the low coral atolls. Mean annual temperatures in Mahé (Victoria) are 26.6°C and 27°C at Aldabra, with only a 3°C seasonal variation. In the mountainous granitic islands, temperature decreases with increasing altitude. Humidity is usually around 75–80% and varies little with the season. Humidity does vary with altitude and the mountains are often shrouded with mist for long periods.

In all the granitic islands, rainfall reaches a maximum in summer. Altitude and aspect strongly influence the amount of rain received (rainfall increases with altitude and is higher on north-facing slopes). Average annual rainfall on Mahé varies from 1,846mm at Anse Royale on the coast to 3,250mm at Salazie on the slopes of Morne Seychellois. Most of the mountainous interior receives in excess of 2,500mm of rain per year. Similarly, at Praslin, the rainfall at Côte d'Or (2,306mm) on the east coast is higher than Baie Ste Anne (2,130mm) on the south coast. Average annual rainfall in the northeastern islands of Bird (1,973mm) and Denis (1,730mm) is twice as high as the southwestern atolls of Aldabra (966mm) and Assumption (867mm). The duration of the dry season (less than 100mm rain) increases southwestwards from only one month at Denis to eight months at Aldabra. The contrast in length of the wet season between the northeast and southwest islands is of fundamental importance in accounting for the striking ecological contrasts that exist amongst the Seychelles islands.

HISTORY

For centuries, the islands of the Seychelles lay hidden in the glossy, blue-black waters of Bahr el Zanj, the ancient Arab name for the tropical ocean extending eastwards from the shores of Africa. Terrifying legends of deep, dark waters, treacherous currents and monstrous waves were born in this mysterious sea. There were stories of strange lands and many islands filled with wondrous plants and peculiar animals, but the exact whereabouts of these mythical places will forever remain a mystery, lost in the cobwebs of time.

From as early as the 7th century, Arabs in their stately dhows plied the trade routes between Arabia, India and Africa. Forts and settlements were created on the east coast of Africa from Mogadishu (Somalia) southwards to Sofala in Mozambique for trading in slaves, ivory, gold and other precious metals. With the seasonal southeasterly trades and northwesterly monsoons, the Arab sailors visited the Comoros and Madagascar, so it is quite conceivable that the Seychelles islands were encountered by Arab dhows. In fact, a series of islands in roughly the same position as the Seychelles appeared on Arab documents dated AD851. A cluster of mouldering graves, believed to be those of Arab sailors, has also been found on the island of Silhouette. However, hundreds of years slipped by before the uninhabited, wooded island gems of the Seychelles were revealed to the Western world.

Chronology

851   Islands in the vicinity of the Seychelles appear on Arab documents.
1501   First recorded discovery of the Seychelles by João de Nova.
1502   Amirantes group discovered by Vasco da Gama.
1506   The granitic islands of the Seychelles appear on Portuguese charts as Sete Irmanas.
1609   The first British expedition in the ship *Ascension* lands on Mahé.
17th and 18th centuries
       Plundering pirates roam the western Indian Ocean.
1730   Olivier Le Vasseur, La Buse, the well-known Seychelles pirate, publicly hanged in Réunion.
1742   *Elisabeth* and *Le Charles*, under the captaincy of Lazare Picault, anchored off Mahé.
1744   Lazare Picault's second exploring trip to Mahé and Praslin.

1756	Captain Corneille Nicholas Morphey led an expedition to the Seychelles and the islands were given their present name. A Stone of Possession was laid to symbolise ownership of the islands by France.
1768	Expedition by Marion Dufresne which explored Praslin and discovered the source of *coco de mer* nuts.
1770	First settlers arrived to set up spice gardens on Ste Anne and Mahé.
1788	Jean Baptiste Philogene de Malavois became commandant of the Seychelles.
1792	Chevalier Queau de Quinssy took over as commandant.
1814	The Seychelles officially declared a British colony, administered as a dependency of Mauritius. Queau de Quincy (formerly Quinssy) stayed on as administrator for the British.
1832	Whaling station opened at Ste Anne.
1835	Abolition of slavery.
1841	Main town on Mahé given the name of Victoria.
1862	St Louis avalanche killed 75 people in Victoria.
1890	First Seychelles stamps issued.
1903	The Seychelles became a Crown Colony with Ernest Bickham Sweet-Escott as first governor.
1914–18	World War I. This caused severe economic hardship in the Seychelles. German warship *Koenigsberg* reputedly hides in Aldabra lagoon.
1939–45	World War II. The Seychelles became an important refuelling base for British ships and flying boats.
1940	Seychelles currency replaced coins and notes from Mauritius.
1948	First elected representatives in the Seychelles government.
1964	Seychelles Democratic Party and Seychelles People's United Party formed.
1965	Annexation of Farquhar, Desroches and Aldabra as part of the British Indian Ocean Territory.
1967	Universal suffrage introduced in the Seychelles.
1970	Seychelles Constitutional Conference and creation of Legislative Assembly.
1971	International airport opened on Mahé.
1976	The Seychelles became an independent republic. Aldabra, Farquhar and Desroches returned to Seychelles administration.
1977	Armed coup resulting in the Seychelles becoming a single-party state with France Albert Rene as president.
1978	The Seychelles declared their Exclusive Economic Zone.
1982	Aldabra proclaimed a UNESCO World Heritage Site.
1983	Vallée de Mai on Praslin proclaimed a UNESCO World Heritage Site.
1991	Return to multi-party democracy in the Seychelles.
1993	Multi-party elections were held, France Albert Rene took office as president.
2004	James Alix Michel took over as the new president.

Explorers

The great Portuguese admiral, Vasco da Gama, opened up the sea route from Europe to India when he rounded the Cape of Good Hope in 1498. João de Nova, another pioneering Portuguese navigator, followed in his wake and made the first recorded discovery of the Seychelles in 1501 when he came upon a group of low coral islands, which were named in his honour. However, in 1824 they were renamed the Farquhar group after Sir Robert Townsend Farquhar, the first British governor of Mauritius. (A tiny island in the Mozambique Channel is now called Juan de Nova.) On his second voyage to India in 1502, Vasco da Gama encountered another group of coral islands, which were named Ilhas do Almirante in honour of the admiral, and the name Amirantes is still in current use. The granitic islands of the Seychelles appeared on Portuguese charts in 1506 as Sete Irmanas, 'Seven Sisters', but there are no records of what those intrepid mariners found on the islands.

During the 16th and 17th centuries, the race was on between the great seafaring nations to locate and claim all the land they could for their respective countries, and to establish replenishing stations for their ships plying the trade route to India. As a result, Madagascar and the Mascarene Islands of Mauritius, Réunion and Rodrigues became known to the explorers. The Seychelles was left in undisturbed tranquillity until 1609 when the British ship, *Ascension,* under Captain Alexander Sharpeigh, anchored off Mahé. John Jourdain, who was on board the *Ascension,* described in his journal the uninhabited islands, the fresh water, the excellence of the timber and coconuts and the plentiful birds, tortoises and fishes. He commented that the tortoises tasted like beef but looked so ugly before they were cooked that the men refused to eat them! After a ten-day sojourn, the *Ascension* left the islands, which were described as places with nothing to fear except the crocodiles. We can only imagine the exquisite beauty of the pristine islands and, although the secret was out, there was no stampede to visit them, and the earthly paradise was to remain uninhabited for a further 160 years.

Pirates

By the early 17th century, trade between Europe and the East was in full swing, and the islands of the Seychelles were stepping stones in the Indian Ocean. Caravels and Indiamen, laden with silks, rare jewels and exotic spices sailed for the demanding markets of Europe. The East India Company, with headquarters in England and Holland, flourished, and trade with the East reached new heights. The heavy, cumbersome vessels transporting these fabulous cargoes were sitting ducks for pirates and brigands in the Sea of Zanj. The tiny, secluded bays, coves and gentle beaches of the Seychelles were ideal hiding places for these robbers of the high seas. Fine hardwood to repair their boats was plentiful, and an abundance of fresh water, fish and meat from turtles and tortoises provided sustenance for the motley crews.

Pirate 'head office' was set up on the tiny island of Ile Ste Marie off the east coast of Madagascar. This was the meeting place of the rogues, where they would

WRECKS OF THE SEYCHELLES

Modern navigation is a far cry from that of the early explorers who found their way around the Indian Ocean with sun, stars, sextants and leadlines. Over the years, the variable currents and the countless reefs and shoals around the Seychelles have resulted in many craft coming to grief.

One of the earliest was a wooden Portuguese vessel which foundered on Boudeuse Cay in the Amirantes in 1550. Various artefacts have been recovered, including bronze cannons, copper nails, and a coin bearing the royal crest of Portugal. The *Dom Royal*, another Portuguese ship laden with treasures and slaves, ran aground on Astove in 1760. The slaves survived on the island for 26 years before they were eventually recaptured. Some gold coins and silver cutlery, reputedly from the *Dom Royal*, have been salvaged by divers.

In 1763, the French frigate *Heureuse* was wrecked off Providence in the Farquhar group, the start of a long list of ill-fated vessels that have succumbed on this atoll. Others include the British brigantine *Aure* (1836), the French barque *Fédération* (1894), the British schooner *Maggie Low* (1901), the British *Endeavour* (1906), and the Norwegian *Jorgen Bank* (1906) and the *Dagmar* (1907). Other Farquhar islands have also claimed craft, including the SV *St Abbs* which in 1854, en route from London to Bombay, hit a reef. There were only six survivors and an account by one of them, Edward Ross, is held in the Seychelles archives. In 1897, the British ship *Aymestry* went down off Ile Déposé; five years later SS *Hardwick Castle* was wrecked on Farquhar, and *Norden* hit St Pierre in 1906.

The Amirantes claimed the British sloop *Spitfire* at Rémire (1801), the slave trader *La Louise* at Desroches (1809) and SS *Sir Celicourt Antelme* at Marie-Louise (1905). The French coal burner SS *Dot* was wrecked on Alphonse (1873), as was *Tamatave* (1903). Coëtivy claimed the corvette *Eclair* (1787) and the lugger *Alice Adeline* (1906). The whaler *Greenwich* was wrecked off Bird (1833) and *La Perle* succumbed on Plat (1863). The southern islands of the Aldabra group also have their share of wrecks with Cosmoledo claiming *Merry Monarch* (1874), the Norwegian barque *Hamengia* (1913) and, a decade later, the auxiliary schooner *Meredith A White*. In 1915, SS *Glen Lyon* was wrecked on Aldabra, and the lugger *Reve* hit the reefs of Assumption.

Over the years various vessels have disappeared without trace in Seychelles waters, amongst them *Briton*, *Cupido*, *Sea Queen* and *Lord of the Isles*. Others such as *Parachi Pachia* and *Voyageur* have sunk in the precincts of the port of Victoria. The Royal Fleet Auxiliary tanker *Ennerdale* hit a rock about 15km northeast of Victoria in June 1970 and sank. In order to disperse the oil remaining in her tanks, Royal Navy divers placed charges on the vessel and attached the fuses to a helicopter overhead for ignition while the divers raced clear in an inflatable boat! The wreck, which is now a favoured diving site, lies about 2km southwest of Mamelles islet between Mahé and Praslin.

divide up their spoils and indulge in drunken debauchery with the local women. In the Caribbean, the Philip Bros of Amerika company dealt in plundered goods and, as there was so much pirate activity going on in the Indian Ocean, they sent a representative, Adam Baldridge, to expand their business there. Baldridge set up a small shop on a tiny islet at the entrance to the lagoon of Ile Ste Marie, and from there he bought and sold the loot. Very often, the plundered treasures would end up exactly where they had originally been destined, only at a greater cost having passed through many middlemen on the way.

These oceanic hijackers were a rough and brutal lot. Many had turned to piracy to escape the degrading life experienced in the merchant navies of the time. To survive and outwit each other they had to be strong, wily, fearless and bold. A well-known rascal operating out of the Seychelles was a Frenchman, Olivier Le Vasseur, known as La Buse. With his cronies he made a daring raid on a crippled ship lying in the port of Réunion. The ship was loaded with rich treasures: chests of gold and silver, sparkling diamonds, precious pearls and fabulous silks. The Portuguese viceroy and archbishop of Goa were both travelling on board, adding their own ceremonial and religious regalia to the priceless treasure trove. La Buse made off with the treasure but was eventually captured and publicly hanged on Réunion on July 17 1730. Just before he died, he flung a scrap of paper into the air. This contained cryptic clues as to the whereabouts of his hidden treasure, and there is great speculation that it is stashed on Mahé, somewhere in the region of Bel Ombre. To this day, the treasure trove has never been found.

Further clues to pirate activity in the Seychelles linger on in names such as Ile Cachée, Anse Fourban on Mahé, Côte d'Or on Praslin, and Source d'Argent on La Digue. Not all pirates were rogues, however, and Jean-François Hodoul, a corsair operating out of Mahé, gave up his swashbuckling ways and became a most respectable justice of the peace. His name has been given to a tiny island – no more than a clump of casuarinas in the yacht harbour at Victoria, and is also the name of the most easterly point of Aldabra.

Settlers

During the 18th century, Mauritius developed into a thriving island community under the very able direction of an exceptional man, Bertrand François Mahé de Labourdonnais. He was appointed governor in 1735 by the French East India Company, which was running the island with approval from the French courts. He successfully served the French in their India campaign, and his leadership was instrumental in the capture of the town of Mahé on the Malabar coast of India, giving him the right to add Mahé to his name. He transformed the straggling little community on Mauritius into a prosperous settlement. In order to secure more food resources, he fitted out two ships, *Elisabeth* and *Le Charles* and, under the captaincy of Lazare Picault, sent them on a voyage of exploration.

On November 22 1742, almost 150 years after the visit by the *Ascension*, Picault anchored in a superbly beautiful bay off an unknown island. It is presumed to have been Anse à la Mouche on Mahé. There, they found mountains densely covered in tall, straight trees, clear rivers, tumbling waterfalls, a profusion of tortoises, birds and turtles and no sign of human habitation. So overwhelmed were they with this multifarious wildlife, that they simply called the island Ile d'Abondance. Loading up a supply of tortoises and coconuts they returned to Mauritius. De Labourdonnais was impressed with all he heard, and two years later sent Picault back to the islands, this time with a competent mapmaker on board, and instructions to find out all he could about the surrounding islands. On this expedition, Picault named the large island Mahé in honour of the governor, and the entire group of islands he called Iles de Labourdonnais. An island covered in palm trees, a little to the northeast of Mahé (the present day Praslin), was given the name of Ile de Palme although he made no specific reference to the mysterious *coco de mer*.

The French influence

The islands were left in peace for another few years until it was rumoured that the English were about to occupy them. Governor Magon of Mauritius quickly stepped in and, in 1756, sent Captain Corneille Nicolas Morphey in command of two vessels, *Le Cerf* and *Le Benoit*. Mahé was thoroughly explored, and the Iles de Labourdonnais were renamed Sechelles, honouring Vicomte Moreau des Sechelles, the French Comptroller General of Finances ('Sechelles' later became 'Seychelles'). Amid patriotic cries of '*vive le roi!*', gun salutes and a flag-raising ceremony, the islands were formally possessed by France and the French East India Company. A Stone of Possession designed with a *fleur-de-lis* and the crown of Louis XV was set in front of the harbour, near present-day Victoria. Captain Morphey and his two ships sailed away, and the Seychelles continued to exist as peaceful, uninhabited islands.

Exactly 12 years later, another expedition under the patronage of Mauritius reached the verdant islands. Marion Dufresne, in command of two ships, *La Digue* and *La Curieuse,* had been sent on a specific undertaking to exploit the fine timber. There was a more thorough exploration of Ile de Palme which was renamed Praslin after Gabriel de Choiseul, Duc de Praslin, French minister of marine affairs. During the exploration of Praslin, the surveyor, Barre, collected some *coco de mer* nuts, which he took back to Mauritius. The secret source of the fabled nuts had been revealed!

It was not until 1770 that the first wave of settlers arrived in the Seychelles. Brayer du Barré, an entrepreneur, raised enough money to set up a spice-growing industry on the island of Ste Anne. The first group of settlers consisted of 14 Frenchmen, seven slaves, five labourers from Malabar and a lady named Maria. Du Barré remained in Mauritius in relative comfort! At the same time, spice gardens were also being created on Mahé itself at Anse Royale, with seeds procured by Pierre Poivre of Mauritius. Nutmeg, cloves and pepper came from India and cinnamon from Ceylon. Neither venture was particularly successful.

Around this time, the English showed a renewed interest in the islands. In 1778, France decided it was imperative to protect her Indian Ocean assets, and

EXILES IN PARADISE

The Seychelles, because of its remoteness, has long been a dumping ground for various undesirable or politically embarrassing characters. Napoleon deported several Jacobin thugs who tried to assassinate him in Paris in 1800. They spent some time in the Seychelles before being sent on to Comoros. During the 19th century, after the abolition of slavery, British vessels patrolling the waters of the western Indian Ocean captured many Arab dhows still engaged in the illegal practice. Though not strictly exiles, over 2,500 slaves of mainly African origin were released on the Seychelles and formed the basis of the Creole nation.

In 1877, ex-Sultan Abdullah of Perak, who was allegedly involved in the murder of a British person, arrived in the Seychelles with his 37-strong entourage. Several African kings were also exiled on Mahé. King Prempeh of Ashanti and his entourage spent their time at Les Mamelles from 1900. The king discarded his African tribal robes, adopted a Western style of dress, and eventually became a Christian. Members of his party received a Western education and one of his sons even became a priest. When he returned to Africa in 1924 he was clothed in a full morning suit complete with a top hat. He was re-elected Head Chief of the Kumasi tribe on the Gold Coast. Two Ugandan kings, Mwanga, King of Buganda, and Kabalega, King of the Bunyoro, were exiled to the Seychelles in 1901. Mwanga died in 1903 but Kabalega spent 20 years in exile. Mahmood Ali Shirreh, Sultan of the Warsangli tribe of Somaliland, was deported to the islands in 1920 and was held until 1928.

More political outcasts arrived in 1921, in the form of Said Khalil bin Bargash, an Arab who was claiming the throne of Zanzibar. He too had a large entourage, which included his two sons and 19 other hangers-on. A year later, the Egyptian premier, Saad Zaghloul Pasha, and five of his cabinet ministers arrived. They did not stay long as the premier was despatched to Gibraltar for medical treatment. Six Muslim detainees were sent from Aden in 1933, and in 1937 a group of Palestinian freedom fighters were sent to the Seychelles by the British for creating disturbances leading to the death of the district commissioner of Galilea. Their exile was short, and they were repatriated two years later.

Archbishop Makarios of Cyprus spent a year in exile in the Seychelles living in a large house on the Sans Soucis road which is now the home of the American Ambassador. The archbishop used to climb to the summit of Morne Seychellois clad in his flowing black robes. He was also reputedly known for his fine singing in the garden, especially after consuming generous amounts of his favourite wine!

Lt de Romainville was sent to set up a military base on Mahé. By 1786 there were 24 military personnel, four civilians and 122 slaves. Agriculture had almost been abandoned in favour of the indiscriminate felling of timber and purveyance of tortoise and turtle meat to passing ships.

Things started looking up in 1788 when Jean Baptiste Philogene de Malavois took over as commandant. He created law and order on Mahé, and the land was apportioned to married men only! He was the first person to take active steps to control the exploitation of the natural resources. He prohibited the cutting down of trees for firewood and the capture of hawksbill turtles and tortoises, but allowed the harvest of green turtles for personal use only.

Chevalier Jean Baptiste Queau de Quinssy arrived in the Seychelles in 1792 as the French commandant. He guided the Seychelles through the last years of French administration, which included the upheavals caused by the Napoleonic wars. Probably the most difficult time he encountered was during the period when the French and English were alternately laying claim to possession of the Seychelles. Diplomatic de Quinssy reputedly capitulated seven times to the British but reverted to his French allegiance each time the British sailed away. Simultaneously, corsairs with letters of marque from their respective governments entitling them to plunder enemy ships caused havoc on the seas around the Seychelles.

The British influence

Mauritius eventually fell to the British in 1810 and, in 1814, consequent upon the Treaty of Paris, the Seychelles was officially declared a British colony administered as a dependency of Mauritius. De Quincy (the spelling of his name changed) continued as the Seychelles administrator for the British. Most of the French laws remained and the planters continued growing their crops with slave labour. By 1816, the Seychelles had a thriving community with a population of 7,500 of whom 6,600 were slaves. A whaling station was opened on Ste Anne in 1832 introducing a rough element to the population. Grand-scale cotton production in America caused the crash of the industry in the Seychelles and subsequently, in 1840, the era of copra (dried kernels of coconut) production commenced. The British influence started creeping in, and the main town was given the name of Victoria in 1841.

The abolition of slavery in 1835 brought an influx of freed slaves, mainly of African descent, from ships captured by the British. The slaves were liberated in the Seychelles and provided a labour force for the emergent coconut plantations. During the second half of the century, the production of copra dominated the scene with hundreds of thousands of litres of coconut oil being produced annually. Vanilla became an important cash crop outstripping copra in 1899. Cinnamon oil was produced in quantity, and cloves were grown on the hill slopes. On the outer coralline islands, which had the most important coconut plantations, guano mining gained momentum, and turtles were heavily exploited for their meat and shells.

The 20th century

The Seychelles ceased to be a dependency of Mauritius in 1903, and Ernest Bickham Sweet-Escott was installed as the first governor and commander-in-chief. Although the islands were under British jurisdiction, and the English language was used in law and business matters, the French way of life persisted, and French remained the dominant language. But the Seychelles was in for a rough time as the discovery of synthetic essence caused the world price for natural vanilla to fall dramatically. Then, with the outbreak of World War I, ships no longer called for cargoes of coconut oil. Poverty became widespread and crime was rife. Political detainees arrived to spend years in exile. They were a diverse lot – kings from various tribes in Africa, sultans from the Middle East and Zanzibar, the Egyptian premier plus cabinet members, and Arab freedom fighters.

World War II saw the Seychelles playing an important role as a refuelling station for British ships. Seychelles troops were sent to Africa and saw action at El Alamein and Tobruk. Ultimately, though, the war caused continued financial woe in the Seychelles, as did a fall in world demand for coconut oil. After the war the exploitation of the natural resources of the Seychelles continued unabated with millions of seabird eggs taken annually and, as the demand for turtle soup and tortoiseshell ornaments grew, turtles were harvested in large numbers. Patchouli oil for the perfume industry also became an important, but short-lived, product.

The modernisation of the Seychelles began with the first commercial bank opening in 1959. When space exploration became an exciting new phenomenon, even the isolated Seychelles was drawn in. The Americans set up a satellite-tracking station on the mountain above Victoria with two enormous 'golf ball' receivers as part of the station. Although the Americans withdrew at the end of the programme, the 'golf balls' remained for several years before being removed.

The Seychelles did manage to escape a potential disaster during the Cold War. In 1965, Britain, with Anglo-American defence strategy in mind, annexed Farquhar, Desroches and Aldabra as part of the British Indian Ocean Territory. A large airforce base was planned for Aldabra but environmental lobbyists, spearheaded by Julian Huxley, succeeded in overturning the venture, and Aldabra eventually became the world's first coral atoll World Heritage Site in 1982. Since the international airport opened in 1971 linking Mahé with major cities in Europe, tourism has become an increasingly important part of the Seychelles economy.

POLITICS

In common with much of the world, the era of party politics has dawned in the Seychelles, and the government included its first elected representatives in 1948. At that time the franchise was extended to property owners only, and it was not until 1967 that universal suffrage was introduced. Two political parties were formed in 1964. The Seychelles People's United Party (SPUP) led by France Albert Rene was strongly committed to achieving

Seychelles independence, while the Seychelles Democratic Party (SDP), led by James Mancham, was keen to maintain ties with Britain. A constitutional conference in 1970 discussed the future of the Seychelles and set up a 15-member Legislative Assembly. After the election, James Mancham became chief minister, his SDP winning six seats to the five seats of the SPUP. In the 1974 elections, the SDP maintained their slender lead. In June 1976, the Seychelles became an independent republic with colourful Mancham as president and Rene as prime minister of the coalition government. A year later, on June 5 1977, while Mancham was out of the country attending a Commonwealth conference in London, the SPUP staged an armed coup, and the Seychelles became a single-party socialist state with Rene as president. The SPUP was renamed the Seychelles People's Progressive Front (SPPF).

Rene survived several attempted coups of which the most publicised was in November 1981. The responsible mercenaries were arrested, tried and imprisoned in the Seychelles and South Africa. In 1991, there was a return to a multi-party democracy, James Mancham was welcomed back, and eventually a new constitution was produced in June 1993. Multi-party elections were held a month later and Rene defeated Mancham with 59% of the votes. Elections are held every five years, and Rene was returned to office in the 1998 elections and again in 2001. However, on April 14 2004 he retired and handed over to his vice-president, James Alix Michel.

GOVERNMENT AND ADMINISTRATION

The Republic of the Seychelles is a multi-party democracy with a constitution approved by the people in 1993. James Alix Michel is the president and also holds the portfolios of defence, police, internal affairs, finance and economic planning. Vice-president Joseph Belmont is minister of tourism and transport and the foreign minister is Jeremie Bonnelame. There are a further ten departments including education and youth, local government, sports and culture, environment and natural resources, agriculture and marine resources, industry and international business, social affairs and employment. The main opposition party is headed by Wavel Ramkalawan. Local residents and their employers pay a social security tax for services such as healthcare, education and old-age benefits.

The Legislative Assembly is in Victoria; the next presidental election is due in May/June 2006 while the election for the Members of the National Assembly is due in October 2007.

ECONOMY

The Seychelles economy depends largely on fishing (chiefly based on tuna processing) and tourism as earners of foreign exchange. Over 128,000 tourists visit the islands each year. On the home front, agriculture provides a limited amount of food for local consumption, restricted arable land being the controlling factor. Local industries are developing, and the Seychelles government is investigating ways to expand foreign earnings by entering the global business and financial markets and encourages offshore investment in the country.

Tourism

Since 1971 and the opening of the international airport, tourism has been a major earner of foreign exchange, with the industry employing a large percentage of the population. In addition to the obvious jobs in aviation, hotels and restaurants, the spin-off work in the supply of services by tour operators, taxis, car-hire, inter-island ferries, dive operators, guides, souvenir sellers and so on, is considerable. The Seychelles, through government policy, has tried to maintain the charm of the islands, and buildings higher than the coconut palms are rarely permitted. Instead of catering for mass tourism, the Seychelles strives to provide small, exclusive resorts and there are only about 5,000 hotel beds available amongst all the islands. An international convention centre, able to handle meetings for up to 600 delegates, has been built in Victoria near Le Chantier traffic circle.

About 128,000 people visit the Seychelles annually, with the majority of visitors from the United Kingdom and elsewhere in Europe. Package tours are often the most cost-effective way to travel to this safe destination. A number of international cruise ships also visit the islands. Passengers generally spend their days ashore exploring the islands but return to the ship at night. Although most visitors come for the sun, sea and sand aspects of a Seychelles trip, scuba diving, snorkelling, birdwatching, walking in the mountains, cruising and deep-sea angling are particularly alluring.

Fishing

Fishing and related activities are a major component of the Seychelles economy, contributing about half of the country's foreign exchange inflow. The main fisheries sectors are the local artisanal fishery, which targets reef fishes, and the multinational tuna fishery which targets tuna in the widespread waters of the Seychelles Exclusive Economic Zone (EEZ).

The artisanal fishery uses both hook and line and traps, and operates a fleet of some 400 small vessels which, by and large, ply the shallow waters around Mahé, Praslin and La Digue. These vessels include pirogues, whalers, schooners and sport-fishing boats. The major species in the catch are *karang* (trevally), *bourzwa* and *bordmar* (red snappers), *zob* (jobfish), *kaptenn* (emperors), *bonit* (bonito), *vyey* (groupers), *kordonnyen* (rabbitfish) and *makro dou* (mackerel). The average annual catch during the past decade has been around 4,500 tonnes. The lobster fishery was closed in 1997 as stocks had not recovered sufficiently after illegal fishing activity. It was reopened in 1999 and about 5 tonnes are harvested each year. Longline fishing for sharks and swordfish was introduced after the Seychelles government banned the use of gill-nets because of the by-catch of turtles and dolphins.

A fleet of 50 purse-seine vessels fish for tuna in the Seychelles EEZ. The majority of these are registered in Spain and France with only six registered in the Seychelles. The total catch in 2002 was 380,000 tonnes and comprised mainly skipjack and yellowfin tuna, most of which is trans-shipped in Mahé. There is also a foreign longline fishery for tuna in the Seychelles EEZ with the majority of vessels using this technique from Taiwan or Japan.

Port Victoria, with its four berths and one bunker pier, is extremely busy and is the main tuna trans-shipment port in the Indian Ocean. Landed catches go to the Indian Ocean Tuna canning factory which, after expansion, produced 35,000 tonnes of canned tuna in 2002. This factory employs almost half of the estimated 4,500 persons involved in the fishing industry.

Prawn farming started over a decade ago with the first aquaculture ponds built at Coëtivy. There are now some 74 ponds, a hatchery and a processing plant. The entire Seychelles demand for prawns is supplied from Coëtivy and the rest is exported. Giant clam and pearl oyster farming are other aquaculture ventures in the Seychelles and can be seen at Amitié near the airport on Praslin. The pearls are proving popular in jewellery sold to foreign visitors.

Agriculture

The early economy of the Seychelles was based on the production of copra and coconut oil, and remains of the plantations are seen all over the islands. Vanilla, also once important, is still grown in a small way on Mahé and La Digue. Other spices, like cinnamon, continue to be cultivated commercially, and can be purchased at the market in Victoria. Vegetables are grown around Anse Royale and Anse Boileau on Mahé, lettuce and tomatoes being important crops. There are several plant nurseries, and orchids are grown for export and local use in hotel decoration. On the misty mountains slopes of Mahé, tea is a successful crop, and the neatly trimmed bushes can be seen from the Sans Soucis road. Tea is marketed as SeyTé for the domestic market.

Trade, industry and investment

Local industry is poorly developed and, with the exception of the tuna processing plant, a paint factory and Seybrew, there is little manufacturing in the Seychelles. Most processed foods and manufactured items are imported and distributed through the Seychelles Marketing Board. All petroleum products are imported.

The Islands Development Company is a para-statal organisation that maintains coconut plantations and tourist facilities on some of the outlying islands. The Seychelles is, however, set to enter the global economy with tax incentives and many other benefits available to foreign investors. The Seychelles International Business Authority (SIBA), an autonomous corporate body, has been established to co-ordinate international business companies, international trusts, offshore banking and insurance as well as shipping and aircraft registration. They can be contacted at PO Box 991, Mahé; tel: 380800; fax: 380888; email: siba@seychelles.net; www.siba.net. All their services can be accessed through the offices of the Seychelles International Trade Zone (SITZ) located at Roche Caiman. Other investment options include trans-shipment, redistribution and management services.

The Development Bank of Seychelles (tel: 224471; fax: 224274) is geared up to handle the financing of projects in agriculture, fishing, tourism, light industry and the service sectors.

People and Culture

When the earliest explorers discovered the Seychelles, there were no people living on the islands. The first group of 18th-century pioneers comprised French settlers, African slaves and Indian workers. More people from France and Mauritius, as well as many slaves from Africa and Madagascar, came to the islands, and before the abolition of slavery, 90% of the population were slaves. After the abolition of slavery in 1835, shiploads of slaves, previously destined for the world markets, were set free in the Seychelles. Political prisoners from France were dumped on the oceanic islands during, and after, the French Revolution. Although the Seychelles was a British colony from 1815, there was never a great influx of English settlers, and the dominant French influence remained. Indian and Chinese traders arrived at the beginning of the 20th century to take advantage of the developing economy. There was, and still is, an easy-going attitude to love and romance, and relationships between the races are commonplace, giving rise to the cosmopolitan, dusky-skinned Seychellois people. Today's inhabitants are a cheerful mix of every race imaginable, and they are proud to count how many nationalities can belong to one family.

POPULATION

The total population of the Seychelles is about 81,000 with 90% living on Mahé. About 25,000 people live in and around Victoria, and the most populated areas are at St Louis, Bel Air and Mont Fleuri. Other well-populated areas are Bel Ombre, Glacis, Anse Royale and Anse Boileau. Praslin, with 7,103 inhabitants, has no really densely populated areas, although most of the people live around Baie Ste Anne, Grande Anse and Anse Volbert. On La Digue, most of the 1,080 residents live on the west coast between La Passe and Anse la Réunion. The average size of families is five, and 33% of the population is under the age of 18.

The people of the granitic islands are, by and large, employed in government service, tourism, fishing, construction or agriculture. The outer islands are sparsely populated by a special breed of people who are happy with the quiet and isolated lifestyle. The remote islands that are run as coconut plantations have basic communications with Mahé in the form of radio-telephone, but there are virtually no community activities apart from fishing!

LANGUAGE

In the Seychelles there are three languages. Creole is the most commonly spoken language though French and English are widely used and understood, with the latter the language of commerce and law. Creole, a French patois, developed during the slave era with the French plantation owners needing to communicate with African and Malagasy slaves. Much of the Creole vocabulary is similar to French although the grammar is simplified, and words and phrases from other tongues such as Swahili or Arabic have been incorporated.

It is only in recent years that the language has been put into a written form by the Creole Institute, Lenstiti Kreol, located at Anse aux Pins on Mahé. It is a phonetic language so, for example, the French *petit* becomes *pti* in the new written language. School books and reading books for children are now being produced in Creole. The local newspaper, *The Nation*, carries articles in both English and Creole. (See *Appendix 1* for useful Creole words and phrases.)

RELIGION

The French and English brought their religions to the islands and there are two cathedrals on Mahé, the Catholic Cathedral of the Immaculate Conception and St Paul's Anglican Cathedral. About 90% of the people are Catholic, and the cathedral in Victoria is usually packed to capacity every Sunday. Mahé must be the origin of the saying 'dressing up in your Sunday best' – the ladies wear their best straw hats with flowers, the little girls are in their frilly dresses, white socks and shiny shoes, while the men are resplendent in clean, ironed shirts and long trousers. Besides the religious aspect, church is an important social event as it is a gathering place to catch up on the gossip of the week. It is also a respectable place for young people to meet and get together. Anglicans account for 8% of the population and their small cathedral was built on the water's edge in Victoria but, with land reclamation, it is now some distance from the ocean. There are churches on most of the inhabited islands, and even on the smallest islands there will be a tiny church. There is also a smattering of Seventh-Day Adventists.

Some of the Indian community use the beautifully decorated Hindu temple in Quincy Street, Victoria, while the Sheik Mohamed bin Khalifa Mosque in Francis Rachel Street is in daily use for the prayers of the small Muslim community. A Baha'i centre in Praslin, with a commanding view over the harbour, has a following on the island.

EDUCATION

The Seychelles government considers education to be one of its priorities and 20% of the budget is spent on schooling, which is compulsory and free up to the age of 15 years. After this students may continue working towards A-levels for a further two years. Schools are located in most of the larger centres on the three main islands and a regular bus service enables the children to get to school easily. Lessons are conducted in the mother tongue, Creole, but in secondary school, many of the lessons are in English or French because of the lack of more advanced textbooks in Creole. The literacy rate is 87%. Tertiary education is continued at the various polytechnics, and practical subjects that can lead to employment are offered. Diploma courses include health care, design, computers, marine studies, agriculture, mechanics and building techniques. The Seychelles Hotel and Tourism Training School is accommodated in the hills of La Misère, and courses cover the many facets of the hospitality industry. There is no university in the Seychelles, so students have to travel abroad in order to study for degrees.

CULTURE

The cosmopolitan Seychellois have a charming Creole culture which stems from the African, European and Asian roots of people. From the slave background, a camaraderie developed and there was a great sense of sharing which is still noticeable today. In fact, sharing is the essence of the Creole culture – sharing of mixed traditions and languages to build up one culture that is unique to the Seychelles. The slaves brought traditional African and Malagasy cultures encompassing witchcraft and superstition. Some islanders still believe in the power of *gris-gris* and will spend a lot of money consulting the *bonnomm dibwa* (medicine man) when needing to resolve issues such as a lovers' dispute. The *bonnomm* is also believed to have healing powers and will sometimes be consulted in cases of illness.

Families are generally large and everyone seems to be related to, or at least know, everyone else. Children grow up in a most uncomplicated way playing in the gentle waves, going fishing and messing about in little boats. Grandmothers and aunts are always around to take care of the children when parents are at work. There is a free and easy approach to marriage: many couples never marry and partner changes are quite acceptable. Children tend to stay with their mothers, regardless of her partner, and the woman is generally the head of the household as fathers sometimes shirk the responsibilities of child rearing.

Life in the Seychelles is interwoven with the sea. The deep blue ocean with its variable winds and currents is always in sight, and one is never far from the sound of the surf. In the early days, fishing from small boats provided the daily food, and news of the outside world arrived intermittently by ship. Today, more sophisticated communication networks prevail but the old days set the scene for the present laid-back lifestyle. The relaxed islanders do not know the word 'hurry'. Tomorrow, very often, does just as well as today. The Seychellois believe that life is to be enjoyed, and they will find any excuse for a celebration with music, dance and plenty to eat and drink.

Music and dancing

The rhythm of the ocean is mirrored in the lively Creole music which can be sweet and gentle or wild and lively, incorporating the deep-seated pulses of Africa and Madagascar. The drums or *tamtam,* made from a hollowed tree trunk, and the *tambour* with its skin cover are deeply reminiscent of Africa. String instruments, the *zez* and the *mouloumpa* are made from calabashes or bamboo, and create sounds hauntingly suggestive of Madagascar. Nowadays, though the sounds are often made on modern guitars and keyboards, and the music of the younger generation is influenced by country and western and reggae, it still has that evocative Seychelles quality, and the rhythmic beats are a clear invitation to dance.

The *sega*, danced to the rhythm beaten out on a drum, is pure African in origin. Couples dance sensuously facing each other, without touching. Adapted versions of the *sega* are performed for tourists. The traditional *moutya,* derived from the slave days, is a gathering which takes place on the beach by the light of the moon and the stars. A great fire blazes and everyone sits around drinking *kalou*, a potent brew made from the sap of the coconut palm, fermented with sugar. Heat from the fire is used to tighten the goatskin drums. The music gets off to a slow start and the dancing is slow and erotic. As the beating of the drums increases, so does the rhythm of the chanting and, as the men and women reply to each other, so the dancing becomes more provocative and sensual.

The *Kreol* festival

At the end of October each year, the *Kreol* identity is celebrated with a week-long festival. A wide range of events takes place based on music, singing, dancing and the visual arts. Vibrant street performances liven up Victoria, fashion shows are held, school children put on variety shows and the elderly are treated to special teas and lunch outings. Other traditional aspects of Creole life are given a forum, with subjects like Creole cuisine and herbalism coming under discussion. *Lenstiti Kreol* plays an important role in the festivities with plays, poetry readings and literary workshops. The festival week ends with a ball and award ceremonies for the winners of the competitions. Visitors from many other Creole countries descend on the Seychelles and participants from Mauritius, Réunion and Rodrigues join with revellers from some of the Caribbean islands. Madagascar, though not a Creole country, also comes to the party.

Art

Sensual scenery, lush tropical vegetation, glorious beaches and a relaxed harmony between all the people of the islands inspires creative expression in the arts. Many foreigners have also settled in the islands, bringing with them their artistic talents in different forms such as painting, sculpture and batik. Many artistic Seychellois have trained and worked abroad and there are artists scattered throughout the islands. Art is strongly encouraged in the schools and exhibitions of children's art can often be seen in unexpected places.

The National Library building houses a gallery, which is always worth a visit. Studios, galleries and boutiques are dotted all over the islands, and artistic treasures from simple sketches to marvellous collector's items are available. Paintings are often vividly coloured interpretations of the surroundings, and there are drawings of people and local scenes as well as magnificent sculptures in bronze or wood. Creative jewellery made from gold, pearls, shells and other items can be found in boutiques on Mahé and Praslin.

Food

Imagine the freshest seafood, flavoured with coconut milk, garlic, ginger, limes and chillies, and cooked to perfection by chefs who know how to make a thousand different fish dishes! Creole cuisine combines the subtlety of Asian food with the spices of Indian cooking, all moulded by fine French flair. Rice is the staple and fish is eaten almost every day. Soup is a tasty starter and is often made from *tec-tec*, a tiny shellfish. *Bouillon blan,* a fish soup that uses a whole, small fish with loads of garlic, ginger and chilli, is a meal in itself. Salads are made with sweet, little purple onions, tomatoes and crisp *bilimbis* which resemble tiny cucumbers. Millionaire's salad used to be prepared from the heart of the rare *palmiste* palm, but now the heart of the coconut palm suffices. Curries are traditional – usually fish or octopus – and quite delicious. For something really exotic you could try the fruit bat curry which is reputed to be tasty, though not as tender as chicken. Breadfruit, plantain, cassava and sweet potatoes provide alternatives to rice. *Chatinis* or chutneys are side dishes made by grating green papaya or the local fruit known as the golden apple. It can be fried with a little onion and served in fresh lime juice or vinegar with ginger and garlic. Dried fish such as shark or tuna can also be prepared this way. Little chillies are often served on the side – they can be dynamite, so try with caution! Breadfruit, with the addition of island spices and coconut milk, is also used for sweet desserts. Other desserts are prepared from coconut and bananas and are usually very sweet and sticky.

A TYPICAL CREOLE RECIPE: BOUILLON BLAN
as prepared by Philip the boatman on Aldabra

Ingredients
One clean, whole fish of about 1kg
100g purple onions
20g garlic
20g fresh ginger
20ml tomato sauce
50g fresh tomato (if available)
5ml dried thyme
3ml mixed herbs
3ml spice for fish
3ml turmeric
salt and pepper
1litre water

Method
Cut the fish (including the head) into three or four chunks and coat with herbs and turmeric. Pound the garlic and ginger with the salt. Slice the onions and fry gently in a little oil. Add the fish, garlic and ginger, stir and add water. Simmer for about 10 minutes. Add tomato sauce, and about 50g of finely chopped fresh tomato if available. Continue simmering for another 10 minutes. Remove the fish and strain the soup. Remove the bones from the fish and return the flesh to the soup. Enjoy!

Although take-away stalls are well-frequented, eating out is expensive. Many restaurants serve excellent Creole food so tourists can get a taste of the islands. All the major hotels serve international cuisine and various speciality restaurants (Italian, French and Chinese) serve really good and tasty meals.

The national drink is the locally brewed beer, Seybrew which, when chilled, slips down ever so easily! The brewery also makes Eku, a Bavarian type of beer, Celebration Brew and Guinness. The Seychellois drink an amazing amount of fizzy soft drinks, and fruit juices are also readily available.

NATIONAL EMBLEMS

The **Seychelles coat of arms** has been adapted from the original drawn by General Gordon in 1881. The circular, central shield has a tortoise, a *coco de mer*, and a two-masted sailing vessel approaching a granite hill. The shield is flanked by two sailfish above which are heraldic feathers and a silver helmet. Flying over the grand design is a white-tailed tropicbird. A folded ribbon at the base carries the motto *finis coronat opus* ('the end crowns the work'). The **national flower** is the tropicbird orchid. The Creole name is *fleur payanke* and the French call it *fleur paille en queue*. The **national bird** is the black parrot, found on Praslin and Curieuse. The Seychelles **flag** has five bright colours (green, white, red, yellow and blue) radiating out from the bottom left of the flag.

SPORT AND RECREATION

The Seychellois are a sport-loving nation. The government, through the National Sports Council, encourages and promotes sport at all levels and has done much to improve sporting facilities. Some of the more popular sports include soccer, basketball, volleyball, swimming, athletics, cycling, body-building and weightlifting. Participants representing the Seychelles take part in many international competitions and do very well for such a small nation.

There are 35 soccer teams registered with the local federation and matches are played on Thursday evenings and Saturday afternoons. The new stadium in Victoria is the venue for the important matches. There is keen competition between the teams from the Indian Ocean islands, and you don't want to be on a flight with the victorious Seychelles team returning from Madagascar!

Running is also a popular pastime and sponsored runs are held from time to time throughout the year. Running up the hills is no mean feat and only advisable in the early mornings. Amongst the older generation, dominoes is almost the national sport, sedately played outside under the trees and on the pavements.

Sailing and other watersports are popular amongst the Seychellois, and training programmes aimed at young people are run from the yacht club in Victoria. An annual sailing regatta, organised by the Rotary, is held at Beau Vallon and there is a windsurfing race between Mahé and Praslin. For the local people, fishing is a way of life and the sport of game fishing is developing rapidly.

Clubs and associations

Rotary, Round Table and Lions meet regularly and welcome visitors.

Biodiversity

The islands of the Seychelles, as a result of their fascinating, continental past and equatorial, oceanic location, support a wide diversity of terrestrial and marine fauna and flora. In general, the terrestrial plants and animals have links with Africa, Madagascar and Asia while the marine life is largely characterised by species that are widespread in the tropical Indo-Pacific region. There are two UNESCO World Heritage Sites: Vallée de Mai on Praslin, and Aldabra atoll (see pages 142–7 and 201–13).

PLANTS

When Nicholas Morphey made the first detailed account of the vegetation around Mahé in 1756, almost impenetrable mangrove forests lined the shores, coconut palms fringed the beaches and the narrow coastal plains and mountain slopes were covered with dense hardwood forests. Subsequently, there have been several botanical surveys of both the granitic and coralline islands. These have revealed that, at present, there are 766 species of flowering plants and 85 ferns known from the granitic islands, of which 69 are endemic (occur only in the Seychelles). The flora of the drier coralline islands is less prolific, supporting 257 species with 34 endemics.

The impact of man has significantly altered the vegetation on every island although, in some places, patches of natural vegetation still exist. The tall, lowland forests of the coastal plains have been the most denuded of all, but small enclaves still exist on Félicité and Silhouette, and some tiny patches can be found on Mahé. The timber was used for houses, boats and furniture, and the land was cleared to make way for agricultural purposes, mainly coconut and vanilla plantations. Shorelines of the granitic islands have been robbed of their mangroves in many places but magnificent, intact mangrove forests still fringe the inner lagoon of Aldabra Atoll.

Seaweeds and shore plants

The seaweeds of the Seychelles have only recently received scientific attention and there are some 350 species of red, brown and green seaweeds known from the islands. There are eight species of **seagrasses** occurring in lagoons, namely *Cymodocea serrulata*, *C. rotundata*, *Halodule universes*, *Halophila decipiens*, *H. ovalis*, *H. stipulacea*, *Syringodium isoetifolium*, *Thalassia hemprichii* and *Thalassodendron cliatum*. The leafy seagrasses form the major part of the diet of green turtles, and the juveniles of many fishes spend the early part of their lives sheltering and feeding in seagrass beds – veritable nursery areas.

Shore plants, which are generally adapted to survive wind and salt spray, characterise the shores of the islands, and 54 species, mainly of Indo-Malay origin, are found in the Seychelles. The creeping beach convolvulous, *Ipomoea pes-caprae*, with purplish-pink flowers and large, tough leaves, is the first of the beach pioneers and is common on all the islands. The two most commonly distributed plants on the beach crest are the scrambling, shrubby salt bush, *Scaevola sericea*, known locally as *veloutier*, which has clusters of white flowers frequented by sunbirds, and *Tournefortia argentea*, with the Creole name of *bwa tabac*, which has thick, fleshy leaves covered in fine hairs. The ubiquitous **coconuts**, *Cocos nucifera*, and **casuarinas**, *Casuarina equistifolia*, are to be found fringing the shores of all the islands. The origins of both are unclear but mention of the presence of coconuts appears in the earliest records about the Seychelles. Casuarinas were recorded from Aldabra in 1815 but, as these widespread coastal trees were present in Madagascar in pre-European times, and as the seeds are easily dispersed, they could have spread naturally to the neighbouring Seychelles. Noteworthy trees of the shoreline include the Indian almond, *Terminalia catappa*, and the Alexandrian laurel, *Calophyllum inophyllum*, commonly known as the **badamier** and **takamaka**, respectively.

Mangrove forests

Mangroves, *mangliye* in Creole, are evergreen trees which have adapted to growing in muddy, intertidal areas. Special root systems have evolved to withstand periods of inundation and exposure as the tides ebb and flow. Their strangely shaped roots or pneumatophores are, in fact, breathing roots adapted to cope with the lack of oxygen in the waterlogged mud. They can be seen poking straight up through the mud like long pencils or they can be angled with knobbly knee-roots. Many mangroves have sturdy prop- or stilt-roots for support. The seeds of some mangrove species are torpedo shaped and actually germinate on the parent tree. When they drop, they get vertically impaled into the soft mud, and roots can start to develop within hours.

Mangrove forests are a unique and important ecosystem that functions to protect the coast from erosion as well as providing a habitat for all sorts of animals including specialist crabs and snails. Mangroves provide nursery areas for juvenile fishes, shelter for young hawksbill turtles and secluded feeding and breeding grounds for shorebirds and seabirds. On Aldabra, frigatebirds and red-footed boobies nest, side by side, in vast numbers in the mangrove canopy.

Most of the mangroves have all but disappeared from the granitic islands with only tiny patches left on Mahé, La Digue and Praslin. There are still small mangrove-forested areas on Silhouette and Curieuse. Amongst the coralline islands, St Joseph's Atoll, Farquhar, Cosmoledo, Astove and Aldabra still support healthy mangrove communities. Aldabra has an estimated 800ha of these forests, with the largest areas located at Bras Takamaka and Bras Cinq

Cases. The most commonly found species are the white mangrove, *Avicennia marina*, the black mangrove, *Bruguiera gymnorrhiza*, the red mangrove, *Rhizophora mucronata*, and the Indian mangrove, *Ceriops tagal*. In certain restricted areas, *Lumnitzera racemosa*, *Sonneratia alba*, *Heritiera littoralis* and *Xylocarpus granatum* can be found. Mangroves generally have specific zonation patterns on the shore relative to tidal height.

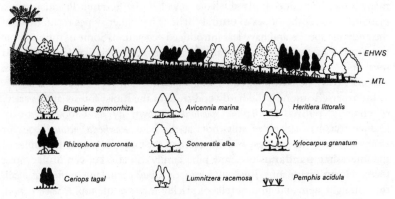

Mangrove tree species and zonation (EHWS: Extreme high water springs; MTL: Mean tide level). Reprinted with permission from Richmond (1997).

Besides mangroves, there are many other plants and trees associated with brackish and freshwater swamps. Reeds, sedges, grasses and water ferns inhabit these areas, which are often shaded by water-loving trees. The beach hibiscus, *Hibiscus tiliaceus*, with golden flowers that turn burnt orange and drop to the ground, are widespread. They are particularly common on the landward side of the mangrove forest at Curieuse. Other conspicuous trees of this area are *Barringtonia racemosa* with long sprays of pale pink flowers, and *Barringtonia asiatica* (Creole *bonnet carre*) with pink, powder puff flowers and large, quadrangular seeds which are dispersed by the sea.

Granitic island vegetation
Coastal plains
The narrow, confined coastal plains of the granitic islands were originally covered in fine, Seychelles hardwood trees like *takamaka* and *badamier*. However, most of the flat land was cleared to make way for plantation agriculture in the late 1800s and the original vegetation only survives in small, isolated pockets. Coconuts, vanilla (*Vanilla planifolia*) and cinnamon, *Cinnamonum zeylanicum*, were extensively planted and they can all be found growing wild, and in profusion. On some of the smaller granitic islands, which are now being conserved, woodland plants like *Pisonia grandis* and tortoise tree, *Morinda citrifolia*, are regenerating well. The human settlements on the islands have generally developed on the restricted flat land near the coast; here, introduced ornamental plants like frangipani, bougainvillea and hibiscus are common.

Mountains

Moving away from the coastal habitat to the mountain slopes and valleys, the vegetation is defined by the amount of rainfall received, and this can vary significantly from area to area. Originally covered in hardwood forests, the lower slopes have been extensively cleared for agricultural purposes. Cinnamon, vanilla and other spices were planted on the hillsides and they, and many other introduced plants, have invaded the terrain. Productive tea plantations cover the slopes of central Mahé. The higher slopes retain more of the endemic species and have less introduced vegetation. Some of the endemic trees in the higher rainfall areas are *Dillenia ferruginea*, known locally as **bwa rouz**, and *Northea hornei*, a tall hardwood tree with a distinctive seed shaped like a monk's cowl, hence the Creole name **kapesin**.

Interspersed amongst the hardwood trees in the moist forests are a variety of endemic **palms**. *Verschafeltia splendida*, known by its Creole name of *latanyenn lat*, has a cone of stilt roots at the base. *Roscheria melanochaetes,* or *latanyenn oban* is the smallest and most rare of the endemic palms. Examples of the interesting **pandanus** or screw pine family can also be seen in the moist forest. Horne's pandanus, *Pandanus hornei*, or *vakwa parasol* in Creole, has a tall, thin, straight stem and an umbrella of prickly leaves at the top. *P. seychellarum*, or *vakwa maron*, has an even more accentuated wigwam of stilt roots.

Mosses and ferns are associated with the moist forests. An endemic fern, *Angiopterus evecta*, with the Creole name *baton monsennyer*, as the unopened fronds resemble a bishop's crook, and the bird's nest fern, *Asplenium nidus*, adorn many trees in the forest. The tree fern, *Cyathea sechellarum*, and the giant fern, *Angiopteris erecta*, favour the darker slopes of ravines traversed by streams.

There are spectacular, drier forests on Praslin, Curieuse and Silhouette. Though much of the original forest was altered by the removal of large *bwa rouz* and *kapesin* trees in days gone by, there are parts that are fairly intact and the prime example of this type of forest is the Vallée de Mai on Praslin. All six endemic palms can be seen in the Praslin National Park, the most spectacular of which is the **coco de mer**, *Lodoicea maldivica*, with its famous, suggestive, double nut. The other five palms, which each have a scientific name and a Creole name, are *Deckenia nobilis* or *palmiste*, *Nephrosperma vanhoutteanum* or *latanyenn milpat*, *Phoenicophorium borsigianum* or *latannyen fey*, *Roscheria melanochaetes* or *latannyen oban* and *Verschafeltia splendida* or *latanyenn lat*. Four species of pandanus thrive in this relatively dry forest, *Pandanus hornei*, *P. sechellarum*, *P. balfourii* and *P. multispicatus*. (More information on the dry forest can be found in the description of Vallée de Mai in *Chapter 6*, pages 142–7.)

Glacis

Glacis is weathered granite and these exposed areas on mountainsides have small pockets of peaty, shallow soil which support a number of interesting plants. The **pitcher plant**, *Nepenthes pervillei*, with its nearest relatives in Madagascar and Asia, is a low-growing, scrambling plant with pitcher-like receptacles that extend from the leaf midrib. The pitcher contains a liquid capable of digesting unsuspecting insects that fall into it. An interesting exception is the small endemic mosquito, *Uranotaenia nepenthes*, which actually breeds in the pitcher! *Pandanus multispicatus* also occurs on the wind-blown, misty *glacis* slopes. Several **orchids** are able to thrive on the *glacis*, and include the endemic Seychelles vanilla orchid, *Vanilla phaleanopsis*, which produces beautiful, waxy-looking, white flowers flushed with pink, on a thick, fleshy, leafless vine. The Seychelles national flower, the tropicbird orchid, *Angraecum eburneum*, is also able to survive on these inhospitable rocky slopes, and can even be found on the dry, craggy limestone *champignon* of Aldabra. *Malaxis seychellarum*, another small orchid which has greeny-yellow or purple flowers, can be found on the rocks or trees. There are another 22 species of orchids, both terrestrial and epiphytic (growing on other plants), but none is particularly spectacular.

Glacis in the drier parts does not have the thick, peaty mats of the moist locations and, though the plant life is similar, there are also some interesting differences. Occurring on the drier *glacis* slopes of Mahé are a few specimens of a most unusual tree, the **jellyfish tree**, *Medusagnye oppositaefolia*. This species is in a plant family all its own, and was thought to be extinct until rediscovered on Mahé in 1970. The flower is small, white and insignificant, and the dry, open fruit resembles a dark jellyfish.

Coralline island vegetation

A beach crest hedge of mostly *Scaevola* and *Tournefortia* characterises the shoreline of the coralline islands, and coconuts and casuarinas fringe many of the beaches. *Suriana maritime*, a low, scrambling coastal shrub with little yellow flowers, is common on the coralline islands and is known as *bois d'amande* in Creole. Two other trees found around the coasts are *Cordia subcordata*, known locally as *bwa porcher*, which has bright orange, bell-shaped flowers, and *Guettarda speciosa* or *bwa cassan*, which has bunches of creamy-white flowers producing a heady fragrance at night.

Pemphis acidula forms dense, impenetrable thickets up to 6m high on Aldabra. It grows in the rocky limestone and is able to withstand the brackish nature of the water. It has small, white flowers frequented by sunbirds. *Pemphis* is also found on Cosmoledo, Astove, Farquhar, Poivre and St Joseph's but does not occur on the granitic Seychelles islands.

Much of the natural forest of the coralline islands was removed for phosphate and guano mining, and later for coconut plantations. However, small patches of these trees surrounded by coconuts can still be found. The most widespread is *Cordia,* while *takamaka* occurs in groves on Aldabra and D'Arros, and is fairly common on many of the other coralline islands. There is also an evergreen mixed scrub cover on the raised limestone atolls with a wide variety of understorey species. Aldabra supports a surprising number of endemic plants including *Pandanus aldabrensis*, the **Aldabra lily**, *Lomatophyllum aldabrense*, and a subspecies of the tropicbird orchid, *Angraecum eburneum* (more details in *Chapter 10*, page 212).

SCIENTIFIC NAMES

The system of scientific names given to animals and plants is best understood if it is regarded as a hierarchical address system in which each species is positioned according to its relationship with other species. At the broadest level, the animal kingdom is divided into phyla which are groups of animals which share a similar overall body plan. Each phylum is then subdivided into more closely related classes, which in turn contain orders, families, and finally genera and species. Each species is allocated a pair of names; in text, these are printed in italics. The first word of the pair is the genus name, while the second, which is always written in lower case, identifies the individual species. Closely related species thus share the same generic names. The specific epithet is meaningless when written alone because many different species in different phyla may have the same specific epithet. For example, the Seychelles warbler, *Acrocephalus seychellenis*, has the same specific epithet as the Seychelles tree frog, *Tachycnemis seychellensis*. So do many other animals and plants of the Seychelles – possibly indicative of poor imagination on the part of museum-bound taxonomists!

This binomial nomenclature was invented by the Swedish scientist Linnaeus in the 18th century, and has been slavishly adhered to by biologists ever since. Unique scientific names (in Latin) are established for every known species, and these are universally recognised, unlike common names, which for the same species may differ from location to location. In this book we sometimes only give the generic name if several species of the same genus are involved. If referring to several species within the same genus, the genus name is abbreviated to the first letter.

As an example, the classification of the emperor angelfish would be as follows:

Phylum	Vertebrata
Class	Osteichthyes
Order	Perciformes
Family	Pomacanthidae
Genus	*Pomacanthus*
Species	*imperator*

Introduced plants

There are trees and shrubs that have been purposely introduced to the Seychelles for erosion control. They include mahogany, *Swietenia macrophylla*, the cocoplum, *Chrysobalanus icaco*, with its edible fruits, and the tall, flat-crowned albizia, *Paraserianthes falcataria*, which has become an invading nuisance. A wilt disease has spread among many of the large trees in Seychelles with most of the sandragons and albizias being affected, as well as many of the *takamakas*. The brown, dead trees make a stark statement against the remaining green of the forest.

Many of the plants introduced for agricultural purposes have become naturalised and are widespread throughout the Seychelles. Coconuts dominated the Seychelles agriculture from the mid-1800s to around 1960 and, though no longer always grown in managed plantations, it is still the dominant species on many of the low coralline islands. Seedlings are grown from the germinating nut and the tree becomes productive after 15–18 years. They bear fruit for about 50 years and each coconut weighs about 1.5–2kg. The Seychellois have a hundred or more uses for coconuts. Fronds provide thatching for walls, roofs and fences while trunks make sturdy timber for furniture. Leaves are used to make hats, bags, baskets, brooms, brushes and mats. Fermenting sap makes a potent toddy, *kalou*, and the growing shoot is a delicious substitute for the *palmiste* in a millionaire's salad. Green coconuts provide a cool, hygienic and refreshing juice that can be drunk straight from the nut. The thick, white flesh of mature coconuts is delicious as a filling snack, and coconut milk squeezed from the grated flesh is an important component of Creole cuisine. Copra is the dried flesh from which coconut oil is extracted, and that too has umpteen uses. Even the dry, brown coconut husks have uses – they make excellent charcoal as well as providing fuel for copra driers or calorifiers.

Cinnamon was once an important crop, with the bark providing cinnamon quills and powder, and the oil, distilled from the leaves, used in the perfume industry. Cinnamon trees are now widespread throughout the mountain slopes of the granitic Seychelles. Vanilla used to account for a significant amount of foreign earnings, but since the manufacture of synthetic essence it has become unprofitable. The vines have become naturalised and can be seen creeping on many of the mountainsides.

Fruits of a great variety are widely grown on the islands. Jackfruit, locally called *zak*, has large, oval, edible fruits growing directly from the trunk. Breadfruit has the wonderful Creole name of *fraipen*, probably because it is so commonly fried and eaten. It has distinctive, palmate leaves and large, round fruits growing from the branches. The story goes that any foreigners eating the fruit will surely return to the Seychelles! Other common fruits include banana, mango, papaya, crispy white jamalac, smelly durian, guava and spicy nutmeg. The market in Victoria is probably the best place to see and sample many of these exotic fruits.

INVERTEBRATES

The various habitats of the Seychelles are home to an amazing variety of creepy-crawlies. Over 3,500 species of insects have been documented, and there is a close association between endemic insects and endemic plants. Beetles are the most well-represented group with about 700 species, followed by some 400 species of flies. One endemic insect of note is the **giant tenebrionid beetle**, *Pulposipes herculaenus*, which is only found on Frégate. The spherical, mud nests of potter wasps are frequently seen but the yellow wasps, with their paper-like hanging nests, should be avoided as they can inflict a nasty sting. The insect faunas of the high granitic islands and low coralline islands are remarkably distinct with less than 10% shared between the two types of islands. Butterflies provide a good example of this, with surprisingly few found in the granitic Seychelles but numerous, brightly coloured species flutter around the islands of the Aldabra group. There are some introduced insect species, most of which have become pests. One of these is the crazy-ant, *Anopolepsis longipes*, which reportedly arrived in Mahé from Southeast Asia in 1962, and is now infesting various seabird colonies.

Large, harmless, orange-legged millipedes are frequently seen on the granitic islands, but be careful of the centipedes as they have a nasty bite. The golden orb spider, *Nephila madagascariensis*, is abundant in the granitic Seychelles and their conspicuous webs are often seen glistening between trees. On Frégate, there is an extremely large, flattened spider, *Amblypige*, which reaches up to 25cm across, as well as a large scorpion, *Chiromachus ochropus*, which is found under rocks or piles of coconut husks. Two species of ticks have been found to parasitise nesting seabirds in the Seychelles and ticks are also found on domesticated animals such as dogs and cattle.

Land and freshwater molluscs in the granitic Seychelles are generally endemic, small and dull in colour, and most survive in the relic forests on the summits of the islands. In the Vallée de Mai on Praslin the large snail, *Stylodonta studeriana*, and the Praslin snail, *Pachnodus praslinus*, can be seen on *coco de mer* palm leaves and stems while the white slug, *Vaginula seychellensis*, frequents the male flowers.

There are 32 species of land and freshwater crabs known from the Seychelles, and these include one endemic freshwater species, *Deckenia alluaudi*, which is found in streams on Mahé and Praslin. The **land crab**, *Cardisoma carnifex* is the most common terrestrial crab, and is widespread through the Seychelles. They are large, nocturnal scavengers that, though they spend most of their lives ashore, must return to the sea to spawn. Similarly, the large robber or **coconut crabs**, *Birgus latro*, also have to return to the sea to spawn. They are the largest terrestrial crabs and can attain 4kg in weight. They have big, strong claws and, when not foraging, shelter between tree roots and in burrows. They feed on a wide variety of plant material as well as scavenging on turtle eggs and hatchlings. They even climb *Pandanus* to feed on the fruits and are able to tear open fallen coconuts.

AMPHIBIANS

Despite the oceanic location of the Seychelles, the continental origin of the granitic islands accounts for the occurrence of 12 species of amphibians (11 endemic). Five of these are true frogs, and include three species of minute, secretive **sooglossids** which live at altitudes exceeding 200m on Mahé and Silhouette. They deposit their eggs in terrestrial nests in moist places, and, upon hatching, the tadpoles of *Sooglossus sechellensis* clamber on to the back of the parent male and remain there until metamorphosing into small frogs. In contrast, in *S. gardineri* no tadpole-carrying occurs, and fully developed froglets hatch from the egg capsules. **Caecilians**, which are specialised, burrowing, legless amphibians, are represented by seven species and they spend their lives hidden in rotten logs and in moist leaf litter. *Hypogeophis rostratus* is ubiquitous through the granitic islands but *Grandisonia brevis* and G. *diminutiva* are endemic to Mahé and Praslin respectively. The tree frog, *Tachycnemis seychellensis*, is found on Mahé, Praslin and La Digue. Interestingly, the green-coloured females deposit their eggs in vegetation over streams and, after hatching, the long-tailed tadpoles drop into the water below. The most wide-ranging frog in the granitic Seychelles is the African species *Rana mascareniensis* which occurs from marshy ground near the coast up into mountain forest. There are no frogs on the outer coralline islands of the Seychelles.

REPTILES

The islands of the Seychelles are surprisingly well-endowed with reptiles, ranging from tiny lizards to giant tortoises. Early explorers documented the occurrence of large crocodiles along the coast of Mahé, but they were hunted to extinction, the only remaining evidence now residing at the natural history museum in Victoria. Smaller, less dangerous relatives proliferate today, and scuttling skinks and gaudy geckos are characteristic of both the granitic and coralline islands.

Lizards

The brightly coloured, endemic *Phelsuma* **geckos**, which are of Malagasy origin, have radiated throughout the Seychelles and various species and subspecies are found in the granitic islands, Amirantes and Aldabra group. A visit to the Vallée de Mai on Praslin will guarantee sightings of green *Phelsuma* geckos (*P. astriata* and *P. sundbergi*) as they scuttle up and down *coco de mer* trunks feeding on insects. These geckos are known as *leza ver* in Creole. The bronze-eyed gecko, *Ailuronyx seychellensis* (*maguya* in Creole), which is active at night, generally hides in crevices and leaf bases of palms during the day. Other lizards widely distributed in the granitic islands are *Phyllodactylus inexpectatus*, chameleons (*Chamaleo tigris*) and *Scelotes* and *Mabuya* **skinks**. The endemic *Mabuya* skinks (*leza sek*) are predators feeding chiefly on seabird eggs and chicks, and the two species *M. sechellensis* and *M. wrightii* are remarkably abundant on islands like Cousin, Aride and Frégate. The *Scelotes* skinks (*S. braueri* and *S. gardineri*) which live in and under leaf litter are also widespread, extending up into the mountains. *Cryptoblepharus boutonii* is a widely distributed gecko inhabiting the shore and tideline of many islands but on Aldabra it extends all over the atoll. *Gehyra mutilata*, the introduced house gecko (*leza disik*), is common on the inhabited islands and can often be seen feeding on insects attracted to lights.

Snakes

Three harmless species of snakes occur on the central granitic islands. The endemic Seychelles **house snake**, *Boaedon geometricus*, is found in forests, coconut plantations, rocky slopes and villages. It is a thick-bodied, short, greyish snake with a white snout and two white stripes behind the eye. It is nocturnal and preys on rats, mice, birds, lizards and frogs. The endemic Seychelles **wolf snake**, *Lycognathopsis seychellensis*, attains 1.2m in length. It is an active, diurnal species found at all elevations and preys on lizards. It has two colour phases, namely 'yellow' when the animal is bright yellow on the underside and brown on top, and 'dark' when it is dark grey with black spots dorsally and a white underside. The **burrowing snake**, *Rampotyphlops braminus*, is a small, dark grey, blind creature that resembles an earthworm. It burrows in damp soil and leaf litter but has also been recorded living in beach sand. This species is broadly distributed outside the Seychelles and was probably inadvertently introduced by man.

Tortoises and terrapins

Giant tortoise populations in the Indian Ocean were first discovered in the 16th century. Subsequently, natural populations were exterminated from all the Seychelles islands except Aldabra by seafarers who ruthlessly exploited the lumbering creatures as a source of fresh meat. The only surviving population was saved by the first lessee of Aldabra, James Spurs, who in 1891 prohibited the killing of the giant tortoises on the atoll. *Geochelone (Dipsochelys) gigantea* is now thriving on Aldabra, and the most recent population estimates are in the region of 100,000 animals, living principally on Grande Terre.

The very existence of these ancient chelonians is limited by food, water, nesting sites and shade from the tropical sun. In order to survive – and avoid literally being cooked in their dome-shaped shells – the tortoises have to seek shade during the day, where they rest in groups under trees and shrubs. When they are out feeding in the early morning and late afternoon they generally orientate themselves so their backs face the sun, thus ensuring that their head, neck and front legs are in shade. The tortoises feed chiefly on grass turf, tree leaves, flowers and fruits.

Most mating takes place from February to May and this is a noisy affair. The heavy male, encumbered by both his and her carapace, climbs on to the female and attempts to curve his tail under her carapace to reach her cloaca. Apparently, the success rate of matings is low! Females nest between June and September, digging holes in the ground at night into which they lay clutches of golf ball-sized eggs enveloped in thick mucous. They then cover the nest with soil, the whole nesting process taking about 11 hours. The period of incubation varies from 73 to 160 days, and the hatchlings emerge from the nest just before the rainy season. They then have to survive the ravages of predators such as coconut crabs, land crabs, rats and birds. The average weight of tortoises on Grande Terre is about 21kg but on Malabar and Picard, where there is more food, they are more than double this weight and reach reproductive condition earlier than those on Grande Terre.

Aldabra tortoises have been translocated to many of the granitic islands, and visitors to Mahé can see captive ones at the Botanical Gardens in

Victoria and in the grounds of several of the hotels. On Curieuse, there is now a thriving tortoise population, and these can easily be viewed on a day trip over from Praslin. There are also free-ranging tortoise populations on Frégate and Cousin.

Three species of freshwater **terrapins** from the genus *Pelusios* have been found in the Seychelles. Although La Digue is regarded as the home of the *tortues-soupapes* as they are known in Creole, *Pelusios seychellensis*, *P. subniger* (star-bellied terrapin) and *P. castanoides* (the yellow-bellied terrapin) are also found on Mahé, Praslin and satellite granitic islands. They are carnivorous but sometimes feed on plants. Extensive draining of coastal swamps is, however, threatening some populations. A captive breeding programme is progressing well on Silhouette at the Nature Protection Trust of Seychelles.

Marine turtles

Four species of marine turtles are known from the Seychelles. Two of them, the leatherback, *Dermochelys coriacea*, and the loggerhead, *Caretta caretta*, although found in other parts of the western Indian Ocean, are rarely seen in Seychelles waters. The **hawksbill turtle**, *Eretmochelys imbricata*, and the **green turtle**, *Chelonia myda*, are widespread throughout the Seychelles, although their populations have been decimated by harvesting for 'tortoiseshell' and meat.

Turtles have a complicated life history that includes both terrestrial and marine phases, and visitors to the Seychelles have the possibility of seeing them in both environments. Mating of turtles occurs at sea, and the females come ashore on sandy beaches to lay their eggs in holes they dig above the high tide mark. The eggs hatch after about two months, and the little hatchlings emerge from the sand to make their way down to the water's edge. On entering the water, the hatchlings are widely dispersed by ocean currents. They then enter the feeding phase, which is largely in coastal waters, and attaining reproductive maturity, start the breeding phase. There are often clear migrations between feeding and breeding grounds. Hawksbill turtles are usually seen in association with coral reefs where they feed on coral polyps and sponges. Green turtles, by contrast, are largely vegetarian and feed on seagrasses and seaweeds.

Both species nest on sandy beaches although the hawksbill appears to prefer more protected beaches. Although the green turtle has been reported to nest year-round, nesting peaks during the southeast trade wind period from June to September, whereas nesting by the hawksbill occurs mainly during the northwest monsoon from October to January. Hawksbill turtles usually attempt to nest under vegetation above the high tide mark and, surprisingly, in the Seychelles have a tendency to nest in daylight hours. Although hawksbill turtles may nest up to five times per season, the average seasonal complement is two, and there is 'site tenacity', with females known to return to the same beach. Hawksbill turtles do not appear to nest annually, and studies of tagged animals on Cousin show inter-season intervals of 2–4 years. Clutch size averages about 170 eggs. Green turtle nesting has been reported at more than 20 islands in the Seychelles, but they have been most studied in the Aldabra group where they nest just above the beach crest in unvegetated sand. Green turtles nest at night, about three times in a season, and show nest site tenacity with a 2–3 year period between nesting. Clutch size is about 125 eggs. Ghost crabs are voracious predators on turtle eggs and hatchlings, while birds frequently attack hatchlings as they make their way to the sea. Feral rats and dogs can also impact turtle populations by digging up nests.

MAMMALS
Terrestrial mammals
Bats are widespread throughout the Seychelles, and two species of endemic bats are found on the granitic islands. The **Seychelles fruit bat**, *Pteropus seychellensis*, spends much of the day roosting in casuarina and albizia trees. Also known as flying foxes, they usually emerge at dusk to feed on soft, sweet fruits. These bats can be quite large, and adult males reach up to 600g. The sheath-tailed bat, *Coleura seychellensis*, is much smaller (only weighing about 10g) and much rarer. They are insectivorous, and roost in caves on the granitic islands. The fruit bat also occurs on the atolls of the Aldabra group, together with three other species of small bats, namely *Taphozous mauritianus*, *Triaenops furculu* and *Tadarida pusilla*.

There have been several species of mammals introduced to the Seychelles over the years. The **tenrec**, *Tenrec ecaudatus*, which is rat-like, light brown in colour with quills on the neck and back, has spread through much of the hill forest where they forage on leaf litter invertebrates and fallen fruit. Rats and mice were introduced during the late 18th century and now occur on most of the islands. Rats cause damage to crops, and also prey on eggs and chicks. Rabbits, cats and dogs have also been introduced and feral cats have been blamed for the decline in several bird species. Domestic pigs, goats, cattle and horses are found on the farms. Feral goats prevent regeneration of natural vegetation and are a problem on Aldabra.

Marine mammals
The distribution ranges of many species of **whales** and **dolphins** include the waters of the Seychelles EEZ. Prior to 1915, sperm whales, *Physeter catodon*, were harvested around Bird and Denis islands on the edge of the Seychelles Bank, and the carcasses were towed to the whaling station on Ste Anne for processing. Recent boat-based and aerial surveys have confirmed that sperm whales and their calves still frequent this area. Humpback whales, *Megaptera novaeangliae*, are sighted from Aldabra during the winter and spring months when these large baleen whales migrate from Antarctica to the tropical waters of the western Indian Ocean for breeding purposes. Bottle-nosed dolphins, *Tursiops truncatus*, Risso's dolphins, *Grampus grisius*, spotted dolphins, *Stenella attentuata*, and the acrobatic spinner dolphins, *Stenella longirostris*, are regularly sighted from vessels traversing Seychelles waters. The strange-looking

vegetarian **dugongs**, *Dugong dugon*, which frequent shallow, tropical lagoons where they feed on seagrasses, used to occur throughout the Seychelles but are now only seen on very rare occasions.

BIRDS

The Seychelles, uniquely positioned in the western Indian Ocean, is home, breeding site and migratory stopover for a wide variety of birds. The Seychelles land birds, with affinities to Madagascar, Asia and Africa, have evolved into new species and subspecies over the millennia, and there are 17 endemic species. Many of the Seychelles islands are globally important seabird breeding colonies, and the majority of the birds nest during the southeast trade wind season, from April to October. Although the actual number of species is relatively low, a staggering number of seabirds breed on the coralline islands. Many can also be seen around the inner granitic islands of Aride, Cousin and Bird. Palaearctic migrants from Europe and Asia stop over in the Seychelles and some stay the entire season, while others are mere passing travellers.

One bird species has become extinct in the Seychelles since man intervened on these fragile islands. Habitat destruction was the main cause of the demise of the green parakeet, *Psittacula eupatria*, but it was also indiscriminately shot as it was believed to devour the crops.

Land birds

It is quite remarkable that, on such a tiny land mass as the Seychelles, there are 17 endemic land-bird species, 12 of which are found on the granitic islands and five in the Aldabra group. The other two dozen species of land birds occurring in the Seychelles are also found in Madagascar and the Comoros, making them endemic to the western Indian Ocean. However, some of the most commonly seen birds are introduced species that have developed successful breeding populations in the Seychelles.

The most commonly seen bird is the **Madagascar fody**, *Foudia madagascariensis*. In the breeding season, the male assumes a glowing orange-red plumage while the female is always a dull streaky brown. The noisy, gregarious **Indian mynah**, *Acridotheres tristis*, is widespread, and the white window patches on the wings are conspicuous when in flight. One of the characteristic bird sounds of the Seychelles is the gentle cooing of the **barred ground dove**, *Geopelia striata*.

The most amazing assortment of birds arrives on the Seychelles islands during seasonal migrations as it is the only landfall in a huge expanse of ocean. They range from Eleanor's falcon to European rollers, tree pipits, hoopoes and barn swallows, as well as a selection of waders such as terek sandpipers, greenshanks and godwits.

Endemic birds of the granitic islands

The national bird, the **Seychelles black parrot**, *Coracopsis barklyi*, is closely related to the Vasa parrots of Madagascar. It is not really black, more of a dark chocolate colour, and can be found on Praslin and Curieuse foraging in the forests for fruits. The **Seychelles blue pigeon**, *Alectroenas pulcherrima*, is a handsome bird, deep blue with scarlet wattles, and it occurs around fruiting trees on the main islands.

One of the most beautiful birds is the **Seychelles black paradise flycatcher**, *Tersiphone corvine*. There are only about 120 birds left, and they are confined to the island of La Digue where they can be seen in the flycatcher reserve and elsewhere on the island. The striking long-tailed male, black all over with a dark blue bill, differs from the female which has a shorter tail, white underparts, a black head and ginger upper parts.

The **Seychelles magpie robin**, *Copsychus sechellarum*, is teetering on the edge of extinction as habitat destruction and introduced cats and rats caused a rapid decline in their numbers. These black-and-white birds spend most of their time grubbing in the leaf litter feeding on insects. The last remaining foothold of the magpie robin was on the island of Frégate but the population reached an alarming low of only 24 birds. Several were relocated to Cousin where they started breeding to the point where the island has almost reached carrying capacity. More recently they have been relocated to Cousine and Aride, where they have settled and are breeding successfully. There are now over 100 magpie robins on four islands. The survival success story, however, belongs to the **Seychelles warbler**, *Acrocephalus seychellensis*. From a mere 29 birds, endangered and on the red data list, there are now several hundred, breeding well and thriving on Cousin, Cousine and Aride. The warbler, a dull olive brown, is easy to see on these islands as it flits through the undergrowth calling and chattering.

One of the rarest birds is the **Seychelles Scops owl**, *Otus insularis*. It is confined to Mahé where it resides in the deep forests of the Morne Seychellois National Park and can be heard making its deep croaking call in the evenings. Little is known about this enigmatic little brown owl, and the first nest was only discovered in 1999.

The **Seychelles white-eye**, *Zosterops modestus*, is a tiny, grey bird with a white eye-ring. They are difficult to find but they frequent degraded woodland. Small groups can be observed at La Misère near the hotel school, and a large population (around 200) was recently found on Conception off the west coast of Mahé, but getting there to see them is extremely difficult. A small group was transported to Frégate, where they are thriving. Another little bird found on the granitic islands is the **Seychelles sunbird**, *Nectarinia dussumieri*. It has a typical, long, curved bill for sipping nectar and the male shows a deep blue iridescence on the throat and breast. The **Seychelles fody**, *Foudia seychellarum*, is dull brown with a large, wedge-shaped bill, but in breeding plumage the male has a bright yellow face. These birds, known locally as the *tok-tok*, scavenge untended seabird eggs, and are confined to Cousin, Cousine and Frégate.

The **Seychelles kestrel**, *Falco araea*, preys on lizards and geckos and is most commonly seen on Mahé on top of buildings or around rock faces. Its call, described as 'ti-ti-ti', gives rise to the Creole name of *katiti*. The widespread **Seychelles turtle dove**, *Streptopelia picturata*, has interbred to a large extent with the Madagascar turtle dove and it is not clear whether any pure forms still exist. The **Seychelles swiftlet**, *Collocalia elaphra*, is the only small swift. They are often seen flying in groups near the mountains of Mahé, Praslin and La Digue where they nest in rocky areas. One of the most commonly heard birds in the forests is the noisy **Seychelles bulbul**, *Hypsipetes crassirostris*, which has an untidy black crest and an orange bill.

Birds of the Aldabra group

Five endemic species are known from the Aldabra archipelago. The last remaining flightless bird of the Indian Ocean is the **Aldabra rail**, *Dryolimnas aldabranus*. Confined to Aldabra, the rails are surviving well on the islands of Picard, Polymnie and Malabar, which are the best places to see these fearless and curious birds. The **Aldabra drongo**, *Dicrurus aldabranus*, black with a forked tail, is a very territorial bird and will even chase the kestrels and crows. The **Aldabra fody**, *Foudia aldabrana*, a nondescript bird (LBJ, or little brown job) can be seen around the settlement on Picard. In breeding plumage, however, the male develops a yellow belly and bright red head, chest and rump. **Abbot's sunbird**, *Nectarinia abbotii*, is found on Cosmoledo, Astove and Assumption but not on Aldabra where the Souimanga sunbird rules the roost. In breeding plumage the male has a green iridescence over the head and chest and a black belly. Despite extensive searches, the **Aldabra brush warbler**, *Nesillas aldabrana*, has not been seen since 1983.

Other land birds common in the Aldabra archipelago share an ancestry with those from Madagascar or Comoros. The **Madagascar sacred ibis**, *Threskiornis bernieri*, with sky-blue eyes, can be seen around the settlement on Picard. Others include the **Madagascar coucal**, *Centropus toulou*, **Madagascar nightjar**, *Caprimulgus madagascariensis*, **Madagacar bulbul**, *Hypsipetes madagascariensis*, and the **Souimanga sunbird**, *Nectarina souimanga*. Only found on Cosmoledo and Astove, the **Madagascar cisticola**, *Cisticola cherina*, is easily seen flitting between the rocky islets.

Shore birds

Also known as wading birds, most of the birds along the shores of the Seychelles are migratory and breed in Europe. These Palaearctic species winter in the southern hemisphere spending the entire non-breeding period in the Seychelles where they frequent both granitic and coralline islands. Whimbrels, *Numenius phaeopus*, plovers, *Pluvialis*, and sandplovers, *Charadrius*, are common, and ruddy turnstones, *Arenaria interpres*, can be seen throughout the year. Flocks of several hundred **crab plovers**, *Dromas ardeola*, occur on Aldabra and Cosmoledo and there are sometimes over a thousand on St François in the Alphonse group. There are usually a couple of these enigmatic birds that breed in the Gulf of Oman, to be found on Mahé and Silhouette.

Seabirds

Eighteen species of seabirds breed in the Seychelles and it is possible to see most of them on the granitic islands of Aride, Cousin and Bird.

Nine tern species breed in the Seychelles and the most spectacular are the hundreds of thousands of **sooty terns**, *Sterna fuscata*, that nest, during the southeast trades, on the low coralline islands and Aride (the only hilltop granitic breeding site). Sooty terns are the most aerial of all birds, spending many years on the wing before reaching breeding maturity. Their mottled eggs are laid on the sand. The most extensive breeding colony is on Cosmoledo with an estimated 1.2 million pairs. Sooty tern eggs are considered a great national delicacy: from 1944 to 1965, one million eggs were collected annually. There were sufficient for the local market and the yolks were also exported. At present, in June each year, some eggs are still collected from Bird and Desnoeufs under the control of the Islands Development Company.

Brown noddies, *Anous stolidus*, and **lesser noddies**, *A. tenuirostris*, are brown-coloured terns and difficult to tell apart at a distance. Both species breed throughout the Seychelles. Up to 170,000 pairs of lesser noddies can breed on Aride in a season. Numbers do fluctuate enormously and are dependent on food supplies. The pure white **fairy tern**, *Gygis alba*, is common on most of the islands. The single, mottled egg is laid in a slight groove on a bare branch, and, as the chick hatches, the feet emerge first and cling on to the branch for dear life. Fairy terns breed throughout the year and can be found on nearly all of the Seychelles islands. The largest tern is the **Caspian tern**, *Hydroprogne caspia*, which has a massive red bill. A few pairs nest on Aldabra, the only known oceanic breeding site in the world. The **swift or crested tern**, *Sterna bergii*, is smaller than the Caspian tern, has a yellow bill and also breeds on Aldabra on rocky *îlots* in the middle of the lagoon. Also breeding on Aldabra is the elegant **black-naped tern**, *S. sumatrana*, which lays its eggs on the bare *champignon*. One of the most beautiful terns is the **roseate tern**, *S. dougalii*, which has accentuated tail streamers and a rosy flush to the breast in the breeding season. These birds breed on Aride, but numbers appear to be declining for no apparent reason. **Bridled terns**, *S. anthetus*, are never seen in large numbers. They can be confused with sooty terns but are seldom seen far out to sea as they generally return to roost at night.

White-tailed tropicbirds, *Phaethon lepturus*, which have long, white tail streamers, fly gracefully around most of the granitic islands. They nest on the ground close to a protective rock or tree trunk. The larger **red-tailed tropicbird**, *P. rubricauda*, is not as easily observed as only a few nest on Aride and most are on Aldabra.

Greater frigatebirds, *Fregata ariel*, and **lesser frigatebirds**, *F. minor*, with their long, angled wings and deeply forked tails, are the most spectacular aerial birds. The males are generally black but the females have more white on the chest. As they take about five to six years to mature, the varying juvenile plumage can cause identification problems. They nest in profusion in the mangroves of Aldabra, cheek by jowl with the unsuspecting red-footed boobies, which they harass until the boobies regurgitate their last meals. As the frigatebirds do not have a good waterproofing system on their feathers, they do not dive into the water. During the non-breeding season, frigatebirds roost on Aride and can be seen soaring over the island.

Boobies belong to the same family as gannets, and three species breed on the outer coralline islands. The most commonly seen is the **red-footed booby**, *Sula sula*, with thousands nesting in the mangroves in the Aldabra archipelago. They are characterised by their distinctive red feet. These birds will spend hours circling a ship at sea, and will often perch on the rigging. The large, ground-nesting **masked booby**, *S. dactylatra*, is not a widespread bird but can be seen in the vicinity of Cosmoledo where it breeds. Also breeding on Cosmoledo is the **brown booby**, *S. leucogaster*, which has a brown chest, and can be confused with young masked boobies.

Wedge-tailed shearwaters, *Puffinus pacificus*, and **Audubon's shearwaters**, *P. lherminieri*, which nest in burrows are seldom seen on land during the day as they spend most of the daylight hours fishing far out to sea.

CORAL REEFS

Coral reefs are the most characteristic feature of the turquoise-blue waters surrounding the Seychelles islands. They are extremely important in ensuring coastal protection, supporting artisanal fisheries and providing the focus for diving tourism. There are three main types: fringing reefs, platform reefs and atolls. Barrier reefs are absent from the Seychelles, although they occur in other parts of the western Indian Ocean.

Reef types

Fringing reefs are associated with the granitic islands of the Seychelles Bank and are most extensive on Mahé and Praslin. There are considerable differences between reefs exposed to the southeast trade winds and those in more sheltered localities. The reefs along the southeast coast of Mahé are continuous and vary in width from 500 to 750m. The reefs along the west coast of Mahé are small and discontinuous, and are mainly found in bays like Baie Ternay and Port Launay. Between the bays, the high granite cliffs drop steeply into the sea and may lack reefs altogether, though some corals grow directly on the granite. On Praslin, the fringing reefs are much more extensive relative to the size of the island. They are widest on the southwest coast where they extend nearly 3km seawards, though elsewhere they may be as narrow as 400m. On La Digue, the reefs are widest on the west coast.

Platform reefs occur at several islands and at Coëtivy and D'Arros large parts of their upper surfaces are covered with land. At Plat and Providence, however, the platform reefs have large shallow lagoons and very little land area. Assumption and St Pierre consist of raised platform reefs which do not exceed 8m above sea level.

There are several true **atolls** in the Seychelles. Farquhar (172km^2) is the largest with the main peripheral reef about 1km wide surrounding a lagoon of about 14m in depth. St Joseph's in the Amirantes is much smaller with the peripheral reef ranging from 0.6–1.2km in width, and surrounding a shallow lagoon of about 6m in depth. The vertical thickness of the coral in the Amirantes has been determined to be about 1km.

The main **raised atolls** of the southern Seychelles are Aldabra,

Cosmoledo and Astove. Aldabra is 34km long and up to 14km across with a rim of raised reef limestone which averages 2km in width. There are four coral-encrusted entrance channels into the lagoon – Grande Passe is 20m deep. The lagoon itself is shallow, and the lagoon floor consists of scoured bedrock with a thin veneer of sediment. The coastal cliffs on the seaward side of these atolls rise about 4m above the level of the reef flat. On Aldabra, there is a conspicuous terrace at about 4m and a higher surface level at about 8m. These features indicate a complex history of submergence and emergence. Geophysical evidence from Aldabra indicates that the coral cap varies between 0.6–1.6km in thickness.

Corals and reef zonation

The western Indian Ocean is a centre for diversity of corals, and some 51 genera of scleractinian or **hard corals** are known from the granitic Seychelles islands and 47 genera from Aldabra. Recent scientific expeditions have recorded a further 40 hard coral species to bring the Seychelles species list to some 161 (excluding *Acropora* species). Hard corals are essentially colonies of polyps living within a communal calcium carbonate skeleton. The colonies can take on many shapes and forms which, amongst others, may be branching, columnar, tabular, encrusting or massive domes. Identification of many of the species requires examination of microscopic features of the skeleton but some of the more well-known species include staghorn coral, *Acropora formosa*, table coral, *Acropora clathrata*, knob-horned coral, *Pocillopora verrucosa*, massive domes of *Porites lutea* and *P. solida*, brain coral, *Platygyra daedalea*, honeycomb corals, *Favites*, and turbinate coral, *Turbinaria mesenterina*. Also easily recognised are mushroom corals, *Fungia scutaria*, which are actually solitary flat polyps, and colourful cup or turret corals, *Dendrophyllia*, which are solitary but grow in clumps on rock surfaces.

Soft corals are also important components of coral reefs and, again, identification to species level often requires microscopic examination of various anatomical features. Some of the more well-known are organ-pipe coral, *Tubipora musica*, dead man's fingers, *Alcyonium flaccidum*, leather corals, *Lobophyton*, soft-lobed corals, *Sinularia*, fleshy mushroom corals, *Sarcophyton glaucum*, thistle corals, *Dendronephthya*, branching soft corals *Nephthea* and stalked soft corals like *Xenia crassa* and *Anthelia glauca*.

Spiral black coral, *Cirrhipathes*, and bushy black coral, *Antipathes*, are other easily recognised corals usually found on deeper reefs together with seafans or gorgonians like *Supergorgia* and *Rumphella*. **Fire coral**, *Millepora*, although not actually a true coral, appears in various forms, and subjects the unwary diver who touches it to an extremely painful sting.

The zonation of the shallow fringing reefs of the granitic islands differs considerably from that on the exposed oceanic atolls. At Mahé or Praslin, if one swims out to the fringing reef from the beach at high tide, one will pass over a rippled sand zone followed by beds of seagrasses. The sand will then become interspersed with cobble ridges, seaweeds like *Sargassum*, *Turbinaria* and *Halimeda*, and large coral colonies of *Acropora*, *Pocillopora*, *Porites*, *Goniatrea*

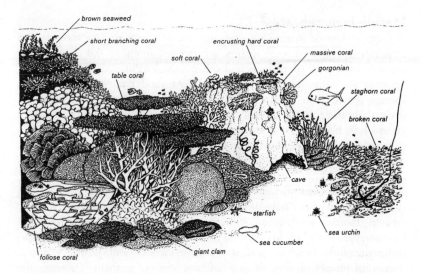

Typical shallow-water coral reef of the western Indian Ocean. Reprinted with permission from Richmond (1997)

and *Favia*. Before reaching the reef edge one will encounter a narrow seaweed ridge with small coral colonies which dries at low tide. The reef edge has a gentle seaward slope and much of the surface is covered with encrusting calcareous algae. The common encrusting corals in this rough water habitat are *Pocillopora*, *Acropora*, *Goniastrea* and *Millepora* (fire coral). On the outer slopes of the reef various species of *Acropora* are dominant, and massive corals like *Porites*, *Favia* and *Leptoria* are more common on the lower slope. Corals decrease rapidly in abundance below 10m depth.

At Aldabra, the zonation of the reef is more vertical. In shallow water from 0–6m there are branching and columnar corals like *Acropora*, followed by a highly diverse zone of soft and honeycomb faviid corals which extends to about 14m depth. Below this, down to about 28m, the reef is dominated by honeycomb faviid corals.

Coral bleaching

During the summer of 1997–98, raised coastal water temperatures throughout the western Indian Ocean (attaining 34°C) led to wide-scale bleaching of corals in the shallow waters surrounding most of the Seychelles islands. This resulted in the death of the coral polyps, followed by colonisation and growth of algae on the remaining coral skeletons. As the corals are dead, boring organisms undermine the colonies, and they slowly break up and become reduced to rubble. Scientific investigations have revealed that corals on the deeper reef walls of many of the southern islands were not as badly affected. Recent reports indicate that regeneration is occurring in some places with settlement of young corals particularly evident around the granitic islands where the corals often grow directly on the granite.

Marine invertebrates

A huge variety of marine invertebrates including encrusting sponges and tunicates (sea squirts), tube worms, crustaceans, molluscs and echinoderms are associated with corals reefs and other coastal habitats of the Seychelles. Sponges are extremely common and diverse, and range from encrusting species growing on granite boulders to huge barrel sponges. Tunicates, particularly the colonial species, are often confused with sponges, and both groups have been poorly studied in the western Indian Ocean. Many species of tubeworm are found on the reefs but the most spectacular is *Sabellastarte sanctijosephi* which has a brightly coloured featherduster-like crown which is quickly retracted into the tube when disturbed by divers.

The **crustaceans** include various types of colourful snapper shrimps (Caridea), coral crabs (Trapeziidae) and anemone crabs (Porcellanidae). Spiny lobsters, *Panulirus versicolor* and *P. longipes*, respectively known as *omar ver* and *omar rouz*, generally hide in caves and crevices in the reef. Ghost crabs, *Ocypode*, frequent sandy beaches, and sunbathing visitors will probably notice numerous holes with little mounds of sand adjacent to them. These are the burrows of ghost crabs, and these swift decapods are most active at night when they can be seen scuttling along the water's edge scavenging for food. Coconut or robber crabs, *Birgus latro*, are sometimes found on the upper shore but generally inhabit beach vegetation, coconut groves and pandanus thickets. Three species of rock crabs (Grapsidae) can be seen scampering over rocky intertidal areas, while on mudflats and amongst mangroves, several species of burrowing fiddler crabs, *Uca*, and marsh crabs (Sesarminae) are found. Male fiddler crabs have a characteristically enlarged claw which they use in waving displays to establish territories and attract females. The marsh crabs typically have equal-sized, bright red or orange claws.

Echinoderms are a noticeable part of the marine fauna in the Seychelles, and most of the 150 species are widespread tropical Indo-Pacific forms. The long-spined black sea urchin, *Diadema savignyi*, is common, particularly where the reefs have been damaged. When diving or wading, care should be taken not to get spiked by their sharp spines as such an injury can be very painful. Slate pencil urchins, *Heterocentrus*, are also found on exposed reefs whilst, in sandy areas, fragile sand dollars, *Echinodiscus*, and heart urchins occur. Sea cucumbers are abundant on reef flats and seagrass beds, and range from the stocky species like *Holothuria nobilis* to long, snakelike species *Synapta maculata* that can attain over 2m in length. Starfishes include large cushion stars, *Culcita*, the long-armed, colourful *Linkia*, and the undesirable and extremely prickly crown-of-thorns starfish, *Acanthaster planci*, which is notorious for its reef-devouring habits. Brittle stars with their snake-like legs are generally difficult to spot and their close relatives, the basket stars, are also usually well-hidden during the day, but at night they creep out and extend their arms into the water column to trap food particles. Similarly, the featherstars are also active at night and also hang on to corals, extending their arms to sieve food from the water.

Marine **molluscs** in the Seychelles are well-represented by about 450 species of bivalves, gastropods (snails) and nudibranchs. Giant clams, *Tridacna*, are some of the most conspicuous bivalves but there are many smaller species in tropical waters. These include *Donax* which are small, wedge-shaped mussels that actively burrow on sandy shores. They are favoured by the Seychellois for *tec-tec* soup. Large conchs (Strombidae), a variety of cowries, *Cypraea*, snow-white egg shells, *Ovula ovum*, green turbans, *Turbo marmoratus*, helmet shells (Cassidae), tritons (Ranellidae), murex shells (Muricidae), olive shells (Olividae), and the poisonous cone shells, *Conus*, are some of the more well-known gastropods occurring on coral reefs. Nudibranchs, which are marine snails without shells, display some of the most striking colours found on reefs, and numerous species including the large (up to 30cm) Spanish dancer, *Hexabranchus marginatus*, are found on the Seychelles reefs. Frequently, while diving you can spot shoals of small squid (Loliginidae) swimming in the water column. Their jet-like propulsion and chameleon-like ability to change colour rapidly make them fascinating subjects to observe. Well-camouflaged octopuses are also sometimes seen hiding in crevices of the reefs.

FISHES

A huge variety of marine fishes is found in the Seychelles waters, and latest lists indicate that nearly a thousand species have been recorded in the area. However, there is only one species of freshwater fish, the endemic Seychelles killifish, *Pachypanchax playfairii*, which is found in streams on some of the granitic islands. Most of the fishes are widely distributed Indo-Pacific species associated with coral reefs, but wide-ranging open water fishes like tunas and billfishes are also common in the oceanic waters of the EEZ. Endemism among fishes in the Seychelles is very low. There are some specific variations in distribution and abundance of fishes amongst the islands which can be related to the availability of suitable habitats, the ability of the species to disperse and the role of human fishing pressure.

Coral reef fish communities are a kaleidoscope of colour, and are characterised by numerous small species from many fish families. They include the butterflyfishes (Chaetodontidae), angelfishes (Pomacanthidae), surgeonfishes (Acanthuridae), damselfishes (Pomacentridae), wrasses (Labridae), cardinalfishes (Apogonidae), goldies (*Anthias*), triggerfishes (Balistidae), filefishes (Monacanthidae) and the majestic Moorish idols, *Zanclus canescens*. These fishes generally swim around the coral heads, often ducking for cover as a snorkeller or scuba-diver approaches. Larger species found on the reefs include snappers (Lutjanidae), parrotfishes (Scaridae), batfishes (Ephippidae), groupers (Serranidae), emperors (Lethrinidae) and sweetlips (Haemulidae). By day, the red soldierfishes and squirrelfishes (Holocentridae) are rarely seen as they hide in caves and crevices but, at night, they emerge to feed on the reef. Shoals of sweepers, *Pempheris*, often form a silvery-brown curtain at the entrance to caves and overhangs. Well-camouflaged species include lizardfishes (Synodontidae), hawkfishes (Cirrhitidae), small gobies (Gobiidae) and blennies (Blenniidae) and other larger poisonous species like stonefish, *Synaceia verricosa*, and scorpionfishes (Scorpaenidae). The magnificent lionfishes, *Pterois*, with their elongate fins, are usually seen hovering nearly motionless over the reef but, beware, they can inflict nasty injuries to unwary divers. Several species of moray eels (Muraenidae) frequent crevices, holes and caves in the reefs, and care should be taken not to stick your hands into such places.

Coral reefs are also home to some of the strangest fishes. Divers are often surprised when they see the elongate, tubular-snouted trumpetfish, *Aulostomus chinensis*, and cornetfish, *Fistularia petimba*, hovering over the reef. Some of the oddities of the reefs include boxfishes and cowfishes (Ostraciidae) with their bodies encased in bony plates, pufferfishes (Tetraodontidae) which, as a defence against predators, can inflate their bodies into spherical balls by swallowing water or air, and porcupine fishes (Diodontidae) which, in addition to being covered with prominent spines, can also inflate their rotund bodies. Whilst on the subject of peculiar fishes, flying fishes (Exocoetidae) cannot be omitted. These fishes, spotted when voyaging between the islands, are characterised by elongate pectoral fins and a forked tail with an enlarged lower lobe. When chased by predators, they erupt from the surface of the water and glide in the air for considerable distances, frequently dipping their beating tails into the water for extra propulsion.

Coral reef fishes also exhibit peculiar lifestyles and associations. For example, the little cleaner wrasse, *Labroides dimidiatus*, removes parasites from other fishes. When diving, stopping to observe the agility and apparent foolhardiness of the wrasse as it nimbly nips parasites from inside the mouths and gill covers of large predators like groupers is a worthwhile diversion. In fact, the wrasses have 'cleaning stations', and one can often see fishes queuing up for the service! Cleaner shrimps provide a similar service. Another interesting association is that of the clownfish and anemone. Clownfish pairs, *Amphiprion*, immune to the stings of the anemones, shelter from predators among the tentacles of their hosts. These fishes attach their eggs to the reef near the anemone, and guard them aggressively until the little larvae hatch out. Look carefully at the shoals of goldies, *Anthias*, over the reef and you will see that the larger ones are more reddish in colour with elongate dorsal and tail-fin filaments. These are the males; the gaggle of other bright-orange goldies are the females in the harems. Interestingly, these fishes are hermaphrodite and capable of changing their sex. If the male is removed, one of the females will change into a male. Similarly, the parrot fishes can also change sex and, as they exhibit colour changes with age and sex, there have been several instances where ichthyologists have actually described juveniles, males and females as separate species!

While scuba diving, take time out from peering at the reef to stop and look up into the water column. You will be richly rewarded as, above the reef, shoals of iridescent blue and gold fusiliers (Caesionidae) provide a breathtaking mobile canopy. Roving predators like jacks and trevallys (Carangidae) could be passing by, and you could even spot a lurking barracuda, *Sphyraena*, waiting for a meal. The pelagic domain is also home to shoals of mackerel, *Rastrelliger kanagurta*, as well as the fast-swimming tunas and billfishes, and underwater sightings of these are always exciting.

The seagrass beds inshore of the reefs provide an important nursery area for juveniles of numerous fish species, and snorkelling in these areas can reveal all sorts of strange and unusual species. Shoals of herbivorous rabbitfishes (Siganidae) and juvenile parrotfishes (Scaridae) are common and goatfishes (Mullidae) with their chin barbels, flattened soles (Soleidae and Cynoglossidae) and flounders (Bothidae) can be spotted in sandy areas around seagrass beds. Some unusual species like elongate pipefishes (Sygnathidae), seahorses, *Hippocampus*, and the strange razorfishes, *Aeoliscus strigatus*, which swim with their heads pointing downwards, find shelter amongst the seagrass. Silvery half-beaks (Hemirhamphidae) also shoal near the surface in sheltered lagoons.

Sharks are plentiful in tropical waters, and around reefs the most likely ones to be seen are the nurse shark, *Nebrius ferrgineus*, the whitetip reef shark, *Triaenodon obesus*, and the blacktip reef shark, *Carcharinus melanpterus*, which has been known to attack man, so do exercise caution. Whale sharks, *Rhincodon typus*, which can exceed 15m in length, occur in the waters around the Seychelles, particularly during the months of August to November. Despite being the largest fish in the sea, their diet consists mainly of plankton which they filter from the water passing over their specialised gills. A dive with these harmless circum-tropical monsters of the deep is an awesome experience.

Various species of **rays** frequent reefs, and some of those most likely to be seen are eagle rays, *Aetobatus narinari*, which seem to glide effortlessly over the reef, and stingrays (Dasyatidae) which usually hide in caves. It is always spectacular to see a manta ray, *Manta birostris*, underwater especially as wing-to-wing they can exceed 6m. When voyaging between the islands one sometimes sees them leaping out of the water and landing with a big splash, a behaviour believed to dislodge persistent parasites.

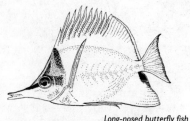

Long-nosed butterfly fish

For a
unique holiday
experience,
you need a
unique
tour operator

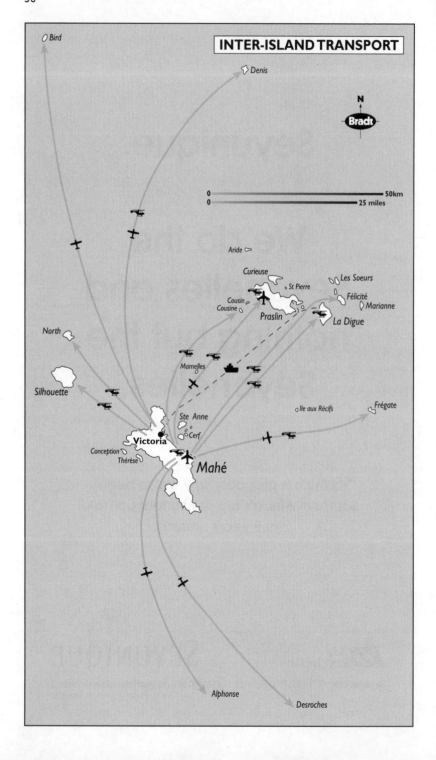

INTER-ISLAND TRANSPORT

N

Bradt

0 ————————————— 50km
0 ————————————— 25 miles

Bird

Denis

Aride

Curieuse

Les Soeurs

St Pierre

Félicité

Marianne

Cousin

Cousine

Praslin

La Digue

North

Mamelles

Silhouette

Ile aux Récifs

Frégate

Ste Anne

Cerf

Victoria

Conception

Thérèse

Mahé

Alphonse

Desroches

Planning Your Trip

The Seychelles, isolated in the crystal-clear, equatorial waters of the Indian Ocean, provides a superb destination for those seeking sun, sea and sand. However, the islands with their Creole culture, as well as unique biodiversity, afford discerning visitors a whole lot more.

WHEN TO VISIT
The equatorial climate is hot all year round, and is governed by the two wind regimes. The southeast trade winds blow steadily from May to October and, during these months, very little rain falls and the days are hot, humid and sunny. The seas are not as calm as during the northwest monsoon period from November to March. The highest rainfall occurs in December and January but don't let that put you off as even when it pours it is not cold. The tropical downpours tend to occur in the afternoons and are short and sharp. Getting drenched in a tropical downpour could be a whole new experience! Seychelles meteorological office; tel: 384070 or 373377.

Public holidays and festivals
Various holidays and festivals may influence the time when you wish to visit the Seychelles – you may especially want to be there then, or you may wish to avoid them altogether! High season times coincide with Christmas and Easter, which also coincide with the Seychelles school holidays. The list of holidays, festivals and special events which follows may help you plan your holiday.

January 1 and 2	New Year
March/April	Easter (dates vary)
May 1	Labour Day
June 5	Liberation Day
June 18	National Reconciliation Day
June 29	Independence Day
August 15	Assumption Day (La Digue Festival Day)
November 1	All Saints' Day
December 8	The Immaculate Conception
December 25	Christmas Day

The *Kreol* Festival is an annual event usually taking place during the last week of October. For this festival, Creole people from several nations get together and celebrate with art, music and dance. Joyful participants come from Mauritius, Rodrigues, Mayotte, Réunion, Madagascar and the Caribbean islands.

Fet Afrik or African Week is celebrated in May. An annual agricultural and horticultural show is held in Mahé in June as is Environment Week which focuses on schools. The Lafet jazz festival featuring musicians from Indian Ocean islands and continental Africa is held in July.

The SUBOIS Underwater Festival caters for international underwater photographers and is held in Mahé each year in October. Various international game-fishing competitions, sailing and windsurfing regattas are also held annually. The Festival de la Mer in September includes the Beau Vallon regatta and the inter-island windsurfing race from Mahé to Praslin.

HIGHLIGHTS

The Seychelles is the ultimate sun, sea and sand destination, and the many beachfront hotels are geared up to cater for idyllic and relaxing holidays. A full spectrum of watersports is on offer at the larger resorts, and the smaller hotels and guesthouses can easily arrange such activities. Good local infrastructure is in place for scuba diving, snorkelling, angling, sailing, birdwatching and hiking, and there are dive centres, watersports operators, charter boats, tour operators and well-trained local guides on hand. Beau Vallon offers the lot!

But there is much more to the Seychelles, and the islands are just asking to be explored. The fantastic scenery and interesting biodiversity are increasingly attracting ecotourists. Entire islands have been set aside as nature reserves and there are marine parks as well as mountain and forest reserves for the nature lover to explore. Experience the magnificent Vallée de Mai, the World Heritage Site that protects the coco de mer on Praslin. Make an expedition to one or more of the tiny satellite islands surrounding Mahé, Praslin and La Digue – some require a whole day while others can be enjoyed in a morning or afternoon.

Besides the scenery and natural history, there are other sides to exploring the islands, particularly on Mahé. Find out about Creole culture, look at the monuments that commemorate important events in the short history of the Seychelles, and delve into the museums and archives. Take an art tour, meet the creative local artists and revel in the vibrant colours of the islands. Sample Creole cuisine or indulge in a sumptuous beach barbecue under the swaying palms on a tiny island. For a taste of the nightlife try your luck at one of the casinos, watch a sega show or drop in at a local disco for some lively island-style dancing. Visitors can even get married on the romantic Seychelles (see opposite).

SEYCHELLES TOURIST OFFICES

Seychelles Tourism Marketing Authority PO Box 1262, Victoria, Mahé; tel: +248 620000; fax: +248 620620; email: seychelles@aspureasitgets.com
France 51 av Mozart, 75016 Paris; tel: +33 1 42 30 02 67; email: info@tourismeseychelles.com

GETTING MARRIED IN THE SEYCHELLES

Fulfilling the romantic notion of getting married in the Seychelles, is relatively easy to arrange, even in a hurry. Marriage ceremonies take place on Tuesday and Thursday mornings at the Civil Status Office in Victoria or at any private venue on week days. To find out all the details contact the Civil Status Office, PO Box 206, Victoria; tel: 383183. For those couples wishing to marry in a church, contact a local priest.

Wedding banns have to be published 11 days prior to the wedding but this period can be shortened to just two days if a special licence costing SR100 is obtained. Copies or originals of certain documents such as passports and birth certificates are required. If either prospective spouse is a divorcee, widow or widower, the death certificate or divorce documents are also required.

Most Seychelles tour operators are able to arrange the entire wedding event for you, including organising photographic and video services, hairdressers and beauticians. The Plantation Club also offers a complete wedding service; tel: 361361; fax: 361333. Creole Holidays has exclusive use of an open-air site at Cap Lazare, an ideal wedding location; tel: 224900.

Germany The Magnum Group, Sonnenstrasse 9, D-80331 Munich; tel: +49 89 23662169; email: seychelles@magnum.de
India India Pvt Ltd, A61 6th Floor, Himalaya House, Kasturba Gandhi, Marg, New Delhi 110001; tel: +91 11 2335 0295; fax: +91 99 2335 0270; email: trac@seychelles.uk.com
Italy Adam & Partner, Via Salaino 12, 20144 Milan; tel: +39 02 439 81675; fax: +39 02 434 00136; email: seychelles@adam.it
Kenya PO Box 437 00606, Nairobi; tel: +254 2 375 2472
South Africa 480 Cork Av, Ferndale 2194; tel: +27 11 791 0300; fax: +27 11 791 0052; email: sto.seychelles@intekom.co.za
Spain Monte Esquinza, 30 bajo dcha, 28010 Madrid; tel: +34 91 702 0804; fax: +34 91 702 2374; email: stomad@attglobal.net
Switzerland Airpass AG, Flughofstrasse 57, 8152 Glattbrugg; tel: +41 43 211 6335; fax: +41 43 211 6344; email: info@seychelles.ch
United Arab Emirates Mohamed Ali Geziry Consultancy, Al Fattan Plaza, PO Box 36345, Dubai; tel: +971 4 286 5586; fax: +971 4 286 5589; email: seychelles@algeziry.com
UK Hills Balfour, 36 Southwark Bridge Rd, London SE1 9EU; tel: +44 020 7202 6363; fax: +44 020 7928 0722; email: seychelles@hillsbalfour.com

RED TAPE
Visas and entry permits
On arrival, it is necessary to have a current passport that is valid for six months after the scheduled date of departure from the Seychelles and a return ticket.

A one-month entry permit will be issued on arrival, and this may be extended for a further two months provided you have proof of funds to cover your stay. Extensions may be obtained from the Immigration and Civil Status Division, Independence House, Victoria (tel: 224030).

Seychelles consulates

Seychelles representation overseas is limited to France and Germany:

France 53 rue François 1er, 75008 Paris; tel: +33 1 47 20 26 26; email: aniskaros@yahoo.com
Germany Bleibtreustrasse 51a, D-10623 Berlin; tel: +49 30 31 90 76 60; email: rasudhoff@t-online.de

Customs regulations

Visitors over 18 years of age have a duty-free allowance of 200 cigarettes or 250g of tobacco, one litre of wine, one litre of spirits, 125ml perfume and 250ml toilette water. Tea, seeds, plants, flowers, raw meat and meat products are prohibited. Drugs such as cannabis, cocaine, LSD and other narcotics are not allowed into the Seychelles and severe penalties are enforced. It is strictly prohibited to take firearms and ammunition, harpoons and spearguns into the Seychelles. A special permit is required for the exportation of *coco de mer*, and a certificate must be obtained from the seller. It is prohibited to export live shells, tortoises and birds, and the possession or exportation of turtles or turtle products is illegal. There is a customs office at the airport (tel: 373777).

EMBASSIES AND CONSULATES

The following countries have diplomatic representation in Mahé:

Belgium Consulate, Victoria House; tel: 224434
China Embassy, St Louis, PO Box 680, Victoria; tel: 266588 or 515888
Cuba Embassy, Bel Eau; tel: 224094
Cyprus Honorary Consul, Turtle Bay, Anse aux Pins; tel: 376215
Denmark Consulate, PO Box 231, Victoria; tel: 224710
France Ambassador, Victoria House. Chancellerie tel: 382500; fax: 382510; Mission de co-opération tel: 382520; fax: 382530; Alliance Française tel: 224968
Germany Honorary Consul, PO Box 132, Victoria; tel: 261222
India High Commission, PO Box 488, Le Chantier; tel: 224489; fax: 224810
Indonesia Consul, 2 Oceangate House, PO Box 31, Victoria; tel: 224835; fax: 225156
Italy Consulate, PO Box 545, Victoria; tel: 224741 or 224465
Madagascar Honorary Consul, PO Box 68, Victoria; tel: 344030
Mauritius Consulate, Anse aux Pins; tel: 376441
Monaco Consulate, Château des Feuilles, Pointe Cabris, Praslin; tel: 233316
Netherlands Consulate, Box 372, Glacis; tel: 261200
Norway Consulate, Victoria House, Victoria; tel: 225366
Russia Embassy, PO Box 632, Le Niol; tel: 266590; fax: 266653
Sweden Consulate, New Port, Victoria; tel: 224710

Switzerland Consulate, PO Box 33, Victoria; tel: 371050
UK High Commission, Oliaji Trade Centre, PO Box 161, Victoria; tel: 225225 or 515052; fax: 225127
USA Consulate, Victoria House; PO Box 251, Victoria; tel: 225256; fax: 225189

GETTING THERE AND AWAY

As the Seychelles are in the middle of the ocean, almost a thousand miles from anywhere, there are only two ways to get there – by air or by sea.

By air

Regular flights link the Seychelles with Europe, Africa and the East. **Air Seychelles**, with its characteristic red, green and white livery and fairy tern logo, is the national carrier. It originally only provided a service from Mahé to Praslin and Frégate with foreign airlines bringing in the tourists. However, in 1983, Air Seychelles launched its first international flight from Gatwick, London, using a DC10 aircraft. Today, Air Seychelles, with its fleet of modern aircraft, links the European cities of London, Paris, Frankfurt, Rome, Zurich and Madrid to Mahé on a regular basis. Other Air Seychelles destinations include Singapore, Mumbai, Dubai and Johannesburg.

Several **other airlines** fly to Seychelles, and these include Air France, Air India, Air Mauritius, Kenya Airways, Emirates Airline and Qatar Airways, but there are many changes taking place in the airline industry. There are also frequent charter flights linking up with package tours and cruise ships.

The busy Seychelles International Airport is located on Mahé, right on the edge of the ocean, just 9km south of Victoria. Constructed in 1971, on land reclaimed from the sea, the international airport terminal buildings are scheduled for major renovations commencing 2005. For international flight enquiries tel: 384400. There is a tourist information office at the airport. Departure tax is now included in the cost of the airline ticket.

Airport transfers

Even though some international flights arrive in Mahé before sunrise, taxis are always available at the airport (SR75 for a ride to Victoria, SR150 to Beau Vallon, plus SR5 for each piece of baggage). An excess is charged at night. There is a bus stop on the main road opposite the airport building. Just cross the road to get a local bus into Victoria (SR3). Buses that stop on the same side of the road as the airport are on their way to the southern part of Mahé.

Airline offices

Air Seychelles Victoria House, PO Box 386, Victoria; tel: 381000; fax: 224305; email: airseymk@seychelles.net
Air India Mahé Trading Building (TSS), PO Box 356, Victoria; tel: 322414; fax: 321366
Air Mauritius Mahé Trading Building (TSS), PO Box 356, Victoria; tel: 322414; fax: 321366
Kenya Airways Huteau Lane, PO Box 288, Victoria; tel: 322989 or 322536; fax: 324162

Inter-island flights

Air Seychelles (Mahé airport; tel: 384405; Praslin airport; tel: 233214) operates regular, and frequent, local inter-island flights to Praslin, Frégate, Bird, Denis, Desroches and Alphonse using Twin Otter, Islander and Trislander aircraft. The domestic luggage allowance is 15kg. Note that some of the island resorts include the transfer from Mahé in their prices but others do not, so it is advisable to check your travel arrangements carefully.

Air Seychelles can also arrange special charter flights. Flights for the Islands Development Company are undertaken to Assumption and Farquhar to supply personnel to the coconut plantations; tel: 375400; fax: 375707.

Helicopter Seychelles (tel: 385858; fax: 373055; email: res@helicopterseychelles.sc; www.helicopterseychelles.com) can take you over to Praslin, La Digue, Silhouette, Frégate, North, Denis, Cousine, Félicité or even to other parts of Mahé. Scenic trips are also available and the Plantation Club has a helipad.

By sea
Ships

Cruise and expedition ships call regularly at the port of Victoria in Mahé, mainly from November to April when the seas are calmer. The larger cruise ships generally only visit Mahé but passengers can be ferried to Praslin and La Digue by local vessels. Expedition cruises with smaller vessels often include the outer islands in their itineraries.

Noble Caledonia 2 Chester Close, London SW1X 7BE, UK; tel: +44 (0)20 7752 0000; www.noble-caledonia.co.uk

Zegrahm Expeditions 192 Nickerson St, 200 Seattle, WA 98109, USA; www.zeco.com. Use a 50-berth sailing ship, *Le Ponant*, for expeditions around the Seychelles islands.

Hebridean Princess (run by Hebridean Island Cruises Ltd) Tel: +44 (0)1756 704704; www.hebridean.co.uk. A larger vessel that also plies the western Indian Ocean waters.

Yacht

Visiting by yacht must be the finest way to explore the fabulous islands of the Seychelles. All visiting yachts must obtain clearance with Customs, Immigration and Health in Victoria, Mahé. Hefty tariffs previously levied on cruising yachts visiting the Seychelles appear to have been rescinded, and current port tariffs for visiting yachts under 20 tonnes are in the region of SR50 per day for stays of more than ten days.

TOUR OPERATORS
UK

Aardvark Safaris Tel: 01980 849160; fax: 01980 849161; email: mail@aardvarksafaris.com; www.aardarksafaris.com

Abercrombie and Kent Travel Tel: 0845 8700 611; email: info@abercrombiekent.co.uk; www.abercrombiekent.co.uk

Cox & Kings Travel Tel: 020 7873 5000; fax: 020 7630 6038; email:
cox.kings@coxandkings.co.uk; www.coxandkings.co.uk
Gane and Marshall Tel: 020 8441 9592; fax: 020 8441 7376; email:
holidays@ganeandmarshall.co.uk; www.ganeandmarshall.co.uk
Naturetrek Tel: 01962 733051; email: info@naturetrek.co.uk;
www.naturetrek.co.uk
Okavango Tours and Safaris Tel: 020 8343 3283; email: info@okavango.com;
www.okavango.com
Partnership Travel Tel: 020 8343 3446; fax: 020 8349 3439; email:
info@partnershiptravel.co.uk; www.partnershiptravel.co.uk
Rainbow Tours Tel: 020 7226 1004; fax: 020 7226 2621; email:
info@rainbowtours.co.uk; www.rainbowtours.co.uk
Realworld-travel Fax: 020 9233 2274; email: enquiries@4real.co.uk; www.4real.co.uk
Reef and Rainforest Tours Tel: 01803 866965; email: mail@reefandrainforest.co.uk;
www.reefandrainforest.co.uk
Roxton Bailey Robinson Worldwide Tel: 01488 689700; email: info@rbrww.com;
www.rbrww.com
Somak Holidays Tel: 020 8423 3000; email: holidays@somak.co.uk;
www.somak.co.uk
Steppes Travel Tel: 01285 650011; fax: 01285 885888; email:
africa@steppestravel.co.uk; www.steppestravel.co.uk
Tim Best Travel Tel: 020 7591 0300; fax: 020 7591 0301; email:
info@timbesttravel.com; www.timbesttravel.com
Time for Africa Tel: 01798 867750; fax: 01798 867796; email:
paddyj@timeforafrica.com; www.timeforafrica.com
Travel Services Seychelles UK Tel: 020 7630 9490; fax: 020 7931 7693; email:
dendy@marketplaces.co.uk; www.tss.sc
The Ultimate Travel Company Tel: 020 7386 4646; fax: 020 7386 4676; email:
enquiry@theultimatetravelcompany.co.uk; www.theultimatetravelcompany.co.uk
Wildlife Worldwide Tel: 020 8667 9158; fax: 020 8667 1960; email:
sales@wildlifeworldwide.com; www.wildlifeworldwide.com

South Africa
SEYUNIQUE Tel: +27 11 453 2933; fax: +27 11 453 0490; email:
reservations@seyunique.co.za
Unusual Destinations Tel: +27 11 706 1991; fax: +27 31 463 1469; email:
info@unusualdestinations.com; www.unusualdestinations.com

USA
Classical Cruises Tel: +1 212 794 3200 or 800 252 7745; www.classicalcruises.com

HEALTH
with Dr Felicity Nicholson
The islands of the Seychelles pose no great health threats, and probably the
worst thing that could happen is sunburn or dehydration. The standard of
living is generally high and there are no awful unsanitary conditions.

LONG-HAUL FLIGHTS, CLOTS AND DVT
Dr Jane Wilson-Howarth

Long-haul air travel increases the risk of deep vein thrombosis. Although recent research has suggested that many of us develop clots when immobilised, most resolve without us ever having been aware of them. In certain susceptible individuals, though, large clots form and these can break away and lodge in the lungs. This is dangerous but happens in a tiny minority of passengers.

Studies have shown that flights of over 5½ hours are significant, and that people who take lots of shorter flights over a short space of time form clots. People at highest risk are:

- Those who have had a clot before – unless they are now taking warfarin
- People over 80 years of age
- Anyone who has recently undergone a major operation or surgery for varicose veins
- Someone who has had a hip or knee replacement in the last three months
- Cancer sufferers
- Those who have ever had a stroke
- People with heart disease
- Those with a close blood relative who has had a clot

Those with a slightly increased risk:

- People over 40
- Women who are pregnant or have had a baby in the last couple of weeks
- People taking female hormones or other oestrogen therapy
- Heavy smokers
- Those who have very severe varicose veins
- The very obese
- People who are very tall (over 6ft/1.8m) or short (under 5ft/1.5m)

Before you go

The only absolute requirement for the Seychelles is proof of **vaccination** against yellow fever when travelling from an infected area (eg: sub-Saharan Africa); it is a good idea to secure the international certificate inside your passport. However, travellers here as elsewhere are wise to be up to date with routine immunisations such as tetanus/diphtheria (ten-yearly), polio (ten-yearly) and hepatitis A. One dose of hepatitis A vaccine protects for about one year, and a booster dose at around this time will extend cover in adults for up to 20 years.

Special circumstances may dictate that other vaccines are advised. For trips of a month or more typhoid vaccine should be considered. If you are intending to work in a hospital/medical setting or closely with children then hepatitis B vaccine is recommended. Similarly, anyone working closely with animals or likely to be more than 24 hours away from medical help should ideally be vaccinated against rabies. Both hepatitis B and rabies vaccines consist of three

A deep vein thrombosis (DVT) is a blood clot that forms in the deep leg veins. This is very different from irritating but harmless superficial phlebitis. DVT causes swelling and redness of one leg, usually with heat and pain in one calf and sometimes the thigh. A DVT is only dangerous if a clot breaks away and travels to the lungs (pulmonary embolus). Symptoms of a pulmonary embolus (PE) include chest pain that is worse on breathing in deeply, shortness of breath, and sometimes coughing up small amounts of blood. The symptoms commonly start three to ten days after a long flight. Anyone who thinks that they might have a DVT needs to see a doctor immediately who will arrange a scan. Warfarin tablets (to thin the blood) are then taken for at least six months.

Prevention of DVT

Several conditions make the problem more likely. Immobility is the key, and factors like reduced oxygen in cabin air and dehydration may also contribute. To reduce the risk of thrombosis on a long journey:

- Take a meal of oily fish in the 24 hours before departure
- Exercise before and after the flight
- Keep mobile before and during the flight; move around every couple of hours
- During the flight drink plenty of water or juices
- Avoid taking sleeping pills and excessive tea, coffee and alcohol
- Perform exercises that mimic walking and tense the calf muscles
- Consider wearing flight socks or support stockings (see www.legshealth.com)
- The jury is still out on whether it is wise to take aspirin.

If you think you are at increased risk of a clot, ask your doctor if it is safe to travel.

doses given a minimum of three weeks apart. In these instances, visit a travel clinic before you go – a full list of current travel clinic websites worldwide is available on www.istm.org/.

Health insurance is advisable, especially should you have to be repatriated for treatment in an emergency. Shop around to make sure that you get the best value for your money, and check the small print carefully.

In the Seychelles

There is no malaria on the islands but, at times, there can be plenty of irritating mosquitoes that can cause uncomfortable itchy bites. You may find sandflies on some of the beaches with washed-up seaweed and seagrasses. If they are troublesome, use an insect repellent as the bites can be very itchy and some people have a mild allergic reaction.

Water is clean and it is quite safe to drink straight from the tap on the main islands, although bottled water is available. The Rochon dam and La Gogue reservoir in the mountains above Victoria supply Mahé with fresh water. Food is usually well prepared and clean, and one seldom hears of upset tummies. But, as so often happens when travelling, your system can take a little while to get used to different types of food and water. The Creole food may be more spicy than your usual home fare. It is important to drink plenty of water to prevent dehydration in the tropical heat.

Sunburn

When visiting the Seychelles you do have to be very careful of the sun, especially if visiting from a cooler European climate. It is very tempting on your first day just to lie in the sun after all those damp, grey, wintry days. Beware! If you are not careful your holiday could be spoilt, to say nothing of later skin cancer problems.

It is wise to build up a tan slowly, using a good sunscreen with a high protection factor, incrementally increasing your time in the sunshine. Wear a sunhat with a wide brim, a light cotton, long-sleeved shirt to protect your shoulders and a floaty sarong to shade your legs. Protection from the sun is not only for ladies, as men are also susceptible – especially on balding pates! If you are on an open boat wearing a swimming costume or shorts, watch your knees and the tops of your feet as they can get red and sore in no time at all. Remember that both water and white sand are reflective, an extra contributory factor to getting sunburnt. So, even if the day is overcast, lather on the sunscreen, renewing it regularly, especially if you are swimming. While snorkelling one can also be very prone to sunburn, particularly on the back of the neck, shoulders and legs, so it's a good idea to wear a T-shirt.

Health care

The main granitic islands have an efficient health-care system, and are within easy reach of Victoria by air or boat. The outlying coralline islands, however, have no hospital facilities. Some may only have a resident warden with the barest emergency bandages and a bottle of mercurochrome, if you are lucky! It should not be a problem as they are right off the tourist track and none but intrepid yachties will visit them. If you are on a cruise ship, you will have your own doctor on board.

The Victoria Hospital in Mont Fleuri is well equipped to handle accidents and emergencies (tel: 388000; clinic hours are Mon–Fri 08.00–16.00; Sat 08.00–12.00; Sun closed). A doctor is available for consultation by tourists with a basic fee of SR150, or SR200 after hours. Some of the hotels have a nurse who is able to give medical advice, and will arrange a hospital visit if necessary. Small clinics with a nurse in attendance are dotted about Mahé at Anse aux Pins, Anse Boileau, Anse Royale, Baie Lazare, Beau Vallon, Béolière, Corgat Estate, English River, Les Mamelles, North Point, Port Glaud and Takamaka. Praslin has a hospital at Baie Ste Anne and a clinic at Grande Anse. There is a small hospital on La Digue and Silhouette has a small clinic.

The emergency telephone number for fire, police or ambulance is 999.

Pharmacies

It is always safest to bring enough of your own medication with you. Medicines on prescription may be obtained from the dispensary at the Victoria Hospital (tel: 388000). There are three pharmacies in Victoria, namely Behram's Pharmacy, Mont Fleuri (tel: 225559); Fock Heng Pharmacy, Revolution Avenue, Victoria (tel: 322751); George Lilam's Pharmacy, Benezet Street, Victoria (tel: 322336). All operate during normal business hours and sell a small range of well-known pharmaceutical products, although anything obscure will probably not be available. No 24-hour pharmacy service is available.

Dentists

There is a dental clinic at the Victoria Hospital, open Mon–Fri 08.00–15.00. Another clinic is at Oceangate House, Independence Avenue (tel: 224852); open Mon–Fri 08.00–16.00. A group of private dentists is located in a building behind Aarti Chambers in Mont Fleuri (tel: 225822).

Optometrists

There is an optometrist, Micock Consulting, in the Aarti Chambers opposite the Victoria Hospital (tel: 321177). Ou Linet in the Codevar in Albert Street is able to repair spectacles, and they also sell contact lens paraphernalia. Pharmacies also sell contact-lens solutions and non-prescription eye drops.

SAFETY

The Seychelles is not a crime-ridden part of the world. However, most of the larger hotels have safety deposit boxes for your valuables like tickets, cash and travellers' cheques. When out and about, use your common sense. For example, it is not wise to leave fancy, expensive camera equipment lying on the back seat of an unattended open Mini-Moke, and even the box at the back is not really secure. Neither is it a good idea to leave a handbag on the beach while you go swimming or snorkelling.

Police stations are situated in Revolution Avenue in Victoria, at Beau Vallon, Mont Fleuri and Anse Royale on Mahé. On Praslin, there are police stations at Baie Ste Anne and at Grande Anse. The police station on La Digue is at La Passe. Policemen wear 'dark blue trousers and a white short-sleeved shirt. Police station telephone numbers are Victoria: 288000; Mont Fleuri: 288000; Beau Vallon: 247242; Anse Royale: 371226; Praslin: 233251; and La Digue: 234251. Dial 999 for fire, police or ambulance.

Women travellers

It is generally safe for women to be out on their own, and travelling on the buses is absolutely fine. Take care not to offend the local people by wearing ultra-skimpy clothes that could be misinterpreted as provocative.

WHAT TO TAKE

Not a lot! As the climate is hot all year round, light cotton clothing is the answer. Generally, a very relaxed atmosphere prevails in the Seychelles, and for ladies, shorts with blouses or T-shirts or a light dress are fine. Many of the hotels do not appreciate swimming costumes in the dining room, and the smarter hotels may suggest that gentlemen wear long trousers in the evening. Other than that, everything is really informal.

A wide-brimmed hat is important, as are sunglasses, plenty of sunscreen with a high sun protection factor and a general moisturising cream. Don't forget your swimming costume. Open sandals or thongs are the most comfortable footwear in a hot climate. If you are thinking of walking on the mountains, a pair of lightweight walking shoes will be adequate. A small torch is always handy, especially when negotiating the path to your chalet in the evening.

The islands are most photogenic so you will need your camera and plenty of film. Film is available from photographic shops and some hotel boutiques but you may not be able to get the brand, speed or type that you prefer, so it is best to bring your own supplies. A polarising filter can be put to good use to cut the glare from your water shots. One-hour processing of print film is possible in Victoria.

If you are into birdwatching, a good pair of binoculars is essential: both 10x40 and 8x32 are good choices. For snorkelling and scuba diving, the dive centres all have good equipment, which can be hired. If you wear spectacles and don't want to go to the expense of having a prescription diving mask made up, a good tip is to silicone the lenses from an old pair of spectacles on to the inside of your mask if you want to see the corals and reef fishes at their best. Still on the underwater scene, if you are planning on scuba diving, do remember to take your certification of proficiency with you.

The Seychelles is a civilised part of the world, so you should be able to get almost anything you have forgotten, although it might be more expensive.

MONEY
Foreign-exchange regulations

There are no restrictions on the amount of foreign exchange brought into the country.

Recently, Seychelles has been suffering from a foreign-exchange deficit and, in an attempt to rectify this, strict foreign-exchange controls are now enforced. Visitors are required to use foreign currency in making payments for hotels and guesthouses, hiring of cars or boats, the service of tour operators or travel agents, patronage of casinos and domestic transfers within Seychelles. Incidental purchases in restaurants outside of hotels, shopping (excluding duty-free shops), petrol and taxi fares are payable in local currency (Seychelles rupees and cents). Exchanging money may be done only at banks, by authorised money dealers at the Seychelles International Airport, or by hotel cashiers, and it is advisable to keep your money exchange receipt. It is a criminal offence to change money with an unauthorised person and it is illegal to enter or leave the country with more than SR2,000 without authorisation. Should you wish to change rupees back into your own currency it can be done provided you show proof of official transactions although it may not be possible to get the currency of your choice. It is thus wise not to change too much cash in the first place: only what you will require for petrol and incidentals.

Local currency

The Seychelles rupee is the currency of the islands and 100 cents constitute one rupee. Coin denominations are five, ten and 25 cents, which are bronze, and one and five rupees, which are silver. The coins each have a natural history subject on the face: five cents – a pandanus, ten cents – a tuna, 25 cents – a black parrot, one rupee – a shell, and five rupees – a *coco de mer* palm. The Seychelles rupee can be abbreviated as SR, R or Rs.

Denominations of the notes are SR10, SR25, SR50 and SR100. They are beautifully designed, all depicting the rich natural heritage of the Seychelles. The SR10 note is currently available in two sizes, the larger being the new one, which can be easily confused with the SR50 note as both are predominantly green.

The exchange rates are published in the daily newspaper, *The Nation*; in April 2005 £1 would cost SR9.55, US$1 SR5.08 and €1 SR5.56.

Banks, ATMs and credit cards

The following banks operate in Victoria: Barclays Bank, Habib Bank, Bank of Baroda, Nouvobanque, Mauritius Commercial Bank (MCB) and Seychelles Savings Bank. Banks are open Mon–Fri 08.30–14.00, Sat 09.00–11.00, and do not close for lunch. On Praslin and La Digue there are branches of Barclays Bank, MCB and Seychelles Savings Bank. ATMs are also available on Mahé, Praslin and La Digue.

Banks at the airport are open only for international flights. It is convenient to change money in the arrival hall while waiting for the luggage to appear on the carousel. Use only official moneychangers. SWIFT and EFTPOS are available for international transfers.

American Express, Diners Club, Visa and Mastercard are widely accepted in the larger hotels, restaurants and shops, but credit cards may not be accepted by some of the smaller establishments, so it is always wise to check first.

Seychelles on a budget

This is easier said than done! However, while most of the accommodation and restaurants in the Seychelles are really expensive, it is possible to have a holiday on the islands without spending a vast amount of money. Package tours often offer the best value as they generally include flights, hotel accommodation and airport transfers. Self-catering accommodation, especially for a couple or family, can be an economical option. On Mahé, the least expensive bed and breakfast establishments are Georgina's at Beau Vallon, Lalla Panzi at Anse aux Pins, and Takamaka at Anse Takamaka. On Praslin, Seaview and L'Hirondelle are the least expensive options. Camping is not permitted in the Seychelles.

Buses provide an interesting and very cheap way to get around Mahé and, to a lesser extent, Praslin. They run regularly during the day with the last service at around 19.00. Over weekends and public holidays the service is reduced. Bicycles can be used on Praslin and La Digue but are only recommended in certain parts of Mahé as many of the roads are very steep and narrow. The schooners operating between the islands are far cheaper options than the fast ferry or air transfers, but you do need time on your hands. The many little stores around the island sell groceries and a great variety of sweet and savoury snacks that do very well for a light lunch, and an icy beer or soft drink bought from these shops will cost half the price of one served in a restaurant. It is not necessary to buy bottled water, as tap water is quite safe to drink. The beaches, snorkelling and wonderful walks on the mountains are free to enjoy!

GETTING AROUND

It is really easy to get around Mahé and Praslin by hire car or taxi. Victoria is the only town with a traffic light! Buses are a good way to see the two larger islands and bicycles are ideal on La Digue. Travel between the islands is a cinch with efficient airplanes, helicopters and many boats. There are no trains in the Seychelles.

Facilities for the disabled

Wheelchairs are available at the airport and at most of the larger hotels. It is advisable to notify the tour agent of any disabilities prior to travelling to ensure that the accommodation is suitable. Depending on the degree of disability, travelling in small boats could be difficult.

Taxis

About 100 taxis are waiting to transport you around Mahé, and a further dozen will take you around Praslin. They operate under the banner of the Taxi Operators Association. The drivers are encouraged to attend regular meetings and talks aimed at improving their knowledge of the islands. Many of the drivers will be happy to take you on a 'conducted tour' and many of them speak English. Apart from the taxi rank in Victoria, taxis are available at all the major hotels, at the airport when international flights arrive, and at the quayside when ferries dock. It is more difficult to get a taxi in the evening but your hotel or guesthouse will be able to arrange one for you. The fares are regulated and the cost of getting from the airport to Beau Vallon is about SR150. Expect to pay an extra SR5 for each piece of luggage.

Car hire

At least 20 car-hire companies operate on Mahé including some of the well-known international names as well as many smaller, local companies. About nine car-hire companies are based on Praslin. Cars range from fun Mini-Mokes to smart chauffeur-driven, air-conditioned, luxury cars. They are usually well maintained. You can expect to pay around €50 per day for a small air-conditioned car. To hire a car, a current driving licence is required.

The Seychellois drive on the left. The speed limit in towns is 40km/h and out of town it is 65km/h except on the new east coast road on Mahé where it is 80km/h. If you see a branch from a tree lying across the road, slow down as it generally indicates some sort of hazard ahead such as a pot-hole, a breakdown or even an accident. Red warning triangles are in short supply.

Buses

Buses are widely used by the residents and, as a ride costs only SR3, are a most economical way to get from place to place. The buses have wonderful natural air conditioning through all the open windows but they do battle up the steep hillsides at times. The bus terminus on Mahé is in Palm Street, Victoria, where detailed timetables are available. Buses run from 05.30 to 19.00 with reduced services on Saturdays, Sundays and public holidays. The bus service on Praslin is not as extensive as on Mahé but is still a useful way to get around. Islander Coach Charter operates a regular coach service between Victoria and the Plantation Club on the west side of Mahé.

Inter-island ferries

An inter-island schooner service plies between Mahé, Praslin and La Digue, and a large, fast, 159-seater catamaran, *Cat Cocos*, links Mahé and Praslin. Various boats can be hired to get to the smaller islands.

Tour operators

The main tour operators in the Seychelles (see pages 62–3) are represented on Mahé, Praslin and La Digue. Several smaller tour companies can also be found in Victoria. The larger operators will efficiently deal with package tours or cruise ships as well as small or even individual tours. All the operators will be able to arrange a variety of day or half-day tours, with or without guides, on all the main islands. They can also organise visits to the different islands with relevant flights or boat transfers. Some of the privately owned islands have their own offices in Victoria and will make all the relevant arrangements necessary for a visit.

ACCOMMODATION

The Seychelles is marketed as an exclusive destination, and visitors pay for the privilege of having secluded beaches and open spaces. There are no high-rise hotels or massive edge-to-edge tourist resorts lining the shores. Neither are there squalid areas with fly-by-night, low-life accommodation. Camping is forbidden in the Seychelles. Although there is no official 'star rating' system there is, generally, a good standard of accommodation in the Seychelles. Places to stay range from large resort-type hotels with casinos to small hotels and guesthouses. Only three hotels have over 200 rooms, and they are all on Mahé, while the largest hotel on Praslin has only 88 rooms. There are also ultra-exclusive lodges set on private islands as well as self-catering and family-run bed and breakfast establishments.

CONVENTION ON INTERNATIONAL TRADE IN ENDANGERED SPECIES OF WILD FAUNA AND FLORA

In 1963, the International Union for the Conservation of Nature (IUCN) called for an international agreement on trade in animal species and their products in response to the impact that increased trade was having on wild populations of many species. Ten years later, the Convention on International Trade in Endangered Species of Wild Fauna and Flora (CITES) was negotiated in Washington DC, and it came into force in July 1975 after ten nations had ratified it. To date, some 150 countries have signed the convention and the Seychelles was one of the early signatories in February 1977.

CITES regulates international trade in animals and plants whose survival may be threatened by trade. CITES operates on a permit system corresponding to species listed on three appendices. Both an import and an export permit are required for the extremely limited trade allowed in Appendix I species such as turtles. Trade in export of Appendix II species only requires an export permit.

The convention is administered via a secretariat based in Geneva and, within party countries, management authorities issue permits based on advice from their scientific agencies. A conference of signatory parties is held every two years to evaluate implementation of the treaty and consider ways to improve efforts. The most recent meeting was held in Bangkok, Thailand, in October 2004.

In the Seychelles, attempts to stop the sale of turtle products (all turtles are CITES species) were only effective when the World Bank and the Seychelles Government funded a programme to curb the tourist-based demand for turtle-shell products and provide artisans with alternative occupations and compensation.

Hotel tariffs are high, and though the service is not always as efficient as it could be, there is always a smile from the laid-back Seychellois. The more exclusive lodges, however, offer unparalleled comfort and luxury with excellent service. While the Seychelles is a lovely destination for those travelling with children, and most hotels generally welcome them, some specifically do not cater for children.

It is very often a more economical option to take a package tour, which will usually include the flight, hotel and airport transfers. For travellers wishing to organise their own itineraries, nothing could be easier as local tour operators are most helpful. Prices quoted for accommodation in subsequent chapters are approximate as costs vary according to season and type of room.

EATING OUT

There is a wide variety of restaurants on Mahé and Praslin. In addition to Creole fare, international cuisine is readily available. **Tipping** is not expected as very often a service charge is added to the bill. However, a tip for extra-attentive service is always appreciated.

Restaurant prices are high. Even on the beach, the least expensive main course will be around SR65; in a smarter restaurant you can expect to pay from SR90 for something simple, with starter and dessert on top.

SHOPPING AND SOUVENIRS

The Seychelles has no big shopping malls but there is an exciting, vibrant and colourful local market filled with exotic fruits, spices and souvenirs. Numerous boutiques and stalls sell a wide variety of tempting articles, and various galleries have some superb artworks including paintings, sculpture and pottery. Classy gold and pearl jewellery, made in Mahé and Praslin, is also available. Antigone Trading sells a good range of books on the Seychelles. Take home the sounds of the Seychelles with local music on CD or tape. Support local handicrafts by purchasing handmade items like dyed batiks and woven mats and hats crafted from coconut palm leaves. Local spices and teas are Seychelles treats, and some perfumes are unique to the islands. The exotic tropical liqueur from the Seychelles, Coco d'Amour, bottled in a jar shaped like the *coco de mer*, is available in many boutiques. Spirit Artisanal concocts various island-style liqueurs from exotic fruits and flowers, and they are available in the market and some small boutiques. It is not advisable to buy the shells and corals offered at the souvenir kiosks as most of them are taken live from the sea, if not in the Seychelles, then in other parts of the world. Turtle- and tortoise-shell artefacts should not be bought as they fall under CITES (see box opposite). Any purchases of *coco de mer* products must be accompanied by the appropriate government certification.

MEDIA AND COMMUNICATIONS
Telephones and internet communications

The Seychelles operates an efficient, worldwide telephone service with direct dialling to most countries. The international code for the Seychelles is 248. Coin and card telephones can be found all over the main islands. Cards are on sale from Cable & Wireless, the post office and many of the smaller shops. **Cable & Wireless** in Francis Rachel Street, Victoria, is open 07.00–21.00 every day for faxes, telegrams, telephone calls and phone cards; tel: 284000. Most of the larger hotels have telephones in the rooms but a high surcharge is often levied. It is much cheaper to use phone cards, which are beautifully designed and come in units of SR30, SR60, SR100 and SR200. For international enquiries dial 151; for local enquiries dial 181 (most of the operators speak English).

The Seychelles has a GSM mobile phone network service with roaming agreements for many countries. Mobile phones can be hired from **Airtel** at the airport (tel: 600 600; email: airtel@seychelles.net), from **Atlas** in Huteau Lane, Victoria (tel: 304 060; email: atlas@seychelles.net) or from Cable & Wireless.

HINTS ON PHOTOGRAPHY
Nick Garbutt and John Jones

All sorts of photographic opportunities present themselves in the islands, from simple holiday snaps to that one-off encounter with an Aldabra tortoise. For the best results, give some thought to the following tips.

As a general rule, if it doesn't look good through the viewfinder, it will never look good as a picture. Don't take photographs for the sake of taking them; be patient and wait until the image looks right.

Photographing people is never easy and more often than not it requires a fair share of luck. If you want to take a portrait shot of a stranger, it is always best to ask first. Focus on the eyes of your subject since they are the most powerful ingredient of any portrait, and be prepared for the unexpected.

There is no mystery about good wildlife photography. The secret is getting into the right place at the right time and then knowing what to do when you are there. Look for striking poses, aspects of behaviour and distinctive features. Try not only to take pictures of the species itself, but also to illustrate it within the context of its environment. Alternatively, focus in close on a characteristic which can be emphasised.

- Photographically, the eyes are the most important part of an animal – focus on these, make sure they are sharp and try to ensure they contain a highlight.
- Look at the surroundings – there is nothing worse than a distracting twig or highlighted leaf lurking in the background. Getting this right is often the difference between a mediocre and a memorable image.
- A powerful flashgun adds the option of punching in extra light to transform an otherwise dreary picture. Artificial light is no substitute for

Media

The daily newspaper, *The Nation*, carries articles in Creole, English and French. It is not available on Sundays or public holidays. *Regar* is a weekly paper available on Fridays.

The Seychelles Broadcasting Corporation (SBC) and Paradise FM provide radio news, music and information in Creole, English and French. The BBC Indian Ocean relay station is located at Grande Anse, and the Far Eastern Broadcasting Association (FEBA) near Anse Etiole broadcasts the gospel far and wide. SBC television broadcasts news and entertainment in Creole, English and French.

RESPONSIBLE TOURISM/GIVING SOMETHING BACK

Responsible tourism can mean many different things. It is about common sense and it hardly needs to be spelled out but it is worth making a few comments. Respect for the host country's culture is high on the awareness

natural light, though, so use it judiciously. Some reserves like Cousin expressly forbid the use of flashguns.

- Getting close to the subject correspondingly reduces the depth of field. At camera-to-subject distances of less than a metre, apertures between f16 and f32 are necessary to ensure adequate depth of field. This means using flash to provide enough light. If possible, use one or two small flashguns to illuminate the subject from the side.

Landscapes are forever changing, even on a daily basis. Good landscape photography is all about good light and capturing mood. Generally the first and last two hours of daylight are best, or when peculiar climatic conditions add drama or emphasise distinctive features. Never place the horizon in the centre – in your mind's eye divide the frame into thirds and either exaggerate the land or the sky.

Film
If you're using conventional film (as against a digital camera), select the right film for your needs. Film speed (ISO number) indicates the sensitivity of the film to light. The lower the number, the less sensitive the film, but the better quality the final image. For general print film, ISO 100 or 200 fit the bill perfectly. If you are using transparencies for home use or for lectures, then again ISO 100 or 200 film is fine. However, if you want to get your work published, the superior quality of ISO 25 to 100 film is best.

- Try to keep your film cool. Never leave it in direct sunlight.
- Don't allow fast film (ISO 800 and above) to pass through X-ray machines.
- Under weak light conditions use a faster film (ISO 200 or 400).

list. In Seychelles, although an easy-going, relaxed lifestyle prevails, it is not a good idea to go into town scantily clad in beachwear. The beaches and surrounds are so lovely it would be a shame to spoil them with litter even though it appears that the residents do just that at times. It is always polite to ask if you may photograph people and, if they refuse, honour their refusal.

Although Seychelles is a developing country, there is not the dire poverty one finds in other parts of the world and social services appear to be doing a good job; there are no beggars or street children, the elderly are cared for and the literacy levels are high. Supporting the local economy by using local stores and smaller independent restaurants is important.

One of the greatest areas of responsibility for tourists in Seychelles is around conservation of the environment. It is the basis on which the country's tourism depends and generates significant foreign exchange for the country. There are codes of conduct for visiting most of the island nature reserves and they have been put in place for the protection of both wildlife and visitors. It is most clearly spelled out when visiting Cousin Special Reserve where the birdlife appears completely unafraid of humans and a respectful distance must be maintained. A similar situation occurs on Aride with the additional aspect of huge numbers of ground-nesting birds making it clearly necessary to keep to the paths to prevent the nests, eggs and chicks from being trampled.

The other sensitive areas are the coral reefs. After the bleaching in 1998, corals are slowly regenerating and it is essential to keep off them, keeping fins well away while diving. The old cliché 'take only photographs and leave only footprints' still holds true, as does 'walk slowly, talk softly'.

Part of the responsibility can be proactive; join one or more of the conservation NGOs or make a donation or, if you prefer, become involved with a children's organisation. The NGOs play a vital and active part in the maintenance and running of many of the island reserves.

Nature Protection Trust of Seychelles (based on Silhouette) POBox 207, Victoria, Seychelles; tel: 323711; email: npts@seychelles.net; http://members.aol.com/jstgerlach
Nature Seychelles, Roche Caiman (affiliated to BirdLife International) PO Box 1310, Victoria, Seychelles; tel: 601100; email: nature@seychelles.net; www.nature.org.sc
Island Conservation Society www.islandconservation.net. This is a very newly formed and worthwhile NGO spearheading the management of Aride.
Seychelles Islands Foundation (administering Aldabra and Vallée de Mai) PO Box 853, Victoria, Seychelles; tel: 321735; email: sif@seychelles.net
National Council for Children Bel Eau; tel:224390; fax: 225688

ACTIVITIES
Diving and snorkelling
The warm tropical waters of the Seychelles are the perfect place to explore the underwater world. But, be warned, you could be spoilt forever! There are countless opportunities for both snorkelling and scuba diving, and the Seychelles can cater for all skill levels from the most timid person trying on a mask for the first time to advanced divers who flinch at nothing and scour the planet for exciting dive locations.

Diving takes place all year round in the Seychelles. The best months for calm, clear water are the inter-seasonal months of March to May and October to December. When the southeast trades are blowing, visibility is usually a bit reduced but pelagic fish increase in abundance, and the wonderful whale sharks arrive. During the northwest monsoon, choppy seas may make access to some dive sites difficult, but calm days intersperse the breezy days and a spot of rain never harmed a diver! There are numerous safe snorkelling sites, and on Mahé, Sunset Beach, Northolme and Port Launay Marine Park offer easy shore access.

Most of the dive operators are located on Mahé or Praslin and the

MARINE PROTECTED AREAS

The Seychelles has designated some 140km^2 of its territory for conservation of marine ecosystems, and the country has the distinction of having established the first marine park in the western Indian Ocean. The Ste Anne Marine National Park, which was proclaimed in March 1973, is probably the best known and, because of its proximity to Mahé, is visited by boatloads of tourists. The park encompasses the islands of Ste Anne, Moyenne, Round, Long and Cerf, together with the adjacent reefs and sea, an area of 15km^2. The park offers a diversity of marine habitats including fringing coral reefs, patch reefs, coral-encrusted granite boulders, seagrass beds, sand flats, intertidal rocks and sandy beaches. Snorkelling is permitted and, if you don't wish to get wet, tours by glass bottom boat set out from the Marine Charter Association jetty in Victoria. Fishing by visitors is prohibited, as is collecting of shells and coral.

The Seychelles Marine Parks Authority was created in September 1996 and is based at Cap Ternay (tel: 378096). It is responsible for the protection and management of all marine reserves, encouraging private investment within the parks (ecotourism), and collecting fees from tourist visitors.

The other areas managed by the Marine Parks Authority include Curieuse, Baie Ternay, Port Launay and the area surrounding Ile Cocos. The Curieuse Marine National Park was established in 1979, and extends from the northeastern shores of Praslin across to, and around, Curieuse and Ile St Pierre. Baie Ternay and Port Launay, adjacent areas at the western extremity of Mahé, were also established as marine parks in 1979; these bays are characterised by fringing reefs which can be viewed by snorkelling or glass bottom boat trips.

Aldabra, a World Heritage Site, serves as a flagship marine protected area and is administered by the Seychelles Islands Foundation. Similarly, the marine areas around Cousin and Aride are protected through the respective efforts of Nature Seychelles and the Island Conservation Society. African Banks, through its allocation to the Ministry of Defence, also offers some protection to the marine life in the area.

Seychelles Underwater Centre has a live-aboard vessel, *Indian Ocean Explorer*, which undertakes expeditions to the Amirantes and Aldabra. Around the granitic islands, a huge number of dive sites, mostly in the 10–30m depth range and requiring access by boat, are frequented by the various dive operators. Many can be dived during all seasons but some sites are specific during the southeast trades or northwest monsoon periods; others require very calm conditions. They include sites on coral reef pinnacles and drop-offs, granite boulders and tunnels, and eerie wrecks. The sites vary in the level of diving skills required, and many can also be dived safely at night.

Dive operators offer scuba-diving training courses under the auspices of the Professional Association of Diving Instructors (PADI), and these range from basic through to advanced as well as various specialist qualifications. Internationally recognised certificates are issued, and a basic open-water course comprises theory lessons, pool training and open-water training. The dive operators can provide full equipment rental and, in addition to single dives, offer packages of dives at different localities which are usually more cost effective.

Seychelles dive operators
Seychelles Underwater Centre Coral Strand Hotel, Beau Vallon; tel: 247357; fax: 344223; email: divesey@seychelles.net. Scuba-diving instruction and a range of diving activities are offered; now a PADI five-star instructor development centre. Operate the live-aboard vessel, *Indian Ocean Explorer*, specialising in diving and ecotourism voyages to the outer islands

Dive Resort Seychelles Plantation Club, Baie Lazare; tel: 361813

Island Ventures Berjaya Beach Resort, Beau Vallon; tel: 247165; fax: 247433; email: info@islandventures.net; www.dive-seychelles.com

Big Blue Divers Vacoa Village, Mare Anglaise; tel: 261106; fax: 247854; email: bigblue@seychelles.net; www.bigbluedivers.net

Les Diable Des Mers Beau Vallon; tel: 247104

Garry & Baptiste Beau Vallon; tel: 764573; email: oceand@seychelles.net

Dive Centre Le Méridien Barbarons, Port Glaud; tel: 378253

Whitetip Divers Paradise Sun Hotel, Anse Volbert, Praslin; tel: 232282; email: whitetipdivers@seychelles.sc

Octopus Diving Anse Volbert, Praslin; tel: 232350; email: octopus@seychelles.net; www.octopusdiving.com

Scubamania Diving Centre Marechiano Hotel, Grande Anse, Praslin; tel: 233875

King Bambo Live-aboard Dive Charters Côte d'Or, Praslin; tel: 232295; fax: 234366

Savuka Diving Centre Coco de Mer Hotel, Praslin; tel: 233900; fax: 233919

Bleu Marine Dive Centre Anse La Blague, Praslin; tel: 232178; fax: 232284

Azzura Pro Dive Anse La Réunion, La Digue; tel: 292535; email: azzura@seychelles.sc

Denis Island Lodge Denis; tel: 321143; fax: 324192

Dive Resort Seychelles Desroches; tel: 229119

Alphonse Water Sports Alphonse; tel: 229040; fax: 229033; email: alphonse@seychelles.net; www.alphonse-island.net

Angling
Big-game fishing around the islands of the Seychelles is possible all year round, and anglers troll the warm, blue waters for the likes of marlin, sailfish, tuna, wahoo, dorado, kingfish and barracuda from a wide range of charter fishing boats. Sailfish are much sought after, and the Seychelles ranks highly

as an international destination for those anglers targeting these magnificent fish. Silhouette, in particular, is the favoured area for sailfishing.

Fishing charter vessels operating in Seychelles waters range in size from 7m runabouts with outboard motors to 15m luxury vessels with inboard diesel engines and all the mod-cons. Those boats operating out of Mahé frequent sites such as North Island, Shark Bank, Silhouette, Hermes, D'An l'Or, Pilot Patches, Tocos, D'An Sud, Topaz Bank and Ile aux Récifs. Further afield, Denis and Bird, as a result of their location on the edge of the Seychelles Bank, offer excellent opportunities on the drop-off into the deep Indian Ocean waters. In fact, several world records for dog tooth tuna caught off Denis have been ratified by the International Game Fishing Association.

Many of the fishing boat operators promote the eco-friendly practice of tag and release, thereby ensuring sustainability of the fish resources. Fly-fishing is also becoming popular, and the Seychelles is gaining a reputation as the finest venue in the world for catching bonefish. Some boats also offer bottom-fishing opportunities to tourists, and the reefs around the Seychelles boast an amazing variety of sought-after reef fishes. Although the Seychelles reef fish stocks still appear to be in reasonable condition, cognisance should be taken of the stock collapses in many other parts of the world where fishing pressure has decimated populations of these relatively sedentary, long-lived, slow-growing species.

The **Marine Charter Association** in Victoria (tel: 322126; fax: 224679; email: mca@seychelles.net) is the place to contact to arrange a fishing trip. Other charter boat operations include:

The Boat House Beau Vallon; tel: 247898; fax: 247955
Striker Coral Strand Hotel, Beau Vallon; tel: 247848; fax: 247797
Ocean Girl Charter Bel Ombre; tel: 713371
Marlin Charters Providence; tel: 373439; fax: 373632; email: marlin@seychelles.net; www.seychelles.net/marlin
Water World Providence; tel: 373766; fax: 373788; email: wworld@seychelles.net; www.seychelles.net/wworld
Vladimir Mahé; tel: 376476; email: rsavycharter@seychelles.sc
Coco de Mer Charter Anse Bois de Rose, Praslin; tel: 233900; fax: 233919
Corsaire Boat Charter Hotel l'Archipel, Praslin; tel: 232138; fax: 232072; email: archipel@seychelles.net
Louis Bedier Anse Volbert, Praslin; tel: 232192; fax: 232356
Cookie-Two Desroches Island Lodge; tel: 229003; fax: 229002
Tam Tam Alphonse Island Resort; tel: 229042; fax: 229041; www.seychelles-flyfishing.com

Cruising

Cruising, by motor boat or sailing yacht, is a superb way to explore the Seychelles, and there are various options available for cruising amongst the inner islands or even venturing further afield to the Amirantes or alluring Aldabra. The **Marine Charter Association** (see above) represents many of the charter vessels, both yachts and game-fishing boats. Their quay, with bar and restaurant in downtown Victoria, is the best place to head for if you are contemplating any sort of boat hire.

The sailing charter business has grown considerably in the Seychelles in recent years, and nowadays numerous vessels are available for bareboat and crewed sailing charters. The two largest operators on Mahé are **Sunsail** (tel: 225700; www.sunsail.com) and **VPM Yacht Charter** (tel: 225676; email: vpmsey@seychelles.net) and both offer monohulls and catamarans. The Sunsail operation is located near the inter-island quay and VPM is located at Angelfish Bayside Marina off Providence Highway. On Praslin, **Dream Yacht Seychelles** (tel: 232681; www.dream-yacht-seychelles.com) operates from the marina near the jetty in Baie Ste Anne and offers a range of monohulls and catamarans. **Coco de Mer Charters** (tel: 233900; email: cocodeme@ seychelles.net) on Praslin have two catamarans available for charter. Generally, yachts can be chartered with crew or as bareboats where those with sailing skills hire the boat for a fixed period of days and cruise unassisted around the islands. In addition, some of the companies allow single clients or couples to reserve cabins on pre-planned cruises. This is particularly useful if one wishes to visit the outer islands like the Amirantes.

The large 'tall ship' sailing schooners *Sea Shell* and *Sea Pearl* (tel: 324026; fax: 322978; email: cruises@seychelles.net), operating out of Victoria, offer day trips and longer cruises around the inner islands for individuals and groups; . The large catamaran *Indiana* operated by Dream Yacht Seychelles offers day sailing trips out of Baie Ste Anne, Praslin.

The best time for cruising is September to December, after the boisterous southeast trades recede and before the unsettled rainy northwest monsoon sets in. April and May are also good months although inter-seasonal winds can sometimes be a bit light for making passage under sail. If you plan on heading to the outer islands, be sure to allow sufficient time to get there and back as well as to enjoy your tropical island destination. For a trip to the Amirantes allow about a week, and Aldabra at least two weeks, preferably more!

The **Seychelles Yacht Club** is conveniently situated adjacent to the Marine Charter Association, and has reciprocity with several foreign yacht clubs. The club has a bar and also offers reasonably priced meals. In Victoria, a few small shops sell chandlery items and Max Sails is a small sail-repair loft in Mont Fleuri, on the road to the airport. Nautical **charts** are, at present, not in stock anywhere in the Seychelles, and anyone cruising around the islands should consider purchasing the definitive cruising guide to the Seychelles by Alain Rondeau, which describes many of the stunning anchorages in fair detail (see *Appendix 2*).

Many motor boats are available for **island-hopping** day trips and they often double up as platforms for game fishing and diving. In addition to those available through the Marine Charter Association, Water World (tel: 373766; fax: 373788; email: wworld@seychelles.net) also offers motor boats for luxury cruising. *La Creole* is a 15m motor vessel available for day charters and excursions; tel: 322414; fax: 321366.

WORLD HERITAGE SITES

In 1972, UNESCO formulated the International Convention for the Protection of World Cultural and Natural Heritage, and over 100 countries, including the Seychelles, have signed and ratified the convention. The purpose of the convention is to ensure international co-operation for the protection and care of the world's irreplaceable heritage. Signatory countries have the responsibility to nominate places that are of outstanding universal value for possible inclusion on the World Heritage Site list. The World Heritage Committee uses a strict set of criteria to assess sites. It meets once a year to consider nominations for the list and, if necessary, remove from the list sites that have been allowed to deteriorate. Once sites are included on the list, the country is required to adopt policies and undertake specific actions to protect, conserve and present to the public these areas of natural and cultural heritage.

The Seychelles has two listed World Heritage Sites. Aldabra Atoll was recognised as a UNESCO World Heritage Site in 1982, and the magnificent palm forest of the Vallée de Mai on Praslin was added to the list in 1983. Both sites are administered by the independent Seychelles Islands Foundation, PO Box 853, Victoria, Mahé; tel: 224030.

Birdwatching

Birdwatching in the Seychelles is a treat and there are many desirable new ticks for your list! It is really easy to get around the main islands and, on Mahé, hiring a car will get you to the Morne Seychellois National Park to look for the Seychelles white-eye and the Scops owl which are notoriously difficult to locate. The other endemic birds can be seen in any of the natural areas and hotel gardens with flowering shrubs. Bird Island, with its vast seabird colonies, is easy to reach from Mahé, and arrangements can be made at their office in Independence Avenue, Victoria (see *Chapter 5*).

On Praslin, the black parrot is the target species, and the best place to see it is in the Vallée de Mai. The walk up to the shelter is often a good route to see the parrots, and look out for sunbirds in the flowering trees. It is also possible to see the parrots around the Coco de Mer Hotel. Cousin and Aride are fabulous places to observe seabirds and you are able to get really close up as they are used to visitors. They are both easily accessible from Praslin (see *Chapter 6*).

Aldabra is the ultimate birding destination in the Seychelles with endemic land birds and great colonies of breeding boobies and frigatebirds. Cosmoledo, too, is an exceptional atoll to visit. There are no tourist facilities on either Aldabra or Cosmoledo, and getting there is difficult and expensive. It is possible to visit these outlying atolls on the *Indian Ocean Explorer*, a live-aboard dive boat operated by Seychelles Underwater Centre (PO Box 384, Victoria; tel: 247357; email: divesey@seychelles.net), based at Beau Vallon on Mahé. Although they are diving specialists, they will gladly accommodate birdwatchers. The accommodation, food and all facilities are good, and they have small inflatable rubber boats perfect for exploring the shallow lagoons.

Nature Seychelles with its UK partner, BirdLife International, is one of the primary organisations concerned with research and conservation of birds and bird reserves. Nature Seychelles newsletter *Zwazo* is published twice a year. Their office is at Roche Caiman (tel: 601100). **The Island Conservation Society** (www.islandconservation.net) is a new organisation, formed in association with the Royal Society for Wildlife Trust, primarily for the protection of Aride. The **Nature Protection Trust of the Seychelles** (tel: 323711; email: npts@seychelles.net) is based on Silhouette and is also concerned with ornithological matters. A quarterly magazine *Birdwatch* covers birding and nature news from the islands.

Part Two

The Islands

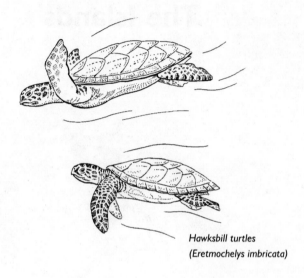

Hawksbill turtles
(Eretmochelys imbricata)

Mahé

Mahé is the largest island in the Seychelles. Granite hills and mountains rise steeply from the sea providing a dramatic backdrop to the irregular coastline. Mahé is 27km long, only 8km wide, and covers an area of 152km². It has a circumference of about 120km with breathtaking bays, intriguing coves and glorious long stretches of soft, white sand. Coconut palms and *badamier* and *takamaka* trees fringe the shoreline creating welcome shade and beautiful vistas.

The highest peak, Morne Seychellois, reaches up to 905m and, even on the hottest day, is frequently bathed in swirling mists. Much of the natural vegetation was destroyed in the early years of Seychelles settlement but the rich soils and high rainfall coupled with keen conservation by the Seychellois have been conducive to a remarkable recovery, and the slopes are now clad with many indigenous trees, ferns, palms and orchids.

A necklace of coral encircles this truly magnificent island, protecting and sheltering the bays and beaches. Every beach or cove of any size or importance is named *Anse*, from the French word for 'cove', and although there may be a small village with a church, school, clinic and shop, it is simply known by its beach name – Anse Royale, Grande Anse, Anse aux Pins, etc. The only town on Mahé, or the whole of the Seychelles for that matter, is Victoria, named in 1841 after the young queen of England.

Mahé is surrounded by groups of satellite islands. Closest to Victoria on the east coast are Ste Anne, Cerf, Moyenne, Round and Long islands. All these are situated within the Ste Anne Marine National Park. Thérèse and Conception are located off Port Glaud on the western side, while Silhouette and North can be seen off Beau Vallon. On a clear day with good visibility, other, more distant islands like Praslin, La Digue, Mamelle and Frégate may be seen.

It is possible to drive almost all the way around Mahé, and there are only a few short stretches in the western and southern extremities with no linking roads. A good system of well-maintained roads has been developed. However, they are not without their dangers. The roads climbing the steep slopes are narrow and twisting with some hairpin bends and few, if any, shoulders. To accommodate the tropical downpours, deep channels have been constructed along the sides of the roads. But, beware, there are no protective barriers, and frequently the white or yellow lines have been worn away and are hardly visible. There is an easygoing attitude among the drivers, who will frequently stop to chat to a fellow driver or pedestrian pal, with scant regard to traffic

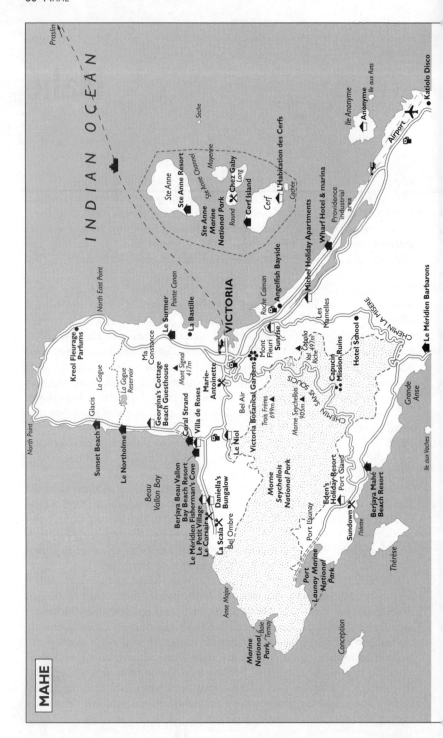

MAHÉ

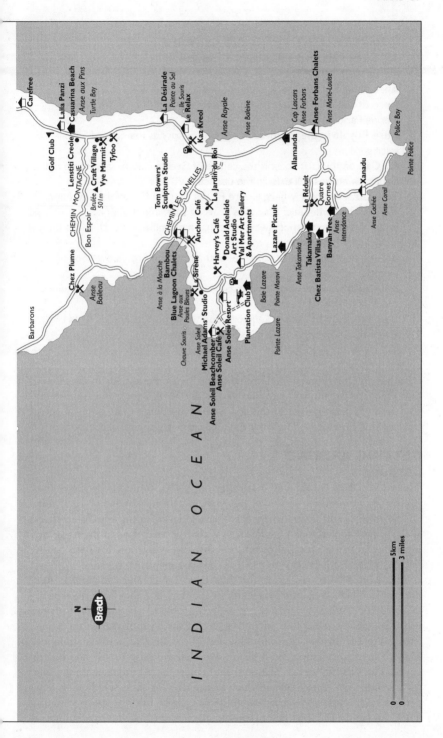

ADMINISTRATIVE DISTRICTS OF MAHE

Anse aux Pins on the east coast is characterised by protective reefs and old coconut plantations.

Anse Boileau is a large agricultural district on the west coast.

Anse Etoile on the coast north of Victoria overlooks the Ste Anne Marine Park.

Anse Royale in the southeast has a long history as the original Seychelles spice gardens.

Au Cap on the east coast is the centre of Creole culture, and some old plantation houses still exist in the district.

Baie Lazare is near where Lazare Picault first set foot in the Seychelles in 1742; the community maintains a strong maritime tradition.

Beau Vallon on the northwest coast has a magnificent beach and is the most popular tourist area.

Bel Air is a residential area in the foothills of Trois Frères overlooking Victoria.

Bel Ombre on the northwest coast is known for its fishing community and reputed pirate treasure trove.

Cascade, located between Victoria and the airport, is noted for its two waterfalls, imposing granite cliffs and Mont Sebert.

travelling in either direction. This, combined with the tourists in their hired cars who are unfamiliar with the geography, makes for some interesting situations. The saving grace, though, is that speeding is not often possible except along Providence Highway, the dual carriageway near the airport.

GETTING AROUND
Car hire

There are at least 30 car-hire companies in Mahé. Some of the larger hire companies have offices in town, but your hotel, guesthouse or local tour operator will be able to arrange car hire for you. Several companies have offices at the airport and are open for business when the international flights arrive. Hire only from a licensed hire company that shows a yellow HV sign on the number plate. It is advisable to take out the extra insurance cover.

The Mini-Mokes are great fun but they are getting old and a little unreliable. They offer little protection in the rain, and they have no reliable lockable boot. While security is not really a problem, it is not wise to leave valuable cameras or clothes in full view, and the lockable boxes on Mini-Mokes are an obvious target for thieves. There are five petrol stations on Mahé, located in Victoria, Beau Vallon, Baie Lazare, Anse Royale and Pointe Larue. The Victoria Service Station is on Francis Rachel Street, adjoining the garden of the law court. The daily newspaper, *The Nation*, is sold here. A new petrol station is under construction in Roche Caiman near the sports stadium. They close in the evenings before sunset, so make sure that you have sufficient

English River in the northern part of Victoria is a rapidly developing district.
Glacis in the north is characterised by spectacular, weathered granite and secluded beaches.
Grande Anse is another agricultural district on the west coast.
Les Mamelles, located inland and south of Victoria, is characterised by several imposing peaks.
Mont Buxton, overlooking Victoria and the east coast is adjacent to English River.
Mont Fleuri, south of Victoria, is home to the hospital, Botanical Gardens and several schools and colleges.
Plaisance is on the outskirts of Victoria between Mont Fleuri and Les Mamelles.
Pointe Larue with the international airport is the gateway to the Seychelles.
Port Glaud, near the western extremity of Mahé, has a waterfall and other fine natural assets.
Roche Caiman is the youngest district and is located on reclaimed land southeast of Victoria.
St Louis includes the central business district of Victoria.
Takamaka in the southwest is well known for its two beautiful beaches of Anse Takamaka and Anse Intendance.

fuel. Fuel costs SR7 per litre. On Mahé, distances are not great, and you will need less than half a tank of petrol for a leisurely circumnavigation. There are pay parking zones in central Victoria and tickets can be purchased from the nearby shops. Remember to drive on the left.

Avis Norman's Car Hire Tel: 224511; fax: 225193; email: avis@seychelles.net; www.avis.com.sc
Hertz Rent a Car Tel: 322447; fax: 324111; email: hertz@seychelles.net; www.seychelles.net/hertz
Sunshine Cars Tel: 225560; fax: 224204; email: sunshine@seychelles.net; www.seychelles.net/sunshine
Mein's Car Hire Tel: 266005; fax: 261169; email: meinscar@seychelles.net
Tropicar Tel: 373336; fax: 373757; email: tropicar@seychelles.net

Local buses

Timetables can be obtained at the central bus station in Palm Street, Victoria; tel: 224550. Whatever destination you choose, the fare will be SR3. Do not choose peak times to sightsee as the buses will be so full of commuters that you probably will not get a good view out of the windows. Few of the buses have bells, and the way to get the driver to stop is to yell '*devant*' very loudly before you need to get off. If you are unsure about where to get off, ask the person you are sitting next to, or the bus driver. Finding the desired bus at the bus station can be a little confusing, as the bus numbers do not correspond with the platform numbers. For example, to get to Beau Vallon, take buses numbered 20, 22 or 24 from platform 9. These buses all pass Beau Vallon en route to Glacis. Bus 20 leaves Victoria at 5 and 35 minutes past the hour, and bus 22 leaves Victoria at 20 and 50 minutes past the hour.

On Revolution Avenue, up the hill past Bel Air Road, there is a bus shelter, and this is a good place to catch the Beau Vallon or Glacis bus mid-morning or afternoon. If you try later at peak hour, the bus will be full and simply drive by without stopping.

There are many routes to get around Mahé, and it will be best for you to consult the timetable and associated map. Most of the buses run more frequently at peak times, but the timetable states that 'times are subject to change without notice'. Once out of the town area you will find 'BUS STOP' painted in large white letters on the road at the relevant stops.

Taxis

An efficient taxi service operates on Mahé. The main taxi rank is in Albert Street, Victoria, not far from the clocktower in the centre of the town (tel: 322279), and shaded by large, flamboyant trees. During lunch hour, two mobile food caravans are open for business, selling hamburgers at SR10, spare ribs, vegetable chow mein or chicken curry for SR20. There are reasonably clean public toilets at the back of the taxi rank.

Other taxis are based at centres around the island, and your hotel or guesthouse will be able to arrange one for you. There are always taxis to meet incoming flights at the airport at all hours of the day or night. They also meet the incoming ferries at the inter-island quay and cruise ships docking at the port. Taxis frequent the major hotels, and it is never a problem to find a taxi during the day, although you may have to telephone for one at night or early in the morning. All registered taxis display a red 'TAXI' sign on the roof and the drivers wear an identification badge. There is an agreed fare structure but it is a good idea to ask the taxi driver to turn on the fare meter at the start of the trip. It should cost about SR150 for a trip from the airport to Beau Vallon.

Drivers belong to the Taxi Drivers Association, and though not all of them speak English very well, many of them will gladly offer to take you on a 'tour' of their island.

Taking a tour

If you feel like having all the arrangements made for you, any of the tour companies in Mahé will be able to set up an interesting tour which could even be a personalised trip, tailor-made to your specific needs. Your expedition could be a simple half-day tour around part of the island, a full-day island tour, a snorkelling trip, an excursion to Praslin, La Digue or one of the other nearby islands or a scenic helicopter trip. Or you might like to hire a guide to take you on one of the mountain walks, or perhaps do an art tour and visit some of the colourful artists.

Many of the tour operators have fairly routine trips on a regular basis. Good guides accompany the tours, and a delicious Creole or seafood lunch is usually part of the deal on a full day out. Shop around to see which operators are offering the tour of your choice.

7°South Kingsgate House, PO Box 475, Victoria; tel: 322682; fax: 321322; email: 7south@seychelles.net; www.seychelles.net/7south

Blue Ocean Travel Providence; tel: 71577; fax: 374286; email: blueoceantravel@seychelles.sc

Creole Holidays Kingsgate House, PO Box 611, Victoria; tel: 280100; fax: 225817; email: resvnta@seychelles.net; www.creoleholidays.sc

Mason's Travel Revolution Av, PO Box 459, Victoria; tel: 288888; fax: 324173; email: masons@seychelles.net

Sea Shell Travel Agency Trinity House, PO Box 186, Victoria; tel: 324361; fax: 324274; email: seashell@seychelles.net

Travel Services Seychelles Mahé Trading Building, PO Box 356, Victoria; tel: 322414; fax: 322401; email: tss01@seychelles.net

Tourist information

The **Tourist Information Office** is in Independence House in Victoria. There you can pick up a good map of the main granitic islands as well as all the information you may need for getting around.

Inter-island travel

By air

Air Seychelles (tel: 381000; fax: 224305; email: info@airseychelles.com; www.airseychelles.com) operates a regular and frequent service to Praslin. Most of the flights to the other islands are generally included in package tours, as few, if any, cater for day visitors. The Air Seychelles office is in Victoria House close to the clocktower in Francis Rachel Street. Visit them to make reservations, and see also page 000.

Helicopter Seychelles (tel: 385858; fax: 373055; email: res@helicopterseychelles.sc; www.helicopterseychelles.com) can take you over to Praslin, La Digue, Silhouette, Frégate, North, Denis, Cousine, Félicité or even to other parts of Mahé. Scenic trips are also available and the Plantation Club has a helipad.

By sea

The most efficient way to get to Praslin is on *Cat Cocos*, the Australian-built 159-seater catamaran that regularly shuttles between Victoria and Baie Ste Anne, Praslin. The journey takes about an hour and payment by tourists is in foreign currency only. It costs US$40 or €40 one way on the main deck and US$45 or €45 on the upper deck Club Lounge which also has a small sun deck. Complimentary coffee and biscuits are served to Club passengers, while a bar in the main deck lounge sells drinks and snacks. Videos are shown in both cabins, which are fully air conditioned. There is an office at the inter-island quay; tel: 324843/44.

CAT COCOS SCHEDULE				
Days	Depart Mahé	Arrive Praslin	Depart Praslin	Arrive Mahé
Mon–Thu, Sat	07.30	08.30	09.00	10.00
	16.00	17.00	17.30	18.30
Fri	07.30	08.30	09.00	10.00
	16.30	17.30	18.00	19.00
Sun	10.30	11.30	15.00	16.00
	16.30	17.30	18.00	19.00

La Digue can be reached by using *Cat Cocos* over to Praslin and then the schooner for the short hop across to La Digue. The traditional inter-island schooners also ply between Mahé, Praslin and La Digue on weekdays. *Dauphin Noir* (tel: 234013) departs Mahé on Mondays and Tuesdays at 11.00, and departs La Digue the next day at 04.30; *Clarte* (tel: 234254) departs Mahé Mon–Fri at 11.30 and departs La Digue at 05.00 the following day. No one seems to answer the telephone and there are no reservations – just arrive at the quay. Tickets can be purchased on board in foreign currency only and cost US$10 one way. Remember to take something to drink as there are no refreshments on board. Excursions to the islands in the Ste Anne Marine Park can be arranged at the Marine Charter Association or through one of the tour operators with fees payable in foreign currency only.

The **Marine Charter Association** is on the sea side of 5th June Avenue in Victoria. They cater for boat charter needs and from their quay you will be able to arrange a snorkelling trip to the islands of Ste Anne and Cerf. The **Seychelles Yacht Club**, next to Marine Charter, is for members only, although it does have reciprocity with other yacht clubs.

WHERE TO STAY

Mahé offers a wide selection of large resorts, small hotels, guesthouses and self-catering establishments. All the larger hotels, and many of the smaller ones, have a watersports and dive centre, a swimming pool, satellite channel TV, DVD/CD facility, IDD telephone, minibar, safe and hairdryer. The bedrooms are generally air conditioned, but the smaller guesthouses may only have ceiling fans. Accommodation is listed according to area and prices are quoted in euros and are approximate for standard rooms. The cost will vary according to the season and type of room. Tour operators are frequently able to quote better prices and tour packages are often the most economical way to go.

Victoria

There are no hotels or guesthouses in the centre of Victoria, and the closest guesthouses are about a ten-minute walk from town.

Sunrise Hotel Mont Fleuri; tel: 224560; fax: 225290; email: sunrise@seychelles.net; www.seychelles.net/sunrise-hotel. Close to town, the hospital and Botanical Gardens. The 16 double rooms are en suite and air conditioned. Six of the rooms have attached kitchenettes so self-catering becomes an option. However, on request, Mrs Chung Faye, the charming manager, is able to provide all meals. She is an excellent cook and the delicious meals are Creole/Chinese in flavour. Bed and breakfast € 90 double, € 65 single; meals per person € 15.

The Wharf Hotel and Marina Providence; tel: 670700; fax: 601700; email: thewharf@seychelles.net; www.wharfseychelles.com. The hotel opened in 2004 and is very conveniently situated midway between the international airport and Victoria on the east coast of Mahé. There is a 4-bedroom penthouse with all the luxuries and 15 other bedrooms, 8 with a marina view and 7 with mountain views. The beautifully appointed hotel has a marina bar and a smart restaurant (La Buse), beauty salon, massage centre, shop, PADI dive centre and a swimming pool. The marina has a slipway and berthing facilities for 40 yachts on either a short- or long-term basis. € 201 per double room per night, bed and breakfast.

Le Sans Soucis Guesthouse Sans Soucis; tel: 225355; fax: 225352; email: sansouci@seychelles.net. This small guesthouse with only 3 rooms is located on the mountain road about 5 minutes' drive from Victoria and within walking distance of some of the fine nature trails and mountain walks. There is a swimming pool, car-hire service and guidance on some of the excursions. € 101–150 per double room per night, bed and breakfast.

Rose Garden Sans Soucis; tel: 225308; fax: 226245; email: rosgardn@seychelles.net; www.seychelles.scd/rosegarden. This old colonial house, in a large garden high on the mountainside with expansive views of the Trois Frères Mountain, has 5 spacious suites, a large swimming pool and a restaurant. Being higher, it can be a little cooler and has a quiet ambience. € 90–151 per double room per night, bed and breakfast.

Hilltop Guesthouse Serrett Rd, St Louise; tel: 266555; fax: 266505. About a 5-minute drive from the centre of Victoria, this 8-roomed establishment is owned by Mrs Fonseka of the Marie Antoinette Restaurant. € 50–74 per double room per night, bed and breakfast.

Northwest
Hotels
Le Méridien Fisherman's Cove Bel Ombre; tel: 677000; fax: 620900; email: reservations@lemeridien.sc; www.fishcove.lemeridien.com. This recently upgraded and refurbished 5-star hotel, which re-opened in July 2004, has a gracious ambience. The spacious rooms, each opening on to a sea-facing balcony or terrace, are beautifully decorated with mirrors reflecting the Indian Ocean. The reception area has cascading waterfalls, shop and spa and the new boardwalk leading to the Sunset Pavilion offers the best views of Beau Vallon Bay. There are 2 restaurants offering seafood, Mediterranean and local cuisine. A free-form swimming pool is set on the beachfront; a floodlit tennis court and non-motorised watersports are available. 70 rooms and suites; € 401–500 per double room per night, bed and breakfast.

Berjaya Beau Vallon Bay Beach Resort and Casino Beau Vallon; tel: 287287; fax: 247943; email: bhrseysm@seychelles.net; www.seychelles.net/berjaya. A large hotel with 232 rooms of varying grades from standard to a presidential suite, it is located on Beau Vallon Beach and offers a wide variety of watersports (Island Venture Dive Centre) as well as a large swimming pool adjoining the beach. The hotel features several restaurants – fine Cantonese cuisine at Le Canton, tasty Italian fare at the Pizzeria, the Parrot Restaurant serves traditional theme dinners and the Teppanyaki offers a traditional Japanese grill. Three bars are available and live bands regularly provide musical entertainment. Uncle $am's Dollar Room Casino is well frequented by visitors and residents. €251–300 per double room per night, bed and breakfast.

Le Northolme Hotel and Spa Glacis; email: northolme@seychelles.sc. This famous old hotel (see page 118) has been completely rebuilt incorporating all the most up-to-date amenities.

Coral Strand Beau Vallon; tel: 621000; fax: 247517; email: info@coralstrand.sc; www.coralstrand.com. This large hotel is superbly located on Beau Vallon Bay. It features a pool and several restaurants including the Mahek, well known for its authentic Indian cuisine. A variety of watersports are available and Teddy's Glass Bottomed Boat has an office here near the pool. €151–200 per double room per night, bed and breakfast. The hotel is scheduled for renovation.

Sunset Beach Hotel Glacis; tel: 261111; fax: 261221; email: sunset@seychelles.net; sunset-beach.com. The newly refurbished hotel is located on a spectacular small rocky peninsula and takes full advantage of views in both directions across the tiny bays to lush, dense vegetation, granite boulders and a beautiful secluded beach. The décor is most attractive with thatch and high ceilings, open-air eating facilities and a superbly sited swimming pool. The restaurant offers Creole, French and international cuisine. There is an unhurried atmosphere, palms and thatched umbrellas. Snorkelling from the beach is easy. 29 rooms, $301–350 per double room per night, bed and breakfast.

Coco d'Or Hotel Beau Vallon; tel: 247331; fax: 247454; email: cocodor@seychelles.sc; www.cocodor.sc. In a quiet road, 5 minutes' walk from the Beau Vallon Beach, the rooms of this attractively refurbished hotel all have a private balcony and air conditioning. The restaurant features Creole cuisine while snacks and drinks are served around the pool or at the Latanier bar. €169 per double room per night, bed and breakfast.

Small hotels, guesthouses and self-catering apartments

Le Petit Village Bel Ombre; tel: 284969; fax: 247771; email: lepetit@seychelles.net; www.lepetitvillage.com. This luxurious small self-catering establishment has 2 double bedroom apartments and 8 spacious studios. The air-conditioned log cabins are very well equipped with open-plan kitchen and living areas and en-suite showers; all open on to a garden almost on the water's edge and are serviced daily. Enjoy a sunset on the deck looking over to Silhouette or have a barbecue under the palm trees. Kayaks are available free of charge and other activities can easily be arranged by Paul and Karen, the friendly and efficient managers. A courtesy bus is available for airport transfers and, if convenient, for trips into town. All the amenities of the big Beau Vallon hotels are a mere 5 minutes away by car or bus. Snorkelling is great off the beach; turtles and spotted eagle rays are often seen drifting by. Meals can be arranged on request. Two of the best restaurants on Mahé, La Scala and Le Corsair, are within walking distance and the local small shops are close by. €201-250 per room per night.

Daniella's Bungalows Bel Ombre; tel: 247212; fax: 247784; email: daniella@seychelles.net; www.daniellasbungalows.com. 12 simple but comfortable bungalows set in a verdant garden with a small stream. Each bungalow has a private veranda and fans help to keep cool. Breakfast is served on the veranda of the main house and evening meals can be provided on request. The bungalows are located on the mountainside of the main road and are only a few minutes' walk from Beau Vallon. 12 rooms. €101–150 per double room per night, bed and breakfast.

Augerine Guesthouse Beau Vallon; tel: 247257; fax: 247257; email: augerine@seychelles.sc. The guesthouse is in the same small road as the Berjaya Beau Vallon Bay Beach Resort, almost on the beach. There are 4 comfortable rooms each with air conditioning, a small fridge and en-suite bathroom. €100–150 per double room per night, bed and breakfast.

Beau Vallon Bungalows Beau Vallon; tel: 247382; fax: 247955; email: bvbung@seychelles.net; www.seychelles.net/bvbung. Located in the centre of Beau Vallon Bay within easy walking distance to restaurants, shops, watersports centres and the bus stop. 12 comfortable bungalows have the self-catering option. Meals can be served on request. €75–100 per double room per night, bed and breakfast.

Panorama Relais des Iles Beau Vallon; tel: 247300; fax: 247947; email: panorama@seychelles.net; www.seychelles.net/panorama. This small, 10-room hotel is in a prime location only a few metres away from the Beau Vallon Beach and close to all the amenities of the area. €95 per double room per night, bed and breakfast.

Romance Bungalows Beau Vallon; tel: 247732; fax: 247797; email: romance@seychelles.net; www.seychelles.net/romance. There are 6 rooms in this small establishment located in the middle of Beau Vallon with all the amenities a short walk away. €75–100 per double room per night, bed and breakfast.

Villa de Roses Beau Vallon; tel: 247455; fax: 248136. This small, immaculate, family-run guesthouse surrounded by well-tended gardens is in a quiet road just a 3-minute stroll from the beach. Bed and breakfast and self-catering options are available. 8 rooms, €75–100 per double room per night, bed and breakfast.

Georgina's Cottage Beach Guesthouse Mare Anglaise; tel: 247016; fax: 247945; email: georgina@seychelles.net; www.the-seychelles.com/georgina. Father and son Mervyn and Patrick La Porte will warmly welcome you to this good-value, no-frills guesthouse, a mere 10m from Beau Vallon Beach. The rooms are simple, each with a bathroom and a ceiling fan. A well-equipped communal kitchen is for the use of all the guests. There are restaurants, hotels and a dive centre within easy walking distance and several small shops are close by; the bus stop is outside the gate. Breakfast is served on the veranda. 5 rooms, €60 per room per night, bed and breakfast.

Pti Payot Mare Anglaise; tel: 261447; fax: 261094; email: loulou@seychelles.net; check. There are 3 self-catering chalets, on the hillside close to the Beau Vallon Beach, each with air-conditioned bedroom, living area, kitchen and a veranda with views across the sea. €101–150 per double room per night, bed and breakfast.

Southeast and southwest
Large hotels
The Banyan Tree Anse Intendance; tel: 383500; fax: 383600; email: reservations-seychelles@banyantree.com; www.banyantree.com. This large and beautiful hotel has

been created in the colonial, Creole style of architecture with furnishings influenced by Indonesia and West Africa. The 36 luxurious secluded private villas are set far apart in lush vegetation overlooking Intendance Beach, either on the beachfront or higher up on the hillside. Each self-contained villa has its own pool and outside pavilion, the bedrooms are stunning and the bathrooms have wide windows facing out to sea. The central area of the hotel houses the restaurants, Saffron with Thai and southeast Asian specialities and Au Jardin d'Epices serving international and Creole cuisine. An open bar area serves a variety of drinks and snacks throughout the day. Meals can be served in the villa or on the beach. A gallery offering Banyan Tree products is available. There is a magnificent spa located in a secluded spot. Attention to detail is extraordinary with orchids and soothing scents, fine muslin drapes and glass walls. Therapists are specially trained in Thailand and India and offer a wide range of pampering treatments, some of which can be done in your villa. There is also a well-equipped gym and small conference room. An electric buggy will take you around the sprawling resort grounds and a 4WD will collect you from the airport. €1,050 per villa per night.

Plantation Club Resort and Casino Baie Lazare; tel: 386868; fax: 386883; email: rm@plantationclub.sc; www.plantationclub.com. Enormous traveller's palms that are native to Madagascar flank the entrance to this large 200-room hotel, and dark *glacis* forms a spectacular boundary to the right of the well-tended gardens: a 180-acre coconut plantation looking out on to a fine 1km stretch of beach. Each of the split-level, luxurious bedroom suites faces the sea or the freshwater lake. There are 3 restaurants, several bars and an enormous swimming pool. Large or small groups are well catered for as there is the flexibility of using different venues in the spacious public areas. Extensive facilities include a health centre, floodlit tennis courts, watersports, a diving centre and a children's club. Nightly live entertainment plus Planters Casino (open 20.00–02.00; slots 12.00–02.00) for roulette, blackjack and poker. The lily-covered lake is home to the rare yellow bittern, a bird that skulks in the vegetation, and a group of giant Aldabra tortoises are in a pen nearby. Antonio Filipini has a wood-sculpturing studio in the hotel grounds. €201–250 per double room per night, bed and breakfast.

Le Méridien Barbarons Barbarons; tel: 378253; fax: 378484; email: reservation@lemeridien.sc; www.lemeridien-barbarons.com. Large, spacious rooms all have their own private terrace. Facilities include swimming pool, tennis courts and beach volleyball. Three restaurants offer excellent Creole and international cuisine. Guests are entertained nightly with programmes of music and dancing. The hotel is scheduled for refurbishment. €251–300 per double room per night, bed and breakfast.

Berjaya Mahé Beach Resort Port Glaud; tel: 385385; fax: 378117; email: bmbsm@seychelles.net; www.seychelles.net/berjaya. This rambling old hotel is perched high on spectacular granite cliffs with stunning sea views and all 173 rooms are sea facing. The hotel has a large swimming pool, a health centre with sauna and massage, several restaurants and bars. The sprawling gardens are filled with tropical shrubs and palms and lead down to a private lagoon. Watersports available. €201–250 per double room per night, bed and breakfast.

Small hotels, guesthouses and self-catering

Casuarina Beach Hotel Anse au Pins; tel: 376211; fax: 376016; email:
casuarina@seychelles.net. This is a nicely relaxed and typically Seychellois
establishment only 5km away from the airport but with a glorious beach and shady
gardens. Each of the 20 rooms has a terrace and a sea view. The food is Creole and
Italian with plenty of fresh seafood. € 101–200 per double room per night, bed and
breakfast.

Le Relax Hotel and Restaurant Anse Royale; tel: 371515; fax: 371900; email:
helpdesk@lerelaxhotel.com; www.lerelaxhotel.com. Perched on a hill overlooking
the lovely Anse Royale and Souris Island, the hotel is only 2 minutes from one of the
best snorkelling sites at Fairyland Beach. The hotel offers 5 deluxe rooms and 4
standard rooms each with minibar, air conditioning, fan, TV, tea and coffee maker.
Breakfast can be served in the room or by the pool. This small hotel has many
facilities including internet, swimming pool, gym, beauty salon and body therapy
centre; babysitting and secretarial services are also available on request. They will go
out of their way to make your stay comfortable. € 101–150 per double room per
night, bed and breakfast.

Allamanda Hotel Anse Forbans; tel: 366266; fax: 366175; email:
amanda@seychelles.net; the-seychelles.com/allamanda. This small, 10-room hotel is
located in a modern, plantation-style house in a quiet part of southeastern Mahé. The
well-appointed, air-conditioned rooms are spacious and comfortable with sea and
beach views. The hotel is famous for its Sunday Creole buffet lunch served in an
open-air, beach-side shelter. Tour groups often stop in here for a good Creole lunch.
€ 158–229 per double room per night, bed and breakfast.

Anse Soleil Beachcomber Anse Soleil; tel: 361461; fax: 361460; email:
asbeachr@seychelles.net; www.beachcomber.sc. This quiet, 10-room hotel is ideally
located on a small, secluded, very beautiful beach with good snorkelling and
swimming. The road leading down to the hotel is a bit rough but don't be put off
because even a small car will manage it. Bed and breakfast and half board are offered.
The hotel is next door to the Anse Soleil café. € 120 for two people, bed and
breakfast.

Anse Soleil Resort Anse Soleil; tel: 361090; fax: 361435. The 4 houses used to
belong to the American tracking-station personnel and are now owned by Andrew
who runs them as a very comfortable self-catering establishment. Conveniently close
to restaurants and a large hotel, they are perched high on the hillside overlooking
Anse à la Mouche. There are different configurations to suit couples or families.
Living areas are comfortable with TV and music centre, floors are shiny cool granite
and the kitchens are well-equipped. Each spacious house has a private patio and lawn.
Andrew will prepare meals on request and will also do the airport transfers. € 70 for 2
people, € 100 for 4 people.

Val Mer Resort Baie Lazare; tel: 381555; fax: 361159; email:
valmer@seychelles.net; www.valmerresort.com. There are 14 light and airy studio
or 2-bedroom apartments; all are air conditioned with a good range of appliances.
The resort is adjacent to the Gerard Devoux Art Gallery and is conveniently located
close to a large hotel, beaches and restaurants. € 101–150 per double room per
night, bed and breakfast.

Xanadu Anse Cachée; tel: 366522; fax: 366344; email: xanadu@seychelles.net. There are 8 beautifully designed wooden chalets in lush gardens nestling into the steep hillside, each with a patio and every mod-con in the kitchen. A pool, restaurant serving excellent Creole cuisine and a private beach are available. €151–200 per double room per night, bed and breakfast.

Takamaka Residence Anse Takamaka; tel: 366049; fax: 366303; email: infobox@seychelleshotel.com; www.seychelleshotel.com. This small, no-frills hotel with 10 rooms is close to the lovely beach of Anse Takamaka. The outdoor restaurant serving good Creole and international food overlooks the lush, tropical garden. €101–150 per double room per night, bed and breakfast.

Island resorts close to Victoria

Anonyme Resort Tel: 380100; fax: 373551; email: anonyme@seychelles.net; www.anonyme.sc. Anonyme, a tiny granitic island only a short distance offshore from the airport has 6 luxury suites and a presidential suite designed for elegance and privacy. Guests can enjoy the pool, gourmet food and snorkelling off the island. €650+ per suite per night, half board.

Sainte Anne Resort Tel: 292000; fax: 292002; office tel: 376786; fax: 376296; email: res.sa@bchot.com; www.sainteanne-resort.com. Part of the Beachcomber Group, this large hotel spreads across a kilometre of the island. The 79 sea-facing villas with over 200m² of living space are private and beautifully appointed with luxurious bathroom, outside gazebo and walled garden. The Royal villa is enormous with 3 bedrooms and private pool. There are several restaurants; the Mont Fleuri, on stilts over a small inlet, is particularly attractive and serves fine gourmet fare. A spectacular infinity pool appears to merge into the sea with Mahé in the distance. A children's centre caters for the youngsters, electric buggies are on hand to transport you around the resort and a wide variety of watersports and a gym are available. If you need pampering, the resort has a luxurious spa using Clarins products. Transfers from Mahé take 20 minutes in a covered boat and depart from a quayside near the Unity Stadium. Helicopter transfers may also be made as there is a helipad at the resort. The boat may also be used, free of charge, by guests wishing to spend a day in Victoria. €750+ per double room per night, half board.

Cerf Island Marine Park Resort Tel: 294500; fax: 294511; email: info@cerf-resort.com; www.cerfresort.com. A small, 5-star boutique hotel with 12 lodges. €600–800 per lodge per night, half board.

L'Habitation des Cerfs Tel: 323111; fax: 321308; email: habicerf@seychelles.net. Designed as a plantation house, this small, 10-room hotel offers a really quiet and peaceful time on the tiny island of Cerf in the Ste Anne Marine National Park. Snorkelling and diving are available on the coral reefs around the island and the restaurant serves international and Creole meals. There is a free shuttle between Mahé and Cerf which takes 15 minutes. €177 per double room per night, bed and breakfast.

WHERE TO EAT

Most hotels are only too pleased to serve non-residents but, if they are full, they may not be able to accommodate extra guests. It is therefore really important to make a reservation beforehand. Menus are usually biased towards fresh fish and seafood with some chicken and meat, while salads and vegetables are not as prominent, as they are frequently imported. Wines are expensive with nothing available under SR150 per bottle and local beer is about SR20 in a restaurant.

Generally, restaurants are very casual, especially the ones on the beachfront – step off the beach in your swimming gear for lunch or even dinner. Hotels are often smarter; some require men to wear long trousers, not shorts, to dinner. The smaller cafés and restaurants that serve both lunch and dinner often close around 14.30 and re-open in the evening. Restaurants connected to hotels will accept payment only in foreign currency and may give change in rupees. Independent restaurants, however, are not obliged to accept foreign currency and will take Seychelles rupees.

Lunchtime is take-away time and there are many small places where you can find good-value tasty Creole/Chinese food served in a polystyrene box for around SR25. Alongside icy soft drinks and beer, many of the small shops sell a range of samosas, small pies and chilli bites, as well as sweet cakes, which are ideal for an inexpensive lunchtime snack. They are made on a daily basis so are always fresh, but you are not likely to find anything left after 14.00.

Particularly recommended hotel restaurants include the beautiful **Saffron Restaurant** at the Banyan Tree with its Thai and southeast Asian specialities. **Le Canton** at the Berjaya Beau Vallon Bay Resort is an excellent Cantonese restaurant and the **Mahek** at the Coral Strand, famous for its Indian dishes is well worth trying. The following are the major restaurants; other, smaller establishments may be mentioned in the text.

Victoria

Pirates Arms Independence Av; tel: 225001. *The* meeting, eating and drinking place in Victoria for locals and tourists alike. The bar and restaurant have an island-style atmosphere with fans whirring overhead. There is always an enjoyable buzz of activity, especially around lunchtime when tables are at a premium, particularly the ones overlooking the street. The menu is extensive and ranges from club sandwiches and pizza to grilled lobster. Prices are from SR35 upwards, fruit juices cost SR14, local beers from SR18 and pizza SR60. Service is somewhat nonchalant and slow so don't go there if you are in a tearing hurry or literally dying of thirst. It is open every day for lunch and dinner. Around the corner, the Pirates Arms has a take-away counter. Join the locals in the queue but remember it closes at 14.00. Chow mein, chicken curry or sausage and chips are around SR20–25.

Sam's Pizzeria Francis Rachel St, on the first floor of Maison Suleman, opposite the petrol station.

News Café Trinity House; tel: 322999. The latest lunchtime eating place for people working nearby. It is modern, air conditioned and light meals are available.

Gelateria Cristallo Market St. A tempting array of ice-creams (SR7 for a cone) and a selection of snacks that are ideal for a light and inexpensive lunch. Try the coconut ice-cream. Spring rolls are SR4 each and sweet cakes SR4.

Jolie Rose 2 Upper level of Victoria Market. Don't expect scintillating service or an inexpensive drink. It is open for lunch and chicken or fish curry is available from around SR60–90.

Kaz Zanana Gallery Revolution Av, opposite the bus shelter. Owned by the artist, Georges Camille, whose works are on permanent exhibition and are for sale. Light lunches are available. Located in a picturesque little wooden house, the restaurant part is situated at the back in two small rooms and spills out on to a lovely shady veranda. The menu is limited and prices range from SR55 to SR65 for tasty items like smoked fish salad, quiche lorraine, prawns and garlic sauce. Foreign newspapers are available at the bar. Open lunch only.

Marie Antoinette St Louis Rd; tel: 266222. This well-known restaurant is situated in a beautiful wood-and-iron colonial Seychellois house, and Madame Fonseka, the owner, serves superb traditional food in true Creole style. Open for lunch and dinner, closed Sun. Reservations recommended as this is known as the best Creole restaurant in Victoria.

Further afield

La Scala Bel Ombre; tel: 247535. Open for dinner only, closed Sun. Perched high on the granite rocks with great ocean views, this restaurant is famous for its fine Italian food. Homemade pasta is a speciality. Off-road parking.

Le Corsair Bel Ombre; tel: 247171. Open Tue–Sun evenings only. The restaurant is set on the edge of the small fishing harbour of Bel Ombre, and looks like an English Tudor house. It has a lovely ambience created by the very high thatched roof and the tall windows which open out giving views of the tiny fishing boats and lights reflecting on the water. The Italian and Creole food is excellent with generous portions and the fresh fish is particularly good. Expect to pay upwards of SR100 for a main course.

The Boat House Beau Vallon; tel: 247898. A very casual restaurant. The Creole buffet available Tue–Sun evenings is good value at SR115; a wide variety of local salads, vegetables and fruits are served with plenty of fresh fish. On Mon evenings a barbecue is served, mainly meat and fewer salads, SR115.

Al Mare Beau Vallon; tel: 620240. Open 10.00–22.00 daily, but closed Thu. Located on the beachfront with the best sunset views over to Silhouette and North islands; tables are inside or on the patio. The restaurant specialises in seafood but meat and vegetarian meals are also available. An average main course will cost about SR100.

Baobab Pizzeria Mare Anglaise; tel: 247167. This casual, toes-in-the-sand, pizzeria is on the water's edge at the end of Beau Vallon Beach. At low tide some tables are on the beach under the *takamaka* trees. Excellent pizzas are cooked in a huge outdoor oven and the fried fish and chips is good value. Musciaisn sometimes entertain the diners.

La Perle Noire Beau Vallon; tel: 620220. The restaurant looks a little scruffy from the outside, but tables are set on the attractive veranda and the Italian/Creole food is really good. Expect to pay SR100–150 for a three course meal and more for seafood.

La Belle Créole Restaurant in the North Point Centre is open 11.00–22.00 for lunch and dinner. Meals (typical Creole fare) are about SR60–80. On Sun, a buffet lunch is available for SR115 and you may eat as much as you like.

Chez Plume Anse Boileau; tel: 355050. Situated in an attractive house serving reasonable Creole food. Be adventurous and try the bat pâté!

Kaz Kreole Restaurant and Pizzeria Anse Royale; tel: 371680. Closed Mon. This open restaurant is on the beach at Anse Royale and serves pizza and Italian food. Live music and dancing entertains guests on Sat nights.

Vye Marmit Anse aux Pins, tel: 376155. Open daily 12.00–21.30, closed Sun. A most attractive restaurant, in a lovely Creole house, set in the grounds of the craft village. Try their octopus salad. The grilled red snapper is very good and costs SR95.

La Sirène Anse Poules Bleues; tel: 361339. Open daily for lunch 11.30–17.00. A rustic-looking restaurant with great views of the bay serving a wide range of Creole food. Try the roast flying fox (SR80); chicken or fish curry is also good as is the grilled fish.

Le Jardin du Roi Anse Royale; tel: 371313. Open daily 10.00–16.30. Once you have made a tour of the spice gardens and looked at the museum, try one of their fresh fruit drinks, snack on a delicious sweet or savoury crêpe or be extravagant and have a tasty spiced ice-cream. The menu is small and uses the spices grown on the plantation. The 3-course plantation lunch on Sun is worth trying.

Anse Soleil Café Baie Lazare; tel: 361700; mobile: 511212. Open daily for lunch. It is worth making the trip down the rather rough road to this rustic, palm-thatched little restaurant. It is a few steps up from the particularly lovely beach and the advantage of the sandy floor is that the tables never wobble. Seafood curry or seafood with ginger is SR85–95, chicken and chips SR60, fish and chips SR55 and two scoops of ice-cream will set you back SR16.

VICTORIA

Victoria, one of the smallest capitals in the world, nestles beneath the imposing granite mountains on the northeast side of Mahé on a ribbon of flat land edging the sheltered bay. It is an interesting little town with typical Creole-style buildings interspersed with more modern architecture. In keeping with the promotion of Creole culture, many of the new buildings follow the traditional style, and some even have a vaguely Indian influence with ornate archways and small tiles. There is a general air of prosperity, new buildings are under construction, the streets are clean, the people appear healthy and well fed, and there are no beggars. However, sometimes the shops simply do not have the specific item that you require as everything has to be imported and foreign exchange is limited.

Victoria is a busy commercial centre, well-serviced by banks, shops and restaurants. Taxis and buses operating from the town centre provide quick and easy connections with the rest of the island. Down at the harbour, the inter-island quay has boats of all descriptions travelling to many of the islands, and the deep-water international quay provides access for large cruise ships and cargo vessels. Located between the two busy quays are the Seychelles Yacht Club and the Marine Charter Association. Unfortunately, the tuna factory is also down on the quayside and, at times, the smell from the processing strongly pervades the air.

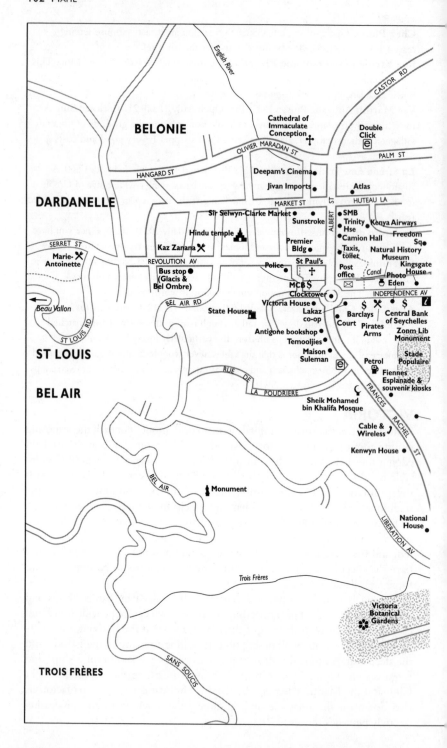

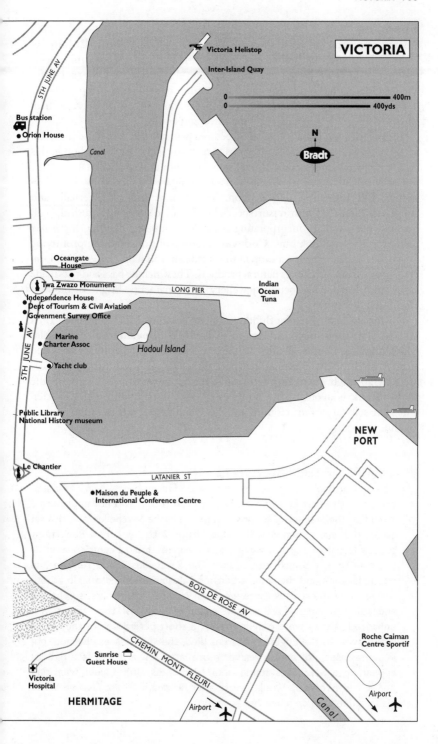

Shopping

There are several souvenir shops in Victoria, including **Antik Colony** on Independence Avenue behind the Pirates Arms which sells charming local products. Souvenir kiosks also line Fiennes Esplanade and the colourful Victoria Market hs wonderful spices and a range of souvenirs (see page 111).

Between Barclays Bank and the law court is **Lakaz Co-operative**, a small shop selling handmade curios, phone cards and books.

Temooljies, on Francis Rachel Street, is a general store and there is a small arcade next to it with a variety of shops. **Antigone** is the tiny bookshop in this arcade, with a wide selection of books dealing with the Seychelles.

Camion Hall, on Albert Street, is a shopping arcade incorporating several outlets. **Ou Linet**, an optical shop, sells contact lens paraphernalia and sunglasses, and they also repair spectacles. **Kreol d'Or** sells beautiful, high quality, gold jewellery incorporating many local subjects like the *coco de mer* palm, tortoises and dolphins. **Codevar**, a non-profit organisation promoting Seychelles handicrafts, has a shop in the arcade, and all items are genuine local crafts made from Seychelles natural products. They include bags and hats made from palm leaf fibres, coconut jewellery and ornaments, bright island-style clothing and postcards.

Downstairs in the Premier Building opposite Camion Hall is the **Sooty Tern** art and craft shop. Beyond Camion Hall, **SMB Supermarket** (Seychelles Marketing Board) offers all the usual supermarket fare. Foodstuffs are imported from Australia, New Zealand, Singapore, Pakistan and South Africa, so prices are generally high. **Jivan Imports**, a little further down the street opposite the **Habib Bank**, is an old, rusty, Creole-style building resounding with character. The store sells fabrics and clothing and the copious wares hang from the ceiling and line the walls.

STAMPS OF THE SEYCHELLES

The first post office opened in Victoria on December 11 1861 as a sub-branch of the Port Louis post office in Mauritius. It was not until April 5 1890 that the first set of stamps was issued in the Seychelles, and this set comprised eight stamps with values from 2 to 16 cents. Reportedly parcels less than 1.5kg in weight cost 2 rupees and 22 cents to send by sea mail to any British destination. The Seychelles was a remote and exotic location and the stamps became valuable to collectors. To add to the rarity of the stamps there were die changes, overprints, surcharges and value changes. Further, the value of many of the stamps was enhanced as they were only in use for a short period before they were withdrawn. As the English monarchs died, the stamp faces changed, but in some cases, not until a year or more later. Edward VII's face did not appear on a Seychelles stamp until 18 months after Queen Victoria's death, and two years would elapse after his death before George V had his face depicted on a Seychelles stamp.

Opposite Jivans, the **Sham Peng Tong Plaza** with the **Bank of Baroda** on the ground floor also has a variety of small shops selling a wide range of bazaar-type goods.

Other practicalities
Post, telephone and internet
The **post office** (open Mon–Fri 08.00–16.00; Sat 08.00–12.00) is on the corner of Independence Avenue and Francis Rachel Street opposite the clocktower. It is an old, granite building with card and coin public telephones situated outside the entrance near the postboxes. Phone cards are on sale here: SR30 for 30 units, SR55 for 60 units, SR105 for 120 units and SR200 for 240 units. It costs SR3 to send a postcard anywhere in the world and the colourful stamps depict the remarkable scenery and natural history of the islands. Aerogrammes can be purchased for SR2.50. There is a special philately counter that sells sets of stamps for collectors (see box below).

Behind the Pirates Arms on Independence Avenue is a small arcade (with public toilets) where there's an internet bureau, **Kokonet** (open Mon–Fri 08.00–18.00, Sat 08.00–12.00, closed Sun; SR10 for 15 minutes). Opposite the pay parking on Francis Rachel Street is a scruffy-looking little lane (La Poudrière) which leads to a building housing **Digitech Internet Bureau** on the first floor (open Mon–Fri 09.00–18.00, Sat 10.00–17.00; SR10 for 15 minutes, SR35 for one hour).

Cable & Wireless is next door to Kenwyn House on Francis Rachel Street. Fax, telegram, telephone and internet services are available (SR11 for 15 minutes, SR32 for one hour). Open daily 08.00–16.00.

The Net internet bureau (ground floor, Sham Peng Tong Plaza, Albert Street; open Mon–Fri 08.00–13.00 and 14.00–17.00, Sat 08.30–13.00)

The Silver Jubilee set issued in 1935 caused a furore when it was discovered that some stamps showed an extra flagpole on Windsor Castle! The random deviants fetched prices way above their value. The next set of stamps issued for the coronation of King George VI sold for such incredibly high prices that the government was able to fund some reclamation work in Victoria. The first photogravure pictorial stamps, depicting typical Seychelles subjects, were issued in 1938, and some of these showed errors and retouching and became sought after by philatelists.

Over the years the natural heritage of the Seychelles has been used to illustrate many of the stamps. Stamps are often issued in commemorative blocks with each set surrounded by an illustrated margin. The outer islands, *Zil Elwannyen Sesel*, had their own sets of stamps issued from 1980. They could be purchased in faraway places like Aldabra and Farquhar and became very valuable. The first set of these had five 2-rupee stamps, each depicting a different type of coral, and the entire set joined together illustrated a coral garden.

charges SR10 for 15 minutes or SR40 for one hour. Next door is Trinity House with **AirTel** at street level. Telephone cards are available for SR50 or SR100. Upstairs, News Café offers refreshments. **MBM Internet** (open Mon–Fri 09.00–18.00, Sat 09.00–13.00; SR10 for 15 minutes, SR40 for 1 hour) is a cool haven to access your emails on a hot day. There is also **Atlas** on Huteau Lane.

Banks
Several of the major banks have branches in Mahé:

Barclays Bank with a convenient ATM is opposite the Natural History Museum on Independence Avenue
Central Bank of Seychelles The large, modern, glass-fronted building is opposite Kingsgate House
Mauritius Commercial Bank (MCB) Albert St, on the corner opposite the post office
Nouvobanque Victoria House, corner of Francis Rachel St and State House Rd, diagonally opposite the post office

Photography
Print film can be processed in a couple of hours at photographic shops on both sides of Independence Avenue. **Photo Eden Kodak Express** is near the Pirates Arms and **Kim Koon** is across the road in Kingsgate House. Camera batteries and various films are sometimes available but it is wise to travel with adequate supplies of your own favourite brands.

Discovering Victoria
The clocktower
The clocktower is the focal point of the town and stands in the middle of the important intersection of Independence Avenue and Francis Rachel Street (Francis Rachel was the first Seychellois soldier to die in the 1977 coup). The silver-painted clock is a replica of that on London's Vauxhall Bridge Road. It arrived in the port in Mahé in 1903. As the clock was being unloaded, the pendulum accidentally fell into the water and was never recovered. Although a new one was made, the clock never chimed, and seldom displayed the correct time. As a millennium treat, a new mechanism was installed, and a local businessman commented 'Its soul is full of memories, it gave freely the time to everyone, to work, play, think or just do nothing.' The clocktower is a good starting point for setting out to explore Victoria on foot.

Independence Avenue
This tree-lined boulevard runs from the clocktower away from the mountain towards the ocean and it is here that banks, restaurants, travel companies and assorted shops and offices are located.

The **Law Court** building on the opposite corner to the post office (see page 105) is elegantly reminiscent of the colonial era. Under the shady trees is a small statue of Queen Victoria, and on the other side of the building is a bust

MONUMENTS

Despite a relatively short period of human settlement, extending over only two centuries, the Seychelles does have some interesting artefacts. Since the introduction, in 1980, of the National Monuments Act, which protects objects of architectural, archaeological or historical interest, about 30 structures have been proclaimed as national monuments. In fact, in terms of the act, any building, grave, or structure erected or used before 1900 must remain undisturbed. Most of the declared national monuments are located on Mahé, though the Roman Catholic churches on La Digue and Praslin, the plantation houses on Silhouette, Farquhar and La Digue, and the doctor's house on Curieuse are on the list. The granite boulders at L'Union Estate on La Digue are the only natural feature to be declared a national monument.

The original Stone of Possession, initially placed on the hillside in present-day Victoria by the French in 1756, is now lodged in the National Museum. It did, however, survive an unsolicited round trip to Europe when a visiting French general took it away to present it to the Paris Museum. Also in the National Museum is the small original statue of Queen Victoria which was unveiled in 1897 to mark her diamond jubilee. A replica is located above the Jubilee Fountain, in front of the Law Court building which dates back to 1887.

The State House, and the cemetery in its grounds where several colonial administrators are buried, also constitute national monuments. The most prominent tomb is that of the last French commandant, Queau de Quincy, who died in 1827. Other national monuments in Victoria include St Paul's Anglican Cathedral, the priest's house at the Catholic Cathedral of the Immaculate Conception, the Bel Air cemetery, the Botanical Gardens, Freedom Square, La Bastille, the Maison du Peuple, the bust of Pierre Poivre and the Bicentennial Monument (Twa Zwazo) with its three crescents symbolising the African, Asian and European origins of the Seychellois people.

Probably the best-known monument is the Victoria clocktower, which was intended as a memorial to Queen Victoria. However, as the Seychelles became a Crown Colony within a few weeks of its unveiling in 1903, the clocktower has become more accepted as a symbol of the gradual advance of the Seychelles to independence than a memorial to a dead queen.

of Pierre Poivre from Mauritius, who was responsible for establishing the first spice gardens on Mahé.

A little further down from the post office on the same side of Independence Avenue is the **National Museum of Natural History** (open Mon–Fri 08.30–16.30; Sat 08.30–12.00). It was originally the Carnegie Library and is now a national monument. The entrance steps are flanked by a replica of a large crocodile on one side and a sad-looking dugong on the other. It is a small, but interesting, museum with historical and cultural exhibits as well as several of environmental interest that inform the visitor about the various ecosystems of the Seychelles. Admission SR10.

If you're in need of refreshments try the **Pirates Arms** (see page 99). Public toilets are located in the arcade behind the Pirates Arms.

Bird Island Lodge has an office in Kingsgate House and the friendly staff will cheerfully make your reservations to visit this amazing seabird breeding island. **Creole Holidays** (see page 91) is located nearby.

Independence House is the large building on the corner of Independence Avenue and 5th June Avenue that houses a variety of offices and shops and the tourist information office. At street level there is a small fountain, and a convenient snack counter that sells samosas, sandwiches, pies and soft drinks. Upstairs there are several government offices including tourism and civil aviation.

The white **Bicentennial Monument** on the roundabout at the intersection of Independence Avenue and 5th June Avenue is known locally as **Twa Zwazo** ('Three Birds') and symbolises the unity of the Seychellois heritage – Africa, Asia and Europe. The enormous sculpture is the work of Lorenzo Appiani, an artist of Italian descent. Independence Avenue continues beyond the roundabout towards the sea and passes the Indian Ocean Tuna factory en route to the inter-island quay, from where the schooners and catamaran depart. **Oceangate House**, a large office block near the roundabout, accommodates the social service departments and a dental clinic. It also has an amusement centre with bar and 190 slot machines. Open 10.00–02.00.

The inter-island quay
Various inter-island schooners and *Cat Cocos* (see pages 91–2) depart from this quay. There are booking offices here for the ferries as well as **Sunsail** and **VPM** yacht charters. Taxis usually await the arrival of *Cat Cocos* from Praslin.

5th June Avenue
This wide road, built on reclaimed land, links the two roundabouts of Twa Zwazo and Le Chantier. Dominating the gardens on the right is a large bronze statue of a man, arms held high, escaping from a broken chain. It is the **Zonm Lib monument** celebrating freedom and liberation from colonialism.

Overlooking the harbour by the Marine Charter Association (see page 92) is a somewhat scruffy-looking restaurant and bar. The curried octopus is especially good value for about SR25.

Hodoul Island is a tiny piece of land in the middle of the yacht basin, covered in casuarina trees and egrets. It is named after Jean François Hodoul, a 17th-century corsair.

The **National Library** (open Mon–Fri 08.30-16.30, closed Wed, Sat 08.30-12.00; admission free) has an impressive façade facing 5th June Avenue but the main entrance to this imposing, modern brick and glass building is in Francis Rachel Street. It houses the public and reference libraries, archives, an art gallery as well as the **History Museum**. Here you can see a variety of artefacts of historical interest including the Stone of Possession, which was originally placed on the island as a formal act by France in 1756. There are photographic portraits of all the British Governors of Seychelles. The **Legislative Assembly** and some government offices are also located in this building.

Le Chantier roundabout has a striking monument with four huge, white sailfish rising out of a fountain. The French name is a reminder that this was once a boat-building yard on the shoreline. Several roads lead off this roundabout.

Chemin Latanier

This is the road leading down to the **New Port**, the deep-water harbour where visiting cruise ships and other large vessels moor. A large model aeroplane and playground are on the left. The **Maison du Peuple** on the right-hand side of Chemin Latanier is a modern building housing the offices of the Seychelles People's Progressive Front and the **International Conference Centre**. The main auditorium can seat up to 600 delegates, while the various smaller rooms can handle 150 to 225 delegates. For bookings contact the Ministry of Tourism and Civil Aviation (PO Box 92, Mahé; tel: 224030; fax: 225897; email iccs@seychelles.net). A large round building on the left holds the offices for Desroches and Alphonse Islands.

Avenue de Bois Rose and Providence Highway

Avenue de Bois Rose is a relatively small road leading off Le Chantier and is the quickest way to the airport as it links into **Providence Highway**, the only dual carriageway in the Seychelles. It has a speed limit of 80km/h and is about the only time you can get into fifth gear! The surrounding area is reclaimed land, and was named Roche Caiman after the crocodiles that used to inhabit the lagoon before the settlers arrived. The large **Unity Sports Stadium** is located along this road and there is a small bird sanctuary incorporating some remaining mangroves near the offices of **Nature Seychelles**, a vibrant NGO headed by Nirmal Jivan Shah that deals with a range of diverse conservation issues (see *Chapter 3, Biodiversity*). The **Seychelles International Business Authority** office can also be found in this area, and the fairly new housing estate is conveniently situated for people working in town. A new modern petrol station is being constructed next to the car wash.

Once on Providence Highway most of the development can be seen on the sea-side of the road, as a shallow lagoon runs the length of the road on the landward side. **Angelfish Bayside** has a small marina, an office for yacht charters and a dive centre. **VPM Yacht Charter** also has an office here. Further on, and set a little way off the road, is **The Wharf Hotel and Marina** (see page 93) which offers sophisticated accommodation as well as a slipway and berthing facilities for 60 vessels. North Island offices are located adjacent to the hotel.

Heading towards the airport, the distinctive red-roofed **church of St Andrew** can be seen on the right above the lush green vegetation of Cascade. The light industrial area of Providence is on the left and it is here that Helicopter Seychelles has its office. The Highway meets up with Chemin Mont Fleuri at the airport.

Chemin Mont Fleuri

This road also leads off Le Chantier roundabout, and is the road to take to the hospital and the Botanical Gardens. The road continues to the airport, and beyond to the south of Mahé. **National House**, on the upper side of the road, houses some government offices. **Liberation Avenue** is a narrow, little road winding up the mountainside of Victoria, and which meets up with Bel Air Road.

The **Botanical Gardens** (open daily 08.00–17.00; entrance fee US$5 or €5) have a good selection of Seychelles indigenous plants as well as numerous introduced species and an orchid house. A map of the gardens, which includes a list of most of the plants, is available at the entrance kiosk

VICTORIA BOTANICAL GARDENS

The Botanical Gardens were started in 1901 by Paul Rivaltz du Pont. As director, he made two sorties to the East where he collected many specimens for the gardens. They were chiefly crop plants but he also brought back many ornamental shrubs and trees. The gardens became part of the Department of Agriculture and du Pont became Director of Agriculture. In this position he was able to maintain his interest in the gardens until he retired in 1934 after making a significant contribution to the botanical knowledge of the Seychelles. The 6ha park, besides being a retreat from the bustle of Victoria, has a fascinating array of plants and houses the Ministry of Health and the Department of the Environment. There is an impressive collection of tropical palms, including the six Seychelles endemic species. A group of bottle palms are on the left near the entrance and Pritchard palms and *coco de mer* palms flank the long driveway. A group of endemic screw pines, *Pandanus hornei*, are at the top end of the gardens close to the cafeteria. Several streams trickle down the hillside and the lawn at the top of the drive leads to a pond with huge-leafed *Alocasias* and water lilies. The cannon ball tree, *Couroupita guianensis*, has pink flowers on the tree trunk, and the large round fruits resemble cannon balls. Nutmeg, cinnamon and allspice trees are dotted about, and there is also a small collection of trees from Aldabra. An orchid house at the top end of the gardens houses a collection of exotic orchids from all over the world. See if you can find the plaque commemorating the environmental time capsule that was buried in the gardens on June 3 1994 and is due to be opened in 2044.

next to the car park. Various souvenirs are available and this is a good place to pick up leaflets describing the various walks on Mahé. Some of the more comprehensive leaflets are SR10 each. This is one of the best places to photograph both male and female *coco de mer* palms as they are out in the open and in good light. Near to a *coco de mer* planted by HRH Duke of Edinburgh during his brief visit to the Seychelles in 1956, is a large pen housing a collection of Aldabra tortoises. The offices of the Department of the Environment are located in the Botanical Gardens. Toilets are on the left of the main path about halfway up the driveway. Le Sapin Cafeteria (open Mon–Fri 09.00–17.00, Sat 09.00–12.00, closed Sun), also at the top end of the gardens, offers hot and cold drinks and snacks, some made from local herbs and fruits. A colony of fruit bats roosts in the tall trees behind the cafeteria.

Victoria Hospital, next to the tranquil gardens, has modern facilities to cater for most health problems (see *Health* in *Chapter 4*, pages 63–7). **Aarti Chambers** is opposite the entrance to the hospital. The Aromatherapy Centre has a salon on the lower level and they will attend to all your beauty requirements, and Shape Health and Fitness Centre is also on the lower level. The privately owned island of Frégate has an office on the upper level. At the back of Aarti Chambers is a private dental clinic.

Francis Rachel Street
This road connects the centre of town with Le Chantier roundabout. **Kenwyn House** is on the left if you are walking from Le Chantier towards town. It is a wonderful example of a typical colonial Creole house built in about 1868. Now a national monument privately owned by Cable & Wireless (next door), it is used as the manager's residence.

Souvenir kiosks line the right-hand side of the road along the tree-shaded **Fiennes Esplanade**, which was once on the seafront. There you will find colourful pareos and shirts, hats made from coconut fibre, and all sorts of other knick-knacks. Resist buying the shells as many are not sustainably harvested out of the sea and many are not even from Seychelles. The **Sheikh Mohamed bin Khalifa Mosque** is opposite the kiosks, and there are several typical old, iron, Creole-style buildings with little, shuttered windows jutting out of the high-pitched roofs. **Stade Populaire** is behind the kiosks and pay car park. This stadium is the venue for large events like soccer matches, holiday parades and school sports events. This part of Victoria is built on reclaimed land.

The large building on the corner of Francis Rachel Street and State House Road is **Victoria House**, home to several embassies, Air Seychelles and the Nouvobanque.

State House Road
This small road leads up to **State House**, the home of the president, which is closed to the public. A square granite building located near the driveway entrance to the house was inaugurated by Sir Ernest Bickham Sweet-Escott in 1902, and was utilised as offices for the various Governors until 1934.

After that it was used by government departments, and served as the National Library for many years before becoming a museum; currently its future is uncertain.

From the car park in State House Road, a walled alley leads into Revolution Avenue between the police station and the Anglican cathedral. It crosses the St Louis River and you can often see cattle egrets and green-backed herons fishing in the clear waters.

Albert Street

Named after Queen Victoria's husband, this street is a continuation of Francis Rachel Street on the other side of the clocktower. To discover more of Victoria continue along Albert Street in a northerly direction, passing the Mauritius Commercial Bank and Travel Services Seychelles (see page 106).

Freedom Square, the large grassy area behind the taxi rank, was formed during the avalanche of 1862 when part of the St Louis hillside slid on to Victoria, killing 75 inhabitants. It was originally known as Gordon Square, after Sir Charles Gordon of Khartoum fame. The present name came into use after the political rallies that were held there during the revolutionary period of the mid-1970s.

Camion Hall (see page 104) is a shopping arcade next to the taxi rank. Opposite is the **Premier Building** where the Seychelles Islands Foundation has its office upstairs (tel: 224030). Further along is the fascinating Jivan Imports (see page 104), where you may meet the owner, Kantilal Jivan Shah, commonly known as Kanti. This ebullient octogenarian is a walking fountain of knowledge when it comes to Seychelles history or anything to do with the wildlife. He is particularly fond of the ladies, and will offer to read your palm and show you his scrapbooks! He has a most comprehensive private library.

Market Street leads off to the left and Huteau Lane to the right.

Olivier Maradan Street

At the end of Albert Street there is an intersection, with Olivier Maradan Street leading off to the left. Located there is the stone **Catholic Cathedral of the Immaculate Conception** which was built in 1900. The grand, almost Spanish-looking building to the left of the cathedral is the priest's residence and is a national monument.

Palm Street

At the Albert Street intersection, Palm Street leads off to the right towards the **bus station** and eventually meets up with the continuation of 5th June Avenue. **Orion Building** on the corner houses several small shops and the head offices of Creole Holidays (see page 91). This is a busy part of town particularly during peak hours.

Huteau Lane

Huteau Lane leads, via a series of bends, to 5th June Avenue. **Atlas** internet service provider is on the left and several fast food outlets are on the right.

They are only open during lunchtime. Around the corner the **Kenya Airways** office is located on the ground floor. A pay parking area is available in this lane.

Market Street

This is the heart of town where the residents do their daily shopping. The music shops are here, and if you want some local Creole music, look out for CDs or tapes by Jean Marc Volcy or Jany Letourdie who are two of the local stars. Coin and card public telephones are located in the middle of this pedestrian walkway. **Sunstroke Shop and Gallery** has a collection of colourful clothing in pure silks and cottons. Upstairs is an art gallery with predominantly silk pictures in brilliant, vibrant colours depicting fishes and birds as well as the life of the Seychellois.

The **Victoria Market** was rebuilt and opened again in June 1999. It is still known as the Sir Selwyn Selwyn-Clarke Market, named after the last British governor of the Seychelles in the late 1940s. The colourful market has a distinctly oriental look about it with a bright turquoise pagoda-style roof and red supporting columns with splashes of yellow and dark blue. An enormous mango tree shades the central square, while frangipani trees with fragrant white flowers scent the air. On the lower level, the fish market has a wide selection of fresh fish including *ton* (tuna), *makrou dou* (mackerel), *vyey* (groupers), *zob* (jobfish), *karang* (trevally) and *bourswa* (snappers). There are always several cattle egrets, locally known as *Madanm Paton,* hanging around the fish, hopping on the counters, and doing a good job of cleaning up all the bits and pieces. Stalls with colourful vegetables, tropical fruits, exotic herbs and tantalising spices are spread out under umbrellas in the central part of the market. Spices are very important in Creole cuisine. Fresh ginger and turmeric (often labelled saffron) are readily available, bottles of hot chillies add a dash of colour, and cinnamon quills and vanilla pods complete the exotic mix. If you can find it, the pure vanilla essence distilled on La Digue is a gourmet's delight. Still on the lower level, Rosie's Flower Shop sells sprays of orchids and huge bunches of fragrant roses out of galvanised buckets. Upstairs are some tiny shops selling touristy things like colourful pareos, paintings and coconut lamps with shades made out of coconut fibres. It is an excellent place to collect gifts and souvenirs. When you are hot and thirsty drop into **Jolie Rose 2**, a café on the upper level (see page 100).

Benezet Street

This is a short alley behind the market that connects Revolution Avenue with Market Street. **Lai Lam Bread Shop and Takeaway** is a popular place, and at lunchtime you can hardly get inside this bakery as so many people crowd in to buy their favourite snacks. Pizzas, quiches, fish and vegetable samosas, sandwiches, rolls and sweet coconut cakes are all available. The takeaway has a mouth-watering range of items around SR25. **Yummy Takeaway** almost next door also has a good selection of Chinese/Creole food at around SR25 per portion.

Revolution Avenue

This is the beginning of the main road going over to Beau Vallon. It starts at the Albert Street intersection at the one and only traffic light, and the first building on the left is the **Anglican Cathedral of St Paul**. It was built in 1857 and, over the years, the small church was enlarged and became a cathedral in 1973. It was completely rebuilt and the new cathedral was consecrated on April 25 2004.

The police station is on the other side of the alley that runs from Revolution Avenue to State House Road. Up the hill is a good place to catch the bus to Beau Vallon or Glacis – but not at peak times when it won't stop.

Kaz Zanana Gallery (open Mon–Fri 09.00–17.00, Sat 09.00–14.00, Sun closed) is opposite the bus shelter. It is owned by the artist, Georges Camille, whose works are on permanent exhibition and are for sale. It has a café open at lunchtime (see page 100). The **Barrel Bar Discotheque** (open Thu–Sun 21.00–03.00) is opposite the bus shelter but slightly closer to town. **Marie-Antoinette Restaurant** (see page 100) is further up the hill on the right as Revolution Avenue curves to the left to become St Louis Road.

Half-day walk

For details of a half-day walking tour of Victoria, see page 126.

DISCOVERING MAHE

Mahé is an island of secluded beaches, long stretches of glistening, white sands and tiny, picturesque coves fringed with tall trees, shady palms and framed by impressive granite boulders. Take the opportunity to explore them and find your own patch of paradise for the day. Soak up the sun-kissed feeling, cool off in the inviting clear, blue water and savour the delights of the underwater world. Don't be lulled into thinking that only the beaches of the Seychelles are to be enjoyed. Take a walk in the mountains, experience the profusion of luxuriant forest greenery, look at plants that exist nowhere else on earth, and be enticed to reach the summit to gaze upon the perfect panorama.

If you are after action and not romantic seclusion, a number of resorts offer thrilling watersports and other activities. Mahé with its luscious beauty is a magnet to artists of all persuasions so visit a sculptor's studio or an artist's gallery and take home a lasting and valuable memento. In between the sun, sand and exploring there will be time to try the local Creole cuisine at a range of restaurants and local stalls. Wherever you go on Mahé you will never feel swamped by huge numbers of tourists, nor will you be trapped in lengthy traffic jams.

The northwest

From Victoria, a road follows the coast around the northern tip of Mahé, a circular route of 20km. However, the quickest way to Beau Vallon is to travel along Revolution Avenue and over to the other side on St Louis Road.

St Louis Road continues from Revolution Avenue and swings to the left, passing the Marie-Antoinette Restaurant and the insignificant Serret Road.

The Chinese Embassy is an impressive white-and-blue-tiled building a little further along on the left in the St Louis area. The narrow road with several hairpin bends passes through residential areas enveloped in lush, tropical vegetation, and there are expansive views across Victoria to the islands in the Ste Anne Marine Park and beyond. One dark, forested road branches off to the left and leads to **Le Niol**. As the road descends towards Beau Vallon, it forks at the police station with the left fork leading to Bel Ombre and the right fork to Glacis.

Beau Vallon

The district of Beau Vallon lies roughly between Vacoa Village resort and the Fisherman's Cove hotel. Beau Vallon Beach is a glorious 3km crescent of gleaming, white sand fringed with *takamaka* trees and coconut palms, and defined by chunky granite boulders at each end. The idyllic bay is sheltered from the southeast trades. Hotels, guesthouses, restaurants, dive centres and souvenir shops nestle in the verdant vegetation, and all share the view of Beau Vallon Bay with fiery sunsets and enticing Silhouette island on the horizon. It is easy to reach the beach from both the Bel Ombre and Glacis roads.

The **Bel Ombre road** begins at the Beau Vallon **police station** and leads off to the left in a westerly direction. Several hotels are on the seaward side of the road and a few guesthouses are situated on the hillside. A large residential area spreads out on the slopes away from the beach. There is a community centre, a lovely old church and cemetery, a few shops and a tiny harbour used by local fishermen.

Berjaya Beau Vallon Bay Beach Resort and Casino (see page 93) is the first hotel on the right after the road divides. Live bands perform here regularly and there is a large swimming pool in the gardens adjoining the beach. Island Venture Dive Centre is located here. There are a few Aldabra tortoises in a pen in the garden near the entrance. The small **Augerine Guesthouse** (see page 95) is down the same road, on the right, next door to a large double-storeyed house but not clearly signposted.

Le Méridien Fisherman's Cove, completely refurbished in 2004, is a large hotel with a gracious ambience and lovely views across the bay (see page 93). The area beyond the hotel is Bel Ombre ('lovely shadow'). An impressive white building houses the Blue Red Disco Centre, which at the time of writing was closed. There are several small resorts with **Bel Ombre Holiday Villas** and **Daniella's Bungalow** offering bed and breakfast. A little further along the coast road **Le Petit Village** is a superior self-catering establishment (see page 94).

Le Corsair, a Tudor-style building looking more like an old English pub than a Seychellois restaurant, is one of the better restaurants in Mahé (see page 100) and overlooks the picturesque Bel Ombre fishing harbour with its colourful collection of small fishing craft. A short way further on are the remains of a local treasure hunt. It is reputed that Le Vasseur, the notorious pirate of the 17th century, stashed away fabulous, plundered treasures in this area. The Cruise-Wilkins family have spent vast sums of money excavating

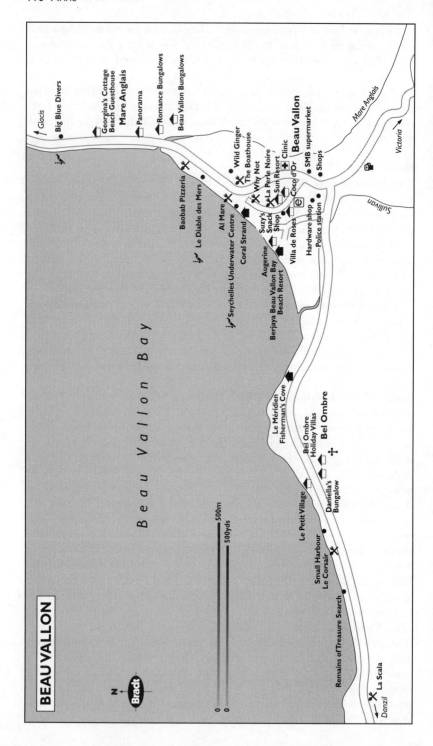

around the rocks and surrounding shore but to no avail. Le Vasseur's treasure trove still awaits discovery.

The road continues along the coast with several small general dealers, houses, a church, a school and a community center. If you are staying in self-catering accommodation, call in at Harold's store as he has a wide selection of essential goodies. **La Scala Restaurant**, another of Mahé's better restaurants (see page 100), is perched high above the road with fabulous sunset views through the tall palms. Parking for their clients is available off road. The Bel Ombre bus route terminates at the restaurant and from here the road narrows becoming quite steep as it continues as Danzil Road. There are a few houses before the road peters out. Two walks commence at this point; one is to Anse Major and the other is the Mare aux Cochons walk (see *Walks on Mahé*, pages 128–9).

If you go back to the police station and take the right fork in the road you will discover the rest of Beau Vallon. Shortly after the road divides you will find a small SMB supermarket and the local clinic. On the left, a narrow signposted road leads to the Coral Strand Hotel and the beach.

Villa de Roses, a charming bed and breakfast and self-catering establishment (see page 95) is set in pretty well-tended gardens on the left and almost next door is **Cyberwave Computing 2000**, an internet bureau (open Mon–Sat 09.00–18.00, Sun 09.00–14.00, SR7 for 15 minutes, SR20 for one hour). **Suzy's Snack Shop**, a little further on, is an excellent place to stop for a quick cold beer or an icy soft drink and a local snack. Suzy sells mini pizzas, fish samosas, little pies and chilli bites as well as sweet cakes. Card and coin public telephones are located here. On the other side of the road you will find the offices of **Tropicar Rent-a-Car**. **Coco d'Or**, a small hotel, is only about 100m from the beach and is close to **Sun Resort** which has a take-away and coffee bar. The **Perle Noire Restaurant** (see page 100) looks a bit shabby from the outside but is worth a visit. The **Coral Strand Hotel** (see page 94) is shortly due for major refurbishment but in the mean time is a large busy hotel with all the usual amenities and several restaurants including the **Mahek** that specialises in Indian cuisine. There is frequently live musical entertainment in the evenings. They are very much at the centre of watersports activities with several operators having facilities in or near the hotel. **Teddy's Glass-Bottomed Boat** (tel: 261125 or 511125) has a little office just by the hotel swimming pool and offers trips round to Baie Tiernay, the marine park. A full-day excursion together with a barbecue lunch will cost €80 and a half day €50.

Seychelles Underwater Centre have their diving operation adjoining the Coral Strand Hotel (see page 94).

From here, the road continues alongside the beach for a little way but it is not a through road. A pedestrian walkway joins the main road to Glacis, and, along this way there are several restaurants. A little further on, and almost on the beach, is the **Al Mare** (see page 100) restaurant with some tables on the sunny patio and the best views of the lovely bay and the two islands on the horizon.

From the Why Not, you will have to backtrack to the main road near the police station to continue in the direction of your choice. Right will lead back to Victoria; left will continue the discovery of Mahé.

The main road to Glacis sweeps down towards the shore through lush forest, and then swings right along the coast. Before reaching the bay, a large notice on the right advertises the art studio of Nigel Henri. Follow the long winding road to his house and studio although he may not be at home as he frequently exhibits his bold, colourful acrylics in Europe and Asia. As you reach the shoreline, stop to enjoy glorious Beau Vallon Beach. Fine white sands stretch out in both directions and Silhouette and North Islands grace the horizon. Bel Ombre and Danzil are away in the greenery to the left, and Glacis is behind giant rocks on the right. Several shops and restaurants are found here.

Le Diable des Mers Dive Centre operates out of a shop next to the **Baobab Pizzeria** (see page 100), a rustic restaurant with sandy floors and a large pizza oven. In fine weather and at low tide, tables may be put out on the beach. **The Boat House** (see page 100) serves a remarkable evening buffet with plenty of fresh fish. **Wild Ginger**, next to the Boat House, sells a wide variety of interesting souvenirs ranging from Creole music CDs to paintings and other handicrafts.

The Mare Anglaise River enters Beau Vallon Bay near there and the area is known as Mare Anglaise. **Romance Bungalows** are tucked into the hillside across the road from the beach and offer bed and breakfast and self-catering options. **Beau Vallon Bungalows and Panorama** provide bed and breakfast accommodation. **Georgina's Cottage Beach Guest House**, a little further down the road next to the bus stop, is the best-value accommodation in Beau Vallon (see page 95).

Further along the road you will find two small general stores that sell everything from beer to toiletries. **Big Blue Divers** have a smart office on the right-hand side of the road and **Pti Payot** is a cheerful self-catering establishment.

Glacis

From here on the area is known as Glacis (*glacis* is the name for the great, weathered granite slopes), and you will see mostly residential properties and a few hotels (see pages 34–5).

Le Northholme Hotel is one of the older hotels on Mahé with a history of colourful clients including writers and film stars like Ian Fleming, Noël Coward and David Niven. It has been completely rebuilt to bring it into line with other five-star hotels without losing its identity. **Sunset Beach Hotel** is very smart and lovely after upgrading. Snorkelling directly from the beaches of these two hotels is easy.

The road hugs the rocky coastline and the scenery is gorgeous with the mountains, secluded beaches and turquoise water. At the northernmost tip of Mahé there is a tiny island, l'Îlot, which is no more than a bundle of rocks. North Point is a relatively undeveloped part of Mahé as the *glacis* hillside is steep and inhospitable.

Above Champignon limestone formation in Passe Gionnet at Aldabra atoll (LM)

Right Pandanus vegetation on Mont Copolia *glacis*, Mahé (LB)

Below Aerial view of St Anne (STO)

Left Source d'Argent beach, La Digue, with characteristic granite boulders (JS)

Below Ile St Pierre (JS)

Kreol Fleurage Parfumes (tel: 241329; email: dag@seychelles.net) is well worth a short visit. Four specially blended perfumes are created here from ingredients typically found on the Indian Ocean islands, namely ylang ylang, vanilla, cinnamon and patchouli. The perfumes are bottled in tiny glass *flaçons*, beautifully encased in Seychelles hardwood, either *bois noir* or *calice du pape*. They sell for €25 each and are available from some boutiques as well as the airport duty-free shops. Opposite the small **Manressa Hotel** a steep, rough road, only for intrepid explorers, leads up the mountain and across to Glacis. The La Gogue reservoir, which was opened in 1979, and used to store excess water from the Rochon Dam, is found here.

In the North Point Centre you will find **La Belle Créole Restaurant** (see page 101) serving typical Creole fare on a daily basis with a special buffet lunch on a Sunday. Continuing south towards Victoria, the area is known as Ma Constance and here you can start to see the changing face of Mahé as the land reclamation islands become so obvious. **Le Surmer Hotel and Restaurant** is located at Pointe Conan. Associated with this establishment is the **369 discotheque**, with karaoke before disco. Open Sat 19.30.

A national monument, **La Bastille**, is near the town and houses some of the national archives, it is also the office of the National Monuments Board. It was built by Mr Jumeau for his daughter and, as it has only one door and from the sea looks like a prison, it was given the name of La Bastille. Completing the northwest loop the road approaches the residential areas of Victoria with good views across to Ste Anne Marine Park.

The southeast

To explore the southeast of Mahé leave Victoria and travel south along the Mont Fleuri Road, past the Botanical Gardens and the Victoria Hospital. This road continues through an old part of town to the airport. An alternative route to the airport is Avenue Bois de Rose from Le Chantier roundabout. The two roads meet a few kilometres before the airport.

A short distance beyond the hospital on Mont Fleuri Road is the **Sunrise Hotel** (see page 93). The Seychelles Polytechnic with several playing fields is next to the road. Another branch of the photographic store **Photo Eden** is located near here (tel: 322457). At the roundabout, La Misère Road leads over to the west coast of Mahé and the south coast road continues towards the airport. **Seypot**, a potters' co-operative, was established in 1981 by graduates from the polytechnic. A range of plates, vases and other items can be purchased from a small showroom.

Lying rotting in the mud near the road is the rusty hulk of a wrecked schooner, *Isle of Farquhar*, once the supply ship to the outer islands. Opposite the Bridge Shopping Centre is **Gallery d'Art**, the Mamelles studio and home of artist **Gerard Devoud**. His vibrantly coloured paintings depict the Seychelles heritage with flair.

Michel Holiday Apartments are well appointed and are near a bus stop, but a little far for an easy walk into town. **Château de Mamelles**, a national monument, is behind the holiday apartments. This imposing house was built in 1804 for the corsair Jean François Hodoul, and is now privately owned.

Seybrew is the local brewery and soft drink manufacturer. Its products are excellent, being made with the sweet waters from the mountains. Seybrew is available in 280ml returnable bottles or as draught in various restaurants. Eku is a Bavarian lager, Guinness is made under licence, and Celebration Brew is fairly new on the market.

Anonyme Island is privately owned and recently seven luxury suites have been built there. The **airport** is approximately 9km out of Victoria and caters for both international and local inter-island flights. **Katiolo**, at Anse Faure, only a little way past the airport, is the hottest disco in town. (A *katiolo* is a small wooden boat very like a pirogue.)

Anse aux Pins

The **Seychelles Golf Club** (tel: 376234), 5km south of the airport, is the only one on Mahé. The nine holes are set under swaying coconut palms with a dramatic backdrop of dark granite mountains. Green fees: nine holes will cost you SR60 and 18 holes SR100, club hire is SR80 and a golf cart is SR20, new golf balls are SR22 each and used balls are SR10.

Casuarina Beach (see page 97) is another older hotel, with a glorious beach and shady gardens where there are a couple of giant Aldabra tortoises. There are numerous other holiday apartments, guesthouses and restaurants along this stretch of coastline including **Carefree Guesthouse** and **La Rousette**.

The **National Institute for Creole Development**, also known as the *Lenstiti Kreol*, is situated in a lovely old house, and has been established to promote the Creole culture of the Seychelles. Schoolbooks and children's books are now being printed in Creole and these are displayed in the foyer. A Creole library is also housed there, and includes many books on the Seychelles heritage, both in French and English. **Maison St Joseph**, the old house, was built by Mr Jumeau in the typical, grand French colonial style.

The **Craft Village** consists of a series of small Creole bungalows. Each has its own speciality handicraft, such as beautifully presented soaps made with coconut oil, glass mobiles, artefacts made from hard coconut shells, locally made clothing and colourful silk paintings, to name only a few. Some of the bungalows function as workshops and you can watch the craftsmen at work.

La Marine Model Boats (tel: 375152) welcomes visitors to its workshop where they build models of old sailing boats. Using naval plans, replicas are made in the finest detail. Because of the time-consuming nature of the business they are not cheap; replicas of small local fishing vessels sell for around SR750 and starting prices for a small ship are around SR3,300. For a fee, they will gladly pack and ship them around the world for you. The craft market is well worth visiting. Open daily 09.00–17.00, closed Sunday. **Vye Marmit** (see page 101) is a beautifully appointed restaurant in a renovated old plantation house. **Tyfoo** is a Chinese restaurant near Le Cap. **Green Valley**

Restaurant and take-away is on the inland side of the road and the **Galaxy Pub and Restaurant** is a little further on.

Anse Royale

Anse Royale is the next embayment on the route to the south, and during the northwest monsoons offers a sheltered and protected curve of beach suitable for swimming. Anse Royale has a couple of small shops, a petrol station, clinic, school, polytechnic, police station and a large community hall. South of the town is the photogenic St Joseph's Church, close to the beach. There are no big noisy hotels but a few small guesthouses and restaurants. Anse Royale is one of the few areas on Mahé with a reasonable amount of flat and fertile land, and there are some flourishing gardens in the area. The long curve of Anse Royale has many small, shaded beaches and secluded coves sheltered by huge granite boulders. It is the ideal place for exploring and having a picnic. As you approach Anse Royale there is a group of rocks near the shore leading to Ile Souris. Snorkelling here is good, but do be aware that at times there can be a fairly strong current running between the coast and the little island.

It was at Anse Royale that the first spice gardens were started in 1772 under the orders of Pierre Poivre from Mauritius. Cinnamon, nutmeg, cloves and pepper were the main crops. The entire plantation was destroyed a few years later, when the French garrison officer guarding the secret spice garden set fire to all the plants when he mistakenly thought an approaching ship was English, and about to take command of the island. By the time it was discovered to be a French vessel, all the trees had been burnt.

La Désirade, situated at Pointe au Sel on the northern end of Anse Royale, has spacious self-catering studio apartments. **Fairyland** is another small guesthouse at Pointe au Sel, with five rooms and a restaurant. **Le Relax**, with six rooms, offers both bed and breakfast and half board. **Kaz Kreol** is a beachfront pizzeria that also serves seafood. On occasions, there is live music with dancing – watch the press for details.

Anse Forbans

One of the undeveloped and very quiet parts of Mahé, Anse Forbans or Pirate's Bay was named on the earliest maps, and was apparently one of the bays used by the 17th-century pirates. You can easily imagine a pirate boat being careened on this beach.

The **Allamanda** (see page 97), named after a bright-yellow flowering shrub, is a small hotel with a restaurant that specialises in a good Creole seafood buffet for tour groups. **Anse Forbans Chalets** are self-catering and set in large gardens with lawns and coconut palms.

The south

After the Anse Forbans chalets, the road swings away from Anse Marie-Louise, and continues inland for about 1km to the village of **Quatre Bornes**. Turn left at this somewhat indistinct junction to get down to Anse Intendance and the southernmost point of Mahé.

Anse Intendance

This must be one of the loveliest and most unspoilt bays of Mahé. Have a picnic under the shady trees and look out for the graceful white-tailed tropicbirds. Note that during the southeast trades, the currents can be dangerous for swimmers. The luxurious, refined **Banyan Tree Hotel** (see page 95) is located down a well-signposted road to the right. Enjoy the best Asian food at the Saffron Restaurant or indulge in their well-appointed health spa.

Continue southwards on the concrete road. **Xanadu** (see page 98) is a secluded and luxurious resort whose beautifully designed wooden chalets enjoy glorious views, and whose gardens are filled with palms and tall trees. The road continues past Anse Corail to Pointe Police, but is closed from there onwards.

The southwest

To explore the southwest go back to Quatre Bornes, turn left and proceed to Anse Takamaka. **Le Réduit**, a small seafood restaurant, is clearly marked on the roadside. Open daily for lunch and dinner; tel: 366116.

Anse Takamaka

This is yet another fabulous, secluded, white, sandy beach fringed with palms. It takes its name from the tall, shady *takamaka* trees. Take care when swimming, as the strong currents can be dangerous at times. Recent incidents indicate that it is unwise to leave valuables on any of the beaches in this area.

Chez Batista Villas and Restaurant at the southern end of the bay overlooks the beach. The attractive restaurant specialises in Creole food. **Takamaka Residence** is one of the lowest priced guesthouses and serves Italian and Creole food. **Lazare Picault Restaurant**, north of the bay, is open daily for lunch and dinner.

Baie Lazare

Continuing close to the coast, you will reach Baie Lazare which is a horseshoe-shaped bay facing south bounded by Pointe Maravi and Pointe Lazare. The **Plantation Club** (see page 96) is the largest hotel in the Seychelles and can be found in the northern corner of this pretty bay. In the garden, a Chinese bittern lurks amongst the waterlilies of the pond, and nearby is a large pen with a group of giant Aldabra tortoises. The **Islander Coach Charter** (tel: 323589) operates a service from the Plantation Club to Victoria, Monday to Saturday.

Antonio Filipini sculpts in wood and his fine creations can be seen at his Plantation Club studio (tel: 510977). The **Valmer Art Gallery and Apartments** are on the main road, opposite the Plantation Club entrance. The gallery exhibits and sells the works of artist Gerard Devoud. His vibrant paintings are bright and colourful depicting different facets of local life. Originals and prints are available and they will be carefully wrapped in protective sleeves for travelling. The newly built, upmarket self-catering apartments are very comfortable. Creole Holidays owns a 65ha nature reserve at Cap Lazare with a palm-thatched Creole-styled village with a range of amenities ideal for weddings, corporate and group functions.

The road continues northward towards Anse à la Mouche and there is a convenient petrol station on the left. **Donald Adelaide's Art Studio** is well signposted, and you can't miss his bright blue, corrugated iron cabin. His original paintings and drawings sell from about SR500 up to SR1,000, while the prints sell for SR300. Opposite **Harvey's Café**, which is open only during the day, a road leads to the **Anse Soleil Resort** (see page 97) comprising several houses set in pretty gardens with lovely views of mountains and the sea. The state of the road deteriorates as you pass **Andrew Gee's Art Studio**. He specialises in silk paintings and his colourful works are on sale here and in various outlets in Victoria and the duty-free shop at the airport. Follow the rough road down the hill till you reach a parking area, shaded under tall trees. Here at Anse Soleil you will find the **Anse Soleil Beachcomber** (see page 97), a small, quiet hotel right on the beach. Find your way to the adjacent **Anse Soleil Café** which is a rustic, palm-roofed beach restaurant with a relaxed ambience. Enjoy the sand under your toes and dine on fresh seafood. The beautiful Anse Soleil beach is fringed with coconut palms and great granite boulders and is good for swimming.

Anse aux Poules Bleues

Michael Adams' Art Studio is on the left at Anse aux Poules Bleues. Palms and thick, creeping vegetation engulf his intriguing old Creole-style building. He is one of the best-known artists in the Seychelles, and his work can be seen adorning book covers and calendars. Much has been reproduced as prints, which are available in various shops in Victoria. Still in Anse aux Poules Bleues, **Pineapple Studio** is on the sea side of the road. This busy little craft factory produces hand-decorated towels, T-shirts and pareos, wooden placemats, coasters, trays and coconut craft. The items are available in the shop here and in many places around the islands.

Anse à la Mouche

Anse à la Mouche is a sweeping shallow bay with warm and sheltered waters. Apparently, Captain Lazare Picault made the first landing here in 1742, under orders from Bertrand François Mahé de Labourdonnaise, the French governor of Mauritius. The bay is named after a ship that ran aground there in 1812. There are several self-catering establishments and restaurants in this area. **Blue Lagoon** self-catering chalets are set in spacious grassy gardens. **Chemin les Canelles** leads off to the right, a little beyond Blue Lagoon, and traverses the island from Anse à la Mouche to Anse Royale (see *Routes across Mahé*, page 124).

Anse Boileau

Anse Boileau is the next bay along the west coast route. Some self-catering establishments are located around the shores of the bay as is the little restaurant

Chez Plume. **Chemin Montagne** is the road off to the right and it winds its way over to the other side of the island (see *Routes across Mahé*, below).

Grande Anse

This is a dramatically beautiful bay with a backdrop of high granite mountains highlighting the soft, silvery sands and turquoise water. Occasionally the sandflies are bad, and at times there can be a strong undertow. Near the bus stop there is a small general store which sells cold drinks. The large **Méridien Barbarons Hotel** (see page 96), an agricultural research station and timber yard are located in Grande Anse. **Chemin la Misère** is the road which leads inland from Grande Anse (see *Routes across Mahé*, below), and the BBC Indian Ocean relay station is opposite the junction.

Port Glaud

This is a small village at the end of the bus route. The sprawling **Berjaya Mahé Beach Resort** (see page 96) has grounds leading on to an interesting beach with rocks and palms. The hotel will arrange excursions over to Thérèse Island. Various watersports are on offer including windsurfing, pedalos, water-skiing, snorkelling, diving and game fishing. **L'Islette**, a small islet a short way offshore, can be reached by foot at low tide. **Eden's Holiday Resort** is the last accommodation along the route. They have eight comfortable self-catering chalets set in lush, tropical forest. It is close to beautiful beaches and good snorkelling. **Eden's Pub**, the last watering hole on that stretch of beach, has two super league pool tables and is open from 10.00 to midnight everyday. The **Sundown Restaurant** is nearby and serves good seafood.

    Chemin Sans Soucis, heading off to the right, is an important road connecting Port Glaud to Victoria (see *Routes across Mahé*, below).

Port Launay

After Port Glaud, the road narrows and eventually threads its way through mangrove forests edging the Port Launay Marine Park. The small beaches are shaded by palms and casuarinas and are protected by many granite boulders. It is fabulous to snorkel directly off the beach in the crystal-clear waters. The road ends at the premises of the Seychelles Youth League.

Routes across Mahé
Sans Soucis
Chemin Sans Soucis

The Sans Soucis road from Port Glaud through the mountains to Victoria is one of the most scenic drives on Mahé and for much of the way you will be driving through the Morne Seychellois National Park. The tall trees are a mixture of indigenous *takamaka* and *bwa rouz*, with introduced cinnamon, mahogany, *bwa zonn* and the feathery-leaved, flat-crowned albizia. *Philodendron* vines creep up many of the trees.

    The **Tea Factory** is only about 4km from Port Glaud. Tea production began in 1966, and the neatly tended tea bushes are visible along the roadside. The factory is open 10.00–16.00 on weekdays and it is possible to purchase some of the delicious, fragrant SeyTé (Seychelles tea) that is produced in five different flavours – vanilla, cinnamon, orange, mint and lemon. The Morne Seychellois walking trail starts about 250m up the hill from the car park at the tea factory.

Capucin Mission Ruins are a reminder of the slave trade as a school was built here by members of the London Missionary Society for the children of slaves set free during the British anti-slavery campaign in the 19th century. It was then known as Venn's Town and operated from 1875 to 1889. Marianne North, the artist, stayed here during her sojourn in Seychelles in 1883. Today, you will see only the moss-covered ruins. A shelter was built when Queen Elizabeth II was entertained to tea during a state visit but there are no tourist facilities. From this remarkable vantage point, one can see over the tea estates and way down to the southwestern parts of Mahé, and may even see white-tailed tropicbirds flying over the green hills.

Val Riche is 4km further on and a signpost indicates the start of the scenic walk. The **Forestry Station** is on the left, and this is the beginning of the Trois Frères walk. You can leave your car in the car park at the forestry station.

Bel Air is a residential area on the outskirts of Victoria and there are several diplomatic homes including the American Embassy, which housed Archbishop Makarios during his year of exile. It is called '1776' and is a privately owned national monument.

Continue along the Bel Air road to the **Rose Garden**, a quiet and secluded small hotel. A little further on is **Thoughts Stained Glass Studio** and the oldest cemetery in Mahé where some interesting characters are buried. Look carefully to find the grave of the corsair Jean François Hodoul.

Bel Air Road descends to an intersection with Revolution Avenue. If you decide to drive into Liberation Avenue instead of continuing into Bel Air there is a panoramic viewpoint. The avenue meets up with Mont Fleuri Road on the south side of Le Chantier roundabout.

La Misère
Chemin la Misère

This is another scenic road that winds through mountains, forests and tea plantations from Grande Anse to Victoria. Characterised by numerous hairpin bends, the views from the route are spectacular.

The **Seychelles Hotel and Tourism Training Centre** has opened in what used to be the American tracking station. Approaching the town there are panoramic views of Baie Ste Anne, and at the viewing point a sadly weathered ceramic map used to indicate the islands seen in the distance.

Bon Espoir
Chemin de Montagne

This road crosses the southern part of Mahé from Anse Boileau to Anse aux Pins. The Bon Espoir **Cable & Wireless** radio communications centre is situated high up in the mountains. Radio links are made from there to all the outlying islands as well as to ships at sea.

Les Canelles
Chemin les Canelles

This interesting road winds over the mountain from Anse à la Mouche to Anse Royale. **Tom Bowers' Studio** is well marked. Tom and his charming wife Ellen will welcome you to his outdoor sculpture studio where his beautiful creations are surrounded by lush vegetation, hundreds of Madagascar fodies and a menagerie of dogs.

   Le Jardin du Roi (tel: 371313, open daily: 10.00–17.30), the first spice garden in Seychelles, is another few kilometres along but it is not particularly well signposted. Look out for an obscure notice painted on the side of a wall of some buildings on the right. These spice gardens and restaurant are well worth a visit. A knowledgeable guide will take you on a conducted tour of the gardens for SR25. Besides cinnamon, cloves, nutmeg, vanilla and pepper there are many medicinal plants under cultivation. There are several enormous *coco de mer* palms, and many other fine examples of indigenous plants. A small museum allows fascinating glimpses into the agricultural past, and the views over the eastern part of Mahé are lovely. The restaurant has a small but tasty menu but it is not the cheapest place. If you feel like really splashing out, try one of their homemade spice-flavoured ice-creams – vanilla, cinnamon or lemon grass. Three scoops in a tall glass will cost you SR45. Open every day for lunch.

INDEPENDENT TOURS FOR CRUISE-SHIP PASSENGERS

Full- and half-day tours are usually arranged for passengers by the cruise-ship's agents in Mahé. These are generally good value as the local guides provide many interesting insights to the Seychellois way of life. However, it is sometimes really nice to escape from organised tours and do your own thing, be it walking, taking a taxi or hiring a car for a drive around parts of Mahé. Taxis are readily available when cruise ships dock, and local tour agents on the quayside are able to arrange car hire very easily. There are several public telephones located close to the pier if you prefer to make your own car-hire arrangements.

Half-day walking tour

Setting off from the ship, walk straight inland to the port exit and customs point. Walk up Chemin Latanier to Le Chantier roundabout, which is easily identified by the four white sailfish pointing skywards. Turn left into Chemin Mont Fleuri and visit the **Botanical Gardens**. It should take about 15 minutes to get there from the ship. Half an hour will allow a quick tour through the gardens, though you may prefer to linger longer. If shopping is high on your agenda, the Botanical Gardens could be missed out, allowing more time to concentrate on the market, shops and souvenir stalls.

   Return to Le Chantier and proceed along Francis Rachel Street. Walking along the right-hand side of the road will be cooler under the trees, and will allow you to browse the stalls on the **Fiennes Esplanade**. Stay on the left side of Albert Street and turn left into Market Street to visit the **Victoria Market**. Return to Albert Street and browse around **Codevar** for handmade crafts. If time is against you, take a taxi from the nearby rank and return to the ship. If you still have plenty of time, however, walk down Independence Avenue, which leads off towards the sea at the clocktower. Drop into the **National Museum of Natural History**, then try out the **Pirates Arms**, the local watering hole. If you are short of time or feeling the heat, this is a good place to pick up a taxi for the return trip to the ship but, if you can manage another 20-minute walk, continue to the **Twa Zwazo** roundabout and turn right into 5th June Avenue. You will pass Marine Charter Association and the yacht club on your left. The **Zonm Lib Statue** will be in the pretty gardens on your right. After the imposing **National Library** building you will be back at Le Chantier roundabout. Turn left into Chemin Latanier to return to the docks.

Half-day driving tours

By doing some creative negotiating, it *might* be possible to hire a car for a half-day period. This would give the option of doing an organised half-day excursion followed by a short time to explore Mahé on your own.

North and central option

The north and central part of Mahé provide an easy and interesting route. Follow the map and drive along the northeastern coastal road. Drop into **Kreol Fleurage Parfumes** for a quick stop and then continue around North Point, through Glacis and on to **Beau Vallon Bay**. There are many places to park the car in the vicinity of the **Boathouse Restaurant** if you wish to do some exploring on foot. A walk along the fine curve of **Beau Vallon Beach** is an excellent way to take some exercise after being on board ship for a few days. Then you can meander on to one of the hotels like **Coral Strand** or **Berjaya Beau Vallon Bay Beach Resort** for refreshments, before going back to the car to continue exploring. Drive up to the junction at the police station, turn right and wend your way to **Bel Ombre**, keeping a lookout for the treasure excavations. The road ends at Danzil, so return to the police station and take the road over to Victoria. As you round the hairpin bends enjoy the spectacular views of Baie Ste Anne and the port (with your ship) way down below. This would be a two- to three-hour round trip, depending on how long you spend on the beach.

Sans Soucis and the west coast option

For a scenic tour through mountains, forests and along part of the west coast locate the **Sans Soucis road** leading from either Bel Air Road or Liberation Avenue. Wind your way through the **Morne Seychellois National Park** and stop at the **Capucin Mission Ruins** for superb views. Pass the **Tea Estate and Factory** before descending to **Port Glaud** on the west coast. Turn right to explore some of the beautiful, small beaches in the **Port Launay Marine National Park**. As the road reaches a cul-de-sac you will have to return to Port Glaud the same way and then continue southwards along the coast past the Berjaya Mahé Beach Hotel, a good place for refreshments. Explore the village of **Grande Anse** and then turn inland at **Chemin la Misère** for a spectacular drive over to the eastern side of Mahé. At the junction with the main south coast road, turn left and in no time you will be back at Le Chantier roundabout and your ship. The round trip should take about four hours depending on how long you tarry on the beach.

Full-day driving tour

With a full day on your hands, the possibilities are endless and depend on your personal preferences. The southern part of Mahé has the most interesting variety of beaches, restaurants and art studios.

Drive out of Victoria and past the airport. At **Anse aux Pins** stop in at the **Craft Village** and **La Marine Model Boats**. Take in some snorkelling at Anse Royale or simply find one of the secluded beaches and enjoy the sand, sun and surf. Drive across to Anse Intendance or Anse Takamaka, and between there and Anse à la Mouche you will find many delightful restaurants serving fine seafood and Creole lunches. This is also the art centre of Mahé with many studios and galleries, such as those of **Michael Adams, Tom Bowers** or **Donald Adelaide,** open to the public. Follow the west coast road, stopping for a swim or a walk on any of the lovely beaches. The most scenic route back to Victoria is over Sans Soucis Road. Enjoy the panoramic views from the **Capucin Mission Ruins**. The road has many twists and turns as it descends into Victoria, and evening views over the bay are particularly lovely as the lights come on in the town and port.

WALKS ON MAHE

Walking is a great way to discover Mahé. Trails have been laid out in different areas of the Morne Seychellois National Park and there is a short trail along part of the northwestern coastline. A series of excellent booklets entitled *Nature Trails and Walks in Seychelles*, describing various walks on Mahé, has been written by Katy Beaver, a resident botanist. They are out of print but some may be available at the Tourist Information Office in Independence Avenue. The Department of Environment has published small leaflets describing the walks and they are available at the Tourist Information Office and the Botanical Gardens entrance office. Most are SR5 but the longer one is SR10. Each one has a good map and description of the trail. They are filled with interesting information about the plants and wildlife that you will encounter en route. Basil Beaudouin, a local guide, can take you on guided mountain walks. You can meet him at the Coral Strand Hotel on Monday evenings at 18.00 to make arrangements for an excursion (tel: 514972).

Beau Vallon to Victoria is an easy walk over the saddle taking about one hour and provides a good introduction to central Mahé and some lovely views.

Danzil to Anse Major is a relatively easy trail beginning at the end of Bel Ombre and follows the coast to a secluded little beach. A great deal of this trail lies within the Morne Seychellois National Park. The noisy chattering birds you are very likely to encounter are the Seychelles bulbuls. Pure white fairy terns and white-tailed tropicbirds can be seen flying along the coastline. Three hours will be sufficient time to walk both ways.

Les Trois Frères are the three peaks overlooking Victoria, and the views from the top are magnificent. It is a steep climb and you should allow two hours from the Sans Soucis Forest Station to the summit. The Forest Station is about 5km from Victoria on the Sans Soucis road. You may park your car there, and follow the trail marked with yellow paint blobs. At the beginning of the route you will notice many introduced plant species like cinnamon, cocoplum and vanilla. Two endemic palm species are common a little higher up along the path.

Val Riche to Copolia is graded medium and should take two hours to the top and down again. The walk starts on the Sans Soucis road about 6km from Victoria. There is a signboard on the left on a bend in the road, and it is just possible to squeeze your car off on to the narrow verge to park. There is a bus stop nearby, though buses are infrequent. The tree-shaded trail is marked with yellow paint. Upon reaching the *glacis* at the top, you will easily see the endemic pitcher plants growing in the shallow soil. Stunning views of the east coast of Mahé and the Ste Anne Marine National Park are the rewards for the climb.

Tea Factory to Morne Blanc begins on the Sans Soucis road about 11km from Victoria, 250m up the hill from the Tea Tavern car park. This walk in the Morne Seychellois National Park is best done in the morning as the first bit is steep and not shaded. It is graded medium and about an hour is needed to reach the top. The mist forest has many unique species, and is an indication of what the islands used to look like before man arrived. Look out for the minute endemic frog, *Sooglosus gardineri*, which makes a surprisingly loud chirping sound and lives in the leaf litter. Again, the superb views from the summit are just rewards for the sweat up the hill.

SATELLITE ISLANDS
Near Victoria
There are several small islands around Mahé which are well worth visiting. Closest to Victoria are the six islands in the middle of the Ste Anne Marine National Park, namely Ste Anne, Cerf, Long, Round, Moyenne and Cachée. All marine life is protected in the park and there is worthwhile snorkelling.

Ste Anne
Ste Anne, the largest of the six islands, and only 4km from Victoria, was the site of the first settlement in the Seychelles. The first motley group of settlers arrived on August 12 1770 from Mauritius to start growing vegetables and spices. Since then, Ste Anne has been home to a whaling station, which operated from 1832 to 1915, a World War II gun battery, and a fuel storage

depot which is still in use. A navigation light is situated on the highest point of the island, Mont Ste Anne at 205m. This little island, 2km long and 1km wide, has two beaches that are important nesting sites for the endangered hawksbill turtle. The 79 villas of the **Ste Anne Resort** are spread along the two main beaches. This five-star resort has all the luxury amenities including fine restaurants and a health and beauty centre.

Cerf

This island is a little smaller than Ste Anne, with the highest point being 108m. It was named after the ship *Le Cerf*, captained by Nicholas Morphey who, in 1756, claimed the Seychelles for France. About 40 people live on Cerf. People wishing to visit the island can arrange to do so at the Marine Charter Association or through the tour operators in Victoria (see page 79). As there is no jetty, you will have to wade ashore. The **Kapok Restaurant** serves good Creole food. Tourist accommodation on the island has recently undergone major renovations.

Cachée

This treasure island, as the name implies, lies southeast of Cerf. It is uninhabited and only about 2ha in size.

Long

Long Island is closed to the public as it houses the prison which has about 100 inmates. It has also been the quarantine station for a long time.

Round

The island was originally a leper colony with dwellings for the patients, a house for the nurse, a chapel and a small prison. **Chez Gaby Restaurant** has been built amongst the ruins, and Mr and Mrs Calais serve the most delicious Creole food using the freshest seafood imaginable. It will take you about 15 minutes to walk around this little island which is covered in verdant forest. Enjoy the lovely sandy cove near the restaurant, and look up into the trees to see some of the enormous fruit bats.

Moyenne

When Brendon Grimshaw, a retired newspaper editor, bought the 9ha island in 1971 it had been deserted for 60 years. The first visitors to Moyenne were no doubt pirates and, despite stories of vast treasures being left on the island, it appears that none have been unearthed. The first known owners of the island were a very young couple, Melidor Louange and Julie Chiffon who, in 1850, somehow acquired Moyenne and lived there for 42 years. They sold it to wealthy Alfred d'Emmerez de Charmoy in 1892. An Englishwoman from Berkshire, Miss Emma Wardlow-Best, lived on the island from 1899 to 1911.

It took Brendon Grimshaw nearly a year to clear a path around the island, and he has since re-established many indigenous trees and shrubs, including Wright's gardenia and the *coco de mer*. The birdlife has flourished and several giant Aldabra tortoises can be found under the shady bushes. It takes about 45 minutes to walk along the path, and the ruins of the two old houses and some very old, possibly pirate, graves can be seen. Mr Grimshaw lives in an old colonial-style house.

The channel between the northern side of Moyenne and Ste Anne is one of the prime snorkelling sites in the marine park.

Off the west coast
Thérèse
This uninhabited 70ha island lies opposite Port Glaud and the Berjaya Mahé Beach Hotel. A fabulous reef, excellent for snorkelling, runs along the main beach of the island. There are stunning views of Mahé from the top of the hill. Day trips to Thérèse can be arranged from the Berjaya Mahé Beach Hotel or from private boat owners at Port Glaud or Beau Vallon.

Conception
Conception rises steeply out of the sea, and has little or no beach, making landing there very difficult; consequently it has never been inhabited. It lies a little south of Cap Ternay off the Port Launay Marine Park, and has some tremendous dive sites at the northeastern end. Covering an area of about 60ha, it has a wealth of undisturbed natural vegetation. Recently, a healthy population of the rare little bird, the Seychelles white-eye, has been rediscovered on Conception. Ornithological research is being carried out with some difficulty owing to the rugged terrain of the island.

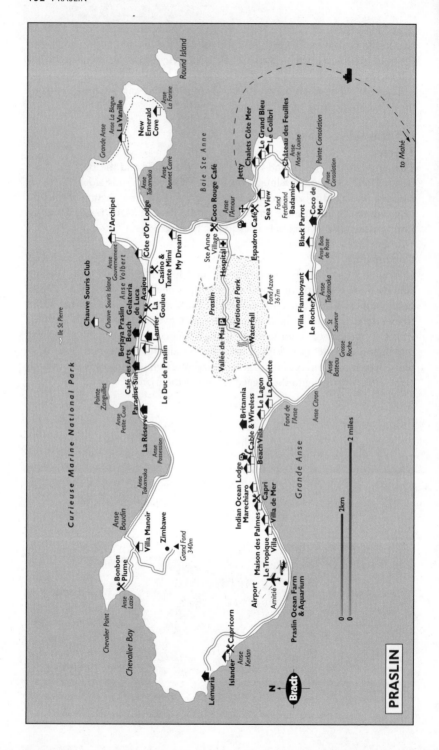

PRASLIN

Praslin

The lovely island of Praslin, home of the *coco de mer* palm, has a gentle, unhurried pace and an ambience of quiet tranquillity. Long stretches of fine, white sand framed by palms and shady *takamakas*; or small, secluded coves bounded by granite boulders, characterise this strangely shaped island which is surrounded by coral reefs. An assortment of islands lie beyond the coral reefs like chunks of emeralds in an azure sea. Mahé, 45km away to the south, is hazy in the distance; Aride, the seabird sanctuary, lies 16km to the north; and enchanting La Digue is located a mere 4km to the east. Curieuse, off to the northeast, is surrounded by its marine park and Ile St Pierre is a jumble of rocks lodged between Praslin and Curieuse. Cousin, an island bird reserve, and privately owned Cousine, lie to the west. Round Island, at the entrance to Baie Ste Anne, and Chauve Souris, a tiny clump of tree-covered rocks just 500m off Anse Volbert, complete the assorted satellite islands.

Areas of great natural beauty surround Praslin but the romantic 'island of palms' is the only place on earth where you will see *coco de mer* palms growing in magnificent profusion. The tall, elegant female *coco de mer* palm produces a huge seed, astonishingly shaped like a female belly and thighs, and the taller male palm has a remarkably phallic-looking flowering catkin. As can be imagined, these erotic shapes have resulted in the perpetuation of many myths and legends.

The first recorded visit to Praslin, when it was covered in virgin equatorial hardwood and palm forests, was made by Lazare Picault in 1744, and he gave it the name of Ile de Palme. Marion Dufresne, leading an exploratory expedition from Mauritius in 1768, named the island Praslin, after Gabriel de Choiseul, Duc de Praslin, the French minister of marine affairs.

Although a large amount of the original forest has disappeared as a result of fires and deforestation, there is still a valley where the remarkable palms are protected and flourish – the Vallée de Mai, a World Heritage Site. There you can enjoy the majestic splendour of the forest and see all six of the Seychelles' endemic palms plus an array of other trees and plants. The nearby island of Curieuse and the proposed new national park on Fond Ferdinand in the south of Praslin are the only other places where *coco de mer* palms can be found growing naturally. Praslin is not only famous for the palms but it is also home to the rare endemic black parrot, and though these birds are never easy to find, they can be seen in any of the natural areas on the island.

Praslin, an island floating in quiet beauty, is second in size to Mahé being 12km long and nowhere more than 5km wide. The highest granite summit, Fond Azore, reaches 367m. Most of the 8,000 people living on the island have tourism-related jobs. Agriculture and fishing are also important aspects of life on Praslin. The village at Baie Ste Anne, less than 2km from the jetty, has a few small shops, banks, post office, school, church and a hospital.

GETTING THERE AND AWAY
By air
The recently rebuilt Praslin Airport at Amitié on the northwestern side of the island must be one of the most attractive airports in the Indian Ocean region with typical Creole architecture, water features, palms and sculptures. There are two restaurants at the airport, Touchdown Restaurant and Touchdown Café, both offering good value fare. There are ATMs and public telephones.

Air Seychelles operates a regular and frequent service to Praslin from Mahé using a 20-seater de Havilland Twin Otter or a six-seater Islander aircraft. Flights shuttle between Mahé and Praslin every 15 minutes during peak times and less frequently otherwise. The short flight takes only 15 minutes and costs €50, one way, which is only €5 more expensive than the upper deck on the *Cat Cocos* ferry. Timetables are available at Praslin Airport (tel: 284666) or at the Air Seychelles office in Mahé (tel: 381000).

Helicopter Seychelles has an office opposite the Air Seychelles check-in counter; all reservations are done at the central office (tel: 385863). Praslin personnel may be contacted at tel: 714832 or via the main office, tel: 385858.

By sea
Cat Cocos, the fast catamaran ferry, takes about an hour to travel between Victoria harbour on Mahé and Baie Ste Anne on Praslin and for non-Seychellois and non-residents, a one-way ticket costs €40 or $40 in the main cabin and €45 or $45 in the upper cabin. There are *Cat Cocos* booking offices on Mahé (tel: 324844), and Praslin (tel: 232616). Payment is required in foreign currency. Cash and major credit cards are accepted.

CAT COCOS SCHEDULE				
Days	Depart Mahé	Arrive Praslin	Depart Praslin	Arrive Mahé
Mon–Thur, Sat	07.30	08.30	09.00	10.00
	16.00	17.00	17.30	18.30
Fri	07.30	08.30	09.00	10.00
	16.30	17.30	18.00	19.00
Sun	10.30	11.30	15.00	16.00
	16.30	17.30	18.00	19.00

FERRY SERVICE PRASLIN–LA DIGUE

Days	Depart Praslin	Arrive La Digue	Depart La Digue	Arrive Praslin
Daily	07.00	07.30	07.30	08.00
	09.00	09.30	09.30	10.00
	10.00	10.30	10.30	11.00
	11.15	11.45	12.00	12.30
Sundays only	12.00	12.30	14.00	14.30
	14.30	15.00	15.30	16.00
	16.00	16.30	16.30	17.00
Mon–Sat	17.15	17.45	17.45	18.15
Sundays only	17.45	18.15	18.15	18.45

There is a regular schooner service over to La Digue, which takes 30 minutes and costs €10 or $10 one way and a return ticket is €19 or $19. As this can be quite a busy service it is wise to reserve your seat (tel: 232329 or 232394). Check in is 15 minutes prior to departure. Payment is required in foreign currency. Cash and major credit cards are accepted.

The harbour is a hive of activity with schooners plying between Praslin, Mahé and La Digue arriving and departing regularly, as well as the *Cat Cocos* ferry with up to 150 passengers at a time. Private charters for birdwatching, deep-sea fishing and pleasure cruising also use the harbour. There is a small covered waiting area, generally quite crowded, where you can shelter from the elements and buy snacks. There are card and coin public telephones. The *Cat Cocos* booking office is also in the building on the jetty. A huge development project is in progress to increase port facilities at Baie Ste Anne and, on completion, there will be adequate berthing for a cruise ship. As part of the large dredging and reclamation project that has taken place, a marina for yachts has been built.

GETTING AROUND

Praslin has a good road around most of the perimeter of the island as well as one crossing the island from Baie Ste Anne to Grande Anse. In the north, there is no road between Anse Lazio and Anse Kerlan, only a few tracks and paths. In the southeast, a dirt road connects the main Côte d'Or road to Anse La Blague.

By bus

There is a regular bus service on Praslin. Bus 61 travels between the jetty terminus and Anse Kerlan. This is a way to get to and from the airport though it is not a very frequent service, operating half-hourly at peak times and hourly at mid-morning and mid-afternoon. Bus 62 travels from the airport along the coastal road past Pointe Consolation to the southwest through Baie Ste Anne village and along the west coast to La Réserve and Anse Lazio. It is not a frequent service either, and is mainly for schoolchildren. For more information, tel: 233258 or 511137.

By taxi

Taxis are available at the airport and at the jetty. All the hotels are able to arrange for a taxi service but, if a taxi is required in the evening or early morning, it is advisable to book in advance.

Car hire

There are several car-hire companies on Praslin and the hotels or guesthouses will arrange to use the nearest one. It is advisable to make your booking in advance.

Austral Car Rental Côte d'Or Praslin; tel: 232015; fax: 232933; email: austcars@seychelles.net; www.australcarhire.com
Grand Bleu Rent-a-Car Anse Kerlan; tel: 233660; fax: 233670
Praslin Holiday Car Rental House 2000, Grande Anse; Tel: 233219; fax: 233011; email: pracars@seychelles.sc
Prestige Car Hire Grande Anse; tel: 233266; fax: 233050; email: dunieville@seychelles.sc; www.hotellagonbaron.com
Standard Car Hire Amitié; tel: 233555; fax: 233163; email: stdc@seychelles.net

Bicycle hire

Cycling is a good way to explore Praslin as the coastal roads are not too undulating and the views are spectacular. Bicycles can be hired in Baie Ste Anne from Sun Bike (tel: 233033), and at Anse Volbert from Côte d'Or Bicycles (tel: 232071). At Amitié, James Collie also has cycles for hire.

Tours on Praslin

Any of the main Seychelles tour operators will be able to take you on a tour around Praslin. **Creole Holidays** has hospitality desks at the major hotels and their office is near the entrance to the airport (tel: 233223). **Travel Services Seychelles** is located at Grande Anse (tel: 233438) and also has hospitality desks at major hotels. **Mason's Travel** is at Grande Anse (tel: 233211). All the hotels, guesthouses and self catering establishments will be able to arrange any tours or boat excursions for you. **Bois Mare Nature Guide** (tel: 513370 or 575733; email: boismare@hotmail.com) is a small independent company run by Victorin Laboudallon who is a specialist nature guide. He is based at Cap Samy.

WHERE TO STAY

Most of the hotels on Praslin have good facilities and many fall into the luxury category and are priced to match. The larger hotels usually feature a watersports and dive centre and have a swimming pool or two. Prices are quoted in euros per person per night for bed and breakfast for two people sharing unless otherwise stated and are approximate for standard rooms. The cost will vary according to the season and type of room. Some establishments are open to a certain amount of negotiation. Tour operators are frequently able to quote better prices and tour packages are often the most economical way to go.

Large hotels

Lémuria Resort Anse Kerlan; tel: 281281; fax: 281001; email:
resa@lemuriaresort.com. This large hotel is set in spacious, well-manicured grounds
around a superb 18-hole Marc Farry golf course. There are 3 restaurants, 4 bars,
tennis courts, swimming pools and 3 lovely beaches. The health and wellbeing centre
uses Guerlain products and has a wide range of treatments and therapies. The Turtle
Club caters for children between 4 and 12 years from 09.00 to 21.00. Lémuria Resort
is the largest hotel on Praslin with 88 villa-type junior suites, 8 senior suites and 8
private pool villas, all finished in sumptuous luxury. The Presidential Suite is more
like a private hotel with its own beach, exclusive staff, chef and security and is
separated from the main hotel by a small river. A helipad is available for helicopter
transfers. Low season cost for a junior villa: €593.

Paradise Sun Hotel Anse Volbert; tel: 293293; fax: 232019; email:
paradise@seychelles.net; www.paradisesun.com. Situated at the end of Côte d'Or on a
lovely part of the beach. Features a large, open, feet-in-the-sand restaurant and bar
almost on the beach. The French Creole-style chalets have all the usual amenities
including tea- and coffee-making facilities and the louvered doors open on to a private
veranda facing the sea. 80 rooms; €401–500.

Berjaya Praslin Beach Resort Anse Volbert; tel: 286286; fax: 232244;
email: bpbfc@seychelles.net; www.seychelles.net/berjaya. The air-conditioned chalets
are set around a swimming pool amidst coconut palms in a lush tropical garden which
leads down to the protected beach. The hotel has facilities for the disabled. A take-
away is located on the beach. 79 rooms; €151–200 per room per night.

Hotel Coco de Mer and Black Parrot Suites Anse Bois de Rose on the southern
coastline; tel: 233900; fax: 233919; email: cocodeme@seychelles.net;
www.cocodemer.com. The Coco de Mer Hotel is located on a narrow terrace with a
small stretch of beach separating it from the exclusive Black Parrot Suites which are
located higher on the hillside. Each room in the hotel has its own private patio or
balcony enjoying great sea views. The small private beach is best at low tide and a free
service also transfers guests to Anse Lazio for the day. The family owns the steep
hillside behind the hotel and the fascinating Jean-Baptiste Nature Trail has been
created, allowing guests to walk through fine pristine forest with views across Praslin at
the top of the ridge. Matt can accompany you and tell you abut the natural history and
a small, informative, well-illustrated booklet is also available from the office. Look out
for the young *coco de mer* palms growing in the garden. Besides the usual watersports
you can play outdoor chess and mini-golf or enjoy a relaxed sundowner in the gazebo
over the water. A casual restaurant is located at the pool while the Hibiscus Restaurant
serves breakfast, lunch and dinner with a special Creole buffet with Seychellois music
and dancing on a Friday night. This family-run hotel provides outstanding, friendly
service. 52 rooms; €301 per double room per night, bed and breakfast.

New Emerald Cove Anse la Farine; tel: 232323; fax: 232300; email:
emerald@seychelles.net; www.emerald.sc. The hotel is accessible only by boat,
making it the ideal island getaway. 49 rooms; €351–400 per double room per night on
half board.

La Réserve Hotel Anse Petite Cour on the northwest side of Praslin; tel: 232211;
fax: 232166; email: lrmk@seychelles.net; www.lareserve-seychelles.com. Situated on a

sheltered, secluded beach with good swimming and snorkelling. The hotel, designed in a relaxed colonial style, has an impressive swimming pool and pool bar and an attractive restaurant on a jetty serving Creole, European and Chinese food. 30 rooms; €351–400 per room per night on half board.

Hotel L'Archipel Anse Gouvernement; tel: 284700; fax: 232072; email: archipel@seychelles.net; www.larchipel.com. This recently refurbished hotel is located at a lovely beach near Anse Volbert at the end of a private road along a lush hillside. Peppermint-coloured L'Archipel offers a gracious ambience, fine cuisine from 2 restaurants and a pool. All the suites and rooms are very spacious and each has its own large veranda and sea views. Disabled facilities are not available. Shorts are not permitted in the cocktail lounge and bar after 19.00, nor in the restaurants for dinner. Free sports include a daily boat trip for snorkelling, canoes and windsurfing. Scuba diving, deep-sea fishing, fly-fishing and excursions to neighbouring islands can be arranged for a fee. €401–500 per double room per night, bed and breakfast.

Acajou Hotel Côte d'Or; tel: 232400; fax: 232401; email: acajou@seychelles.net; www.acajouhotel.com. The long, low attractive buildings are constructed from wooden logs and set in pretty gardens close to the beach. The attractively decorated rooms each have a private balcony with views of the garden and swimming pool. The hotel is within walking distance of the casino. 28 rooms; €201–250 per double room per night, bed and breakfast.

Hotel Marechiaro Grande Anse; tel: 283888; fax: 233993; email: merkler@seychelles.net; www.seychelles.net/marechiaro. Conveniently located less than 10 minutes from either the Vallée de Mai or the golf course at Lémuria. The attractive granite and timber chalets are in lovely gardens with a pool and tennis court. Award-winning Ristorante Capri on the beachfront is famous for its superb Italian and Seychellois cuisines and is a member of the Chaîne des Rôtisseurs. Conference and disabled facilities are available. 25 rooms in 11 chalets; €201–250 per double room per night, bed and breakfast.

Indian Ocean Lodge Grande Anse; tel: 233324; fax: 233911; email: iol@seychelles.net. Situated on the long beach on the western side of Praslin, a central large thatched restaurant offers local and international cuisine. 32 rooms; €201–250 per double room per night, bed and breakfast.

Smaller hotels

Château des Feuilles Pointe Cabris; tel: 290000; fax: 290029; email: reserve@chateau.com.sc; www.chateau.com.sc. Member of Relais & Châteaux. This classy little hotel is located high above the ocean amidst lush tropical vegetation and pink granite boulders and has stunning views to many of the nearby islands. The rooms are well appointed with all mod-cons. A spectacular jacuzzi is situated high up on a headland with an amazing 300° view. The Château has a private helipad enabling guests to fly to and from Mahé or to visit the neighbouring islands. Visits can be arranged to 223-acre Grande Soeur Island which is exclusively for the use of hotel guests over weekends. Enjoy a lunchtime barbecue, snorkelling and swimming at one of the most beautiful of all Seychelles beaches. Grand Soeur is a 20-minute boat ride from Praslin or 5 minutes by helicopter. Children over 8 years of age are accepted. 9 rooms; €401–500 per double room per night, bed and breakfast.

Palm Beach Hotel Grande Anse; tel: 290290; fax: 233090; email: palmbeach@seychelles.sc. This new hotel looks over to Cousin and Cousine islands. The ground-floor rooms are suitable for disabled people with direct access to the beach and swimming pool. The restaurant and bar overlook the sea and Creole and international cuisine are served. 16 rooms; €151–200 per double room per night, bed and breakfast.

Hotel le Duc de Praslin Anse Volbert; tel: 232252; fax: 232355; email: leduc@seychelles.net; www.leduc-seychelles.com. Located a minute's walk away from the Côte d'Or beach, the Duc de Praslin has an open-air restaurant, which overlooks a profusion of orchids and bright bougainvilleas and serves authentic Creole cuisine. 15 rooms; €170-400 per double room per night, bed and breakfast.

Le Colibri Guesthouse Pointe Cabri, Baie Ste Anne; tel: 232302; fax: 232302; email: colibri@seychelles.net. Located high on the hillside, the rooms are simple with a rustic feel and have fantastic views across Baie Ste Anne to Round Island and La Digue; the sunrises are worth getting up for. Evening meals are part of the deal and everyone sits at a long table to enjoy the Creole seafood fare. 13 rooms; €101–150 per double room per night, bed and breakfast.

Hotel du Café des Artes Anse Volbert; tel: 232170; fax: 232155; email: café@seychelles.net. Owned and run by artist Christine Harter on the Côte d'Or beach. The rooms are large, airy and artistically furnished each with a veranda and a charming ambience. There is a convivial beach suite, almost on the sand and ideal for families or friends. Breakfast is served on the beach in fine weather and guests may dine at the local hotels at a preferential rate. There is a small gallery where Christine sells her work. A watersports kiosk is located nearby on the beach. 5 rooms; €180–210 per double room, bed and breakfast.

La Vanille Hotel Anse La Blague; tel: 232178; fax: 232284; email: vanille@seychelles.net. In a quiet corner of Praslin on a lovely beach with good snorkelling and great views over to neighbouring islands. A small restaurant close to the beach serves good Creole food with French flair. 10 rooms; €150–250 per double room per night, bed and breakfast.

Guesthouses and self-catering apartments

Les Villas d'Or Anse Volbert; tel: 232777, fax: 232505, email: villador@seychelles.net; www.seychelles.net/villador. This was voted 'best self-catering establishment of the Seychelles for 2003' and is located on Côte d'Or close to the casino. The spacious, well-appointed villas with all the creature comforts are spread out around the garden ensuring privacy. Guests may request breakfast, which will be served in your villa and dinner is served at Tante Mimi. 8 single villas in units of 2, and 2 twin villas able to accommodate 4 people. €201–250 per double room per night, bed and breakfast.

L'Hirondelle Côte d'Or; tel: 232243; fax: 232243; email: hirondel@seychelles.net; www.seychelles.net/hirondelle. Run by the Vidot family, the beach house has 3 double bedrooms, kitchen, lounge, bathroom and a veranda with sea views of Anse Volbert. The 4 beach apartments each consist of a double bedroom, bathroom and kitchenette, eating area and veranda with a sea view. Good value for a comfortable, no-frills holiday. English, French, German and Spanish are spoken. Beach house, €220 per night for 6 persons; the apartments, €95 for 2 persons. Breakfast can be arranged at €10 per person.

Les Rochers Bungalow Grosse Roche, La Pointe, tel: 233034; fax: 233034. Two bungalows are on a stunning little beach with gorgeous granite rock formations which light up in the sunset. It is a quiet part of Praslin with many small beaches and coves to discover. The family-run Les Rochers Restaurant is nearby and there is also one of the better souvenir shops on the island. €101–160 per double room per night, bed and breakfast.

Mango Lodge Côte d'Or; tel: 232077; mobile: 570454; fax: 232077; email: mango@seychelles.net. Perched on a ridge high above the beach, Mango Lodge offers a penthouse with 2 bedrooms en suite and a wide, open veranda which doubles as a dining area with magnificent views. There are 5 individual chalets and several other rooms. A gas barbecue is available for guests and, if there is a group, a chef from the village can be brought up to prepare your meal. As the Lodge is up a long and steep road it is advisable to have a car. If you are considering a long holiday, prices may be negotiable. They have a connection with Sagittarius Watersports and will make any arrangements for you. 11 rooms; €90–150 per double room per night, bed and breakfast.

My Dream Guesthouse Baie Ste Anne; tel: 232122. Has 2 rooms and is owned by Gilbert who offers to arrange any trips you might require. €70 for 2 people.

Villa Manoir Anse Boudin; tel: 232161; fax: 232161. An inexpensive, simple, self-catering option. Anse Lazio is about a 10-minute walk away and if you are prepared to wait, the buses do eventually arrive. It is at the junction of the road up to Zimbabwe. There are 2 self-catering rooms suitable for a family. €50–74 per double room per night.

Seaview Guesthouse Baie Ste Anne; tel: 232470; fax: 232470. A simple, family-run establishment close to the jetty at Baie Ste Anne. 2 rooms, €50–74 per double room per night.

WHERE TO EAT

Most of the hotels are only too pleased to serve non-residents but, if the hotel is full, they may not be able to accommodate extra guests. It is really important to make a reservation beforehand. Lémuria will not even allow you past the entrance gate unless you have a prior booking. Most of the menus are biased towards fish and seafood with some chicken and meat, while salads and vegetables are not as prominent, as they are frequently imported. The smaller cafés and restaurants that serve both lunch and dinner often close around 14.30 and re-open in the evening. Restaurants connected to hotels will only accept payment in foreign exchange and may give change in rupees. However, the independent restaurants are not obliged to accept foreign currency and will take Seychelles rupees.

Many of the small shops sell icy soft drinks and beer as well as a range of samosas, small pies, chilli bites and cakes which are ideal for an inexpensive lunchtime snack. They are made on a daily basis so are always fresh and you are not likely to find anything left after 14.00. Many of the local eateries are in the form of take-aways. It is a good idea to find out where the Pralinois eat – you just have to get there before they do!

Ristorante Capri at the Marichiaro Hotel on Grande Anse; tel: 283888. A member of Chaîne des Rôtisseurs and the best Italian restaurant on Praslin. Famous for its seafood and pasta, it is expensive. Lovely open-air ambience.

Les Rochers Grosse Roche; tel: 233910. Open for dinner only, Tue–Sat, 19.00–21.00. It serves an à la carte menu with international and Creole cuisine including curried fruit bat. There are only 8 tables. It is very expensive but very good.

Tante Mimi's Restaurant Anse Volbert; tel: 232500. Located above the casino is a large, smart restaurant serving a wide variety of dishes and their authentic Creole dishes are particularly good. Try their special Sunday lunch.

Touchdown Restaurant, upstairs at the Praslin airport; tel: 233655. Open 07.00–23.00. It seems an unlikely place for a good restaurant but it offers reasonable value with starters at SR35, main courses SR75–95, sandwiches and burgers SR24–40. You can also play the slot machines. The Touchdown Café on the ground floor is open 05.00–18.00 and has a good selection of light snacks and coffee.

La Goulou Café Côte d'Or; tel: 232223. A relaxed open-air type of café serving lunch and dinner.

Laurier Guesthouse and Restaurant Anse Volbert; tel: 232241. Open every night, closed Wed. The restaurant, located in the hub of the tourist part of Praslin, has a casual open-air restaurant serving the best Creole buffet and the fresh fish is really good. Some nights guests are entertained to live music.

Bonbon Plume Anse Lazio; tel: 232136. Serves lunch 12.30–15.00, dinner can be arranged by request for a group of 10 or more. The set menu is about SR180 per person.

Gelateria de Luca Anse Volbert has a wide selection of ice-creams for SR7; mango and coconut are our favourites. Snacks are also available.

DISCOVERING PRASLIN

The unhurried pace of life on Praslin is a holidaymaker's dream – beautiful beaches, good snorkelling, many restaurants and the majestic Vallée de Mai to explore. There is not much nightlife although some of the hotels have live entertainment with local bands and singers.

Four routes can be followed to discover the central, western, southern and eastern parts of Praslin.

Central Praslin: Baie Ste Anne to Grande Anse via Vallée de Mai

The crowded jetty is a buzz of activity during the arrival and departure of the ferries. The ticket sales office is located here and a tourist office will assist with any queries. There is a snack shop and even a tiny shop for purchasing the last must-have souvenirs from Praslin.

A long, low wooden building at the beginning of the jetty houses the offices of **Dream Yacht Seychelles** and is associated with a small private marina. Catamarans, monohulls and motor boats are available for charter and provide a picturesque entrance to Praslin. On the hillside the Baha'i Centre overlooks the jetty. From the car park and bus terminus at the Baie Ste Anne jetty the road hugs the coast into the village.

Immediately on the right is **La Port Boutique** (tel: 232262), where the owner is usually found hard at work with her sewing machine producing colourful, handmade clothing, which is also for sale in some hotels. **Praslin Slipway and Engineering** is a little further on and one can generally see a range of vessels undergoing repairs in the shipyard. **Amirs mini market** is on the right with **Brad's Café and Bar** (tel: 232711) close by, open 10.30–21.00. On the left, Mr Albert Durand's **Fabrication de Poisson en Bois** has a workshop oozing old Seychellois character. He makes wooden fishes, turtles and boats and welcomes visitors. His family owns the adjacent **Espadron Café**. They make delicious, smoked sailfish toasted sandwiches and evening meals can also be arranged here. Continuing past residential properties, the road passes **Sea View**, a small self-catering guesthouse, one of the least expensive on Praslin. A cluster of general stores (all named after ladies) is adjacent to it – Mary's has a post box, Cynthia's sells stamps and Adrienne's sells bread, cakes and banana bread. This store opens at 06.00 and is ideal for travellers catching the early ferry to La Digue.

The conspicuous **Baie Ste Anne Church** with its really tall palm trees is on the sea side of the road and there is a bus stop opposite. A convenient petrol station is on the left and is open daily 06.00–20.00. The road passes the police station, the Baie Ste Anne Supermarket with the Comodoro Night Club upstairs, before reaching the village proper. **Barclays Bank** (open Mon–Fri 08.30–14.30, Sat 08.30–11.30) and ATM is on the corner of the road leading to the Vallée de Mai.

To proceed to the Vallée de Mai and Grande Anse turn left at the intersection in the village. **Nouvobanque** with a bureau de change is located on this road in a fairly modern building which also houses the offices of several social services. The green-roofed hospital is on the right, the library on the left and the road climbs slowly uphill past some residential properties until it enters the **Praslin National Park** through a green tunnel of forest. Tall trees, palms and screw pines line the roadside, creeping vines adorn the tree trunks and the undergrowth consists of thick patches of introduced dieffenbachia plants (those green-and-white hothouse plants). About 2km from the village, the bus stop, car park and entrance to the **World Heritage Site of Vallée de Mai**, home of the *coco de mer*, is reached. This is a must-see attraction and is detailed below.

About 500m beyond the park entrance, the picturesque waterfall made famous in the painting by Marianne North can be glimpsed through the foliage on the right side of the road. Unfortunately, there is nowhere to park a car to view this famous waterfall; you simply have to walk along the narrow road. Marianne North was a wealthy English lady and talented artist with a great pioneering spirit. During her travels around the world, she spent some time in the Seychelles in 1883, and did 45 fine watercolour paintings of the islands, including some of Praslin and the *coco de mer*, all of which can be seen in the North Gallery at Kew Gardens, London.

The road descends to the west coast at Fond de l'Anse. The road to the left leads southwards to Anse Consolation and the road to the right goes along the coast of Grande Anse to the airport and Anse Kerlan.

Vallée de Mai

The World Heritage Site of Vallée de Mai is a tiny enclave of 20ha within the Praslin National Park, and is home to some 4,000 *coco de mer* palms. The admission fee is $15 or €15 and visitors receive a fact-filled pamphlet including a map. At the entrance into the reserve there is a thatched shelter showing a detailed map of the area and there are usually a few *coco de mer* nuts with surrounding husks and flowers displayed on a bench. Pick up one of the nuts simply to feel its incredible weight.

The well-maintained paths are clearly marked and easy to follow. In some places they are a little steep with steps, and there are boulders as stepping stones across the streams. The shortest circular route of approximately 1km will take about an hour, allowing plenty of time to stop and examine all the interesting things described on informative plaques placed at various points along the way. Three hours are needed to complete the full north to south circular route, including a visit to the rustic shelter on the northern extremity. From there, the expansive views across the park give an idea of what the entire island must have looked like in its pristine state.

The palpable silence of the forest is likely to be broken by the friendly chattering of Seychelles bulbuls and, if you are lucky, by the noisy whistling calls of a black parrot. If there is a breeze the other noise will be the clashing of the huge leaves of the *coco de mer*. Don't let a little shower of rain put you off visiting the Vallée de Mai as there is a special magic to visiting the valley in the rain. The enormous, thick, corrugated leaves of the *coco de mer* are like giant umbrellas, keeping you relatively dry as they channel the water down the gutter grooves of the leaf stems right down to the base of the trunk. Directly after rain is the most likely time to see the jewel-green female tree frogs, as well as the elusive tenrecs, rummaging around in the leaf litter looking for waterlogged insects.

There is a large car park at the entrance to the Vallée de Mai, and a shop selling books and curios pertaining to the *coco de mer*. Should you wish to purchase one of the extraordinary double nuts, be sure that it has the official certification papers with it, as they are necessary for the exportation of the *coco de mer*. Appealing to the romantic tourist market, an alcoholic liqueur Coco d'Amour is prepared and sold in a bottle resembling the double nut. Toilets are located behind the shop. A **cafeteria** sells snacks and soft drinks. Open daily 08.00–16.30.

The *coco de mer*

Lodoicea maldivica, the *coco de mer*, belongs to the Borassaidae subfamily of the large palm family. It is dioecious, meaning that the male and female flowers are on separate plants. The male palm, which reaches a maximum height of about 30m, towers over the female palm which attains only about 24m. The mature, green, heart-shaped fruit is about 46cm long, and can weigh as much as 20kg, making it the heaviest seed in the plant kingdom. The male catkin can be as thick as a person's arm and roughly 50cm long. It bears small, yellow, fragrant flowers much loved by geckos and slugs. The female inflorescence bears five to thirteen flowers covered by hard, round, brown bracts on a zig-zag axis. Usually only one of the three ovules in each flower

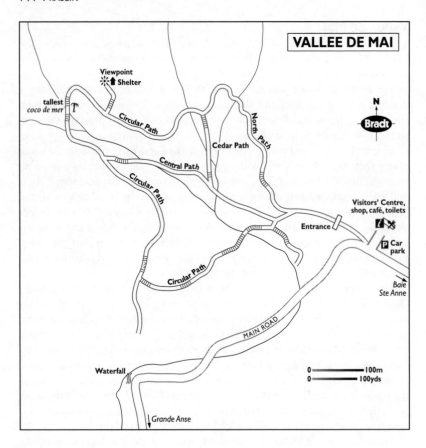

develops into a bilobed nut. Occasionally, however, a trilobed or even a quadrilobed nut may be produced. Usually only three to five fruits on each female inflorescence develop and the fruit takes about seven years to reach maturity on the mother plant. During the maturation period a soft jelly develops inside the nut and, by the time the nut is fully mature, the jelly has become a very hard white kernel. The palm takes at least 25 years from germination until it bears fruit.

When the smooth, green *coco de mer* nut has fallen to the ground, it lies dormant for about six months as the outer husk disintegrates to expose the hard, rough-textured, dark brown nut. The shoot containing the embryo arises from the sinus between the two lobes, and probes into the soft ground before sending down a taproot and lateral roots. It takes almost two years from germination to the emergence of the first leaf. When the protective sheath splits, the enormous leaves on long stalks grow to a span of almost 6m. One of the intriguing aspects about the stability of this tall palm is the tough and fibrous bowl which forms at the base of the trunk. It is about 50cm in diameter and 20cm deep and is perforated by the numerous spreading adventitious roots, which ultimately support the tall and heavily laden tree. Even after the palm has died and decayed, the bowl can remain for up to 60 years and many can be seen along the paths in the park.

Myths and mysteries of the coco de mer

Before 1768, no-one knew the origins of the erotically shaped double-lobed nuts that were occasionally found on the faraway shores of India, Sri Lanka and the Maldives. They were named sea coconuts, and were believed to be the fruits of enormous trees that grew underwater in the great central whirlpool of the oceans. The mystical nuts were intricately carved and inlaid with precious gems, gold and silver and were the prized possessions of kings and rulers – some can be seen in the great museums of Europe. Besides its reputation of having aphrodisiac properties, the kernel of the *coco de mer*, decayed or otherwise, was believed to be a cure for many ailments and an antidote to poisons.

Barre, a surveyor with the Marion Dufresne expedition in 1768, brought the fabulous mysterious nuts to the attention of the world. He found the nuts in the forests of Praslin, and took them back to Mauritius where Pierre Poivre, the botanically minded quartermaster, realised what they were. *Voilà*, the secret of the *coco de mer* was out! General Charles Gordon visited Praslin in 1881 and was convinced that the *coco de mer* was the 'tree of knowledge'. He wrote extensively on his fanciful theories, and contemplated that he had found the original Garden of Eden in the islands of the Seychelles.

Even today the Seychellois have some charming romantic fables about the mysterious palm. Because the male towers so protectively over the female it is reputed that, on nights when the moon is full, the male moves over to the female and they make love. No-one has ever reported on this phenomenon, because, as the story goes, if you witness it, you will be instantly turned into a black parrot!

SEYCHELLES ISLANDS FOUNDATION

Seychelles Islands Foundation (SIF) is a statutory body that was formed in 1979 when the Royal Society handed over the lease and the research station of Aldabra to the government of the Seychelles. The SIF manages and conserves the atoll, which was given World Heritage status in 1982. The unique Vallée de Mai was recognised by UNESCO as a World Heritage Site in 1983 and the management of the Vallée de Mai was tranferred to SIF in 1989. Both the Seychelles world heritage sites are thus managed by one organisation. SIF is largely a self-financing organisation as the revenue from Vallée de Mai covers the running costs of both Aldabra and the *coco de mer* palm forest. Various individuals and private institutions make donations that assist with the financing of these two remarkable natural areas. SIF does an enormous logistical job in providing staff, supplies and equipment to such a remote location as Aldabra as well as co-ordinating the scientific research programmes.

The biodiversity of Vallée de Mai

By a stroke of luck, the Vallée de Mai escaped any kind of degradation and remained a virtually virgin forest until the 1930s when the owner decided to beautify the valley and planted ornamental, fruit and spice trees to create a botanical garden. The government acquired the land in 1948, and started a programme to remove these alien plants and encourage the natural vegetation to regenerate. Cinnamon and allspice trees can, however, still be seen and there are a number of introduced jackfruit trees dotted about. Creeping vines of *Philodendron* and vanilla can be found in profusion, especially near the entrance. Further in, however, the forest is imbued with a pristine, primordial atmosphere.

Huge pre-Cambrian granite boulders are randomly scattered throughout the Vallée de Mai and weathering processes are responsible for leaving smaller rocks broken and jumbled together on the valley floor. Streams burble down the hillsides. Freshwater crabs have burrows in the banks of the streams, and shrimps live in the clear waters. Lichens, algae and mosses colour the rocks, and tiny ferns peep out from between the boulders. The low plant clinging to the edge of many of the pathways is known as gecko foot, *Salpiglossus*, and, according to folklore, has medicinal properties. Orchids, tree ferns, bird's nest fern, *Asplenium nidus*, and a variety of other epiphytic plants adorn many of the endemic trees and palms. Spectacular *Pandanus* screw pines add to the botanical mélange thriving in the Vallée de Mai.

All six species of palms (*latannyen*) endemic to the Seychelles grow in the reserve but the tall erect *coco de mer* is the most spectacular, towering above them all. One of the most useful and important palms is *Phoenicophorium borsigianum*, known by its Creole name of *latannyen fey*. It has broad, undivided leaves and is used extensively for thatching. A roof properly thatched with these leaves will last for 20 years. The most noticeable things about *Verschaffeltia splendida* or *latannyen lat* are the sturdy prop roots at the base of the trunk that support this tall palm. In the adult palm, the broad leaves appear shredded but they are not separate leaflets as in the coconut palm. Both *latannyen lat* and *fey* have sharp, black spines protecting the first two leaves of the young plant so do not take hold of them. *Nephrosperma vanhoutteana* or *latannyen milpat* has leaves divided into smaller leaflets like the coconut. It gets the Creole name from the rippling leaves said to look like a walking millipede. Red berries are borne on a long straight spike, easily visible between the leaves. The *palmiste* or *Dekenia nobilis*, named after the famous Belgian explorer Baron von der Decken, is characterised by flowers that look like long strings of hanging spaghetti. *Roscheria melanochaetes*, or *latannyen oban*, which reaches a height of about 7m is the smallest palm and has a slender trunk. It prefers shady spots and the leaves are red in young palms and dark green in the adult.

Other distinctive plants sharing the valley are the various *Pandanus* or screw pine species. Tall plants with a plethora of stilt roots to support them, they do vaguely resemble the palm family. Very often, though, the leaves have a serrated edge and appear thorny. Horne's pandanus, *Pandanus hornei*, has a single trunk supported by a tight cone of stilt roots, and a crown of leaves. The Seychelles pandanus, *Pandanus sechellarum*, has so many thick prop roots that it is difficult to see which is trunk and which is root. Pandanus fruits are usually round or oval with many segments.

Two magnificent endemic trees are *Dillenia ferruginea*, known as *bwa rouz*, and *Northea hornei*, the *kapisen*. The scientific name of the *kapisen* honours both Marianne North, the artist, and John Horne, the botanical director of the Pamplemousse Gardens in Mauritius.

Walking along the paths, you have to be very observant to see some of the small but interesting creatures that dwell in this remarkable palm forest. The bright green tree frogs, *Tachycnemis seychellensis*, usually rest horizontally flattened against palm leaves, and you often see their shadows at eye level on the underside of the leaf. It is a good idea to use binoculars to examine the male catkins of the *coco de mer* as both the chunky bronze-eyed geckos, *Aeluronyx seychellensis*, and the more slender green geckos, *Phelsuma*, are often seen amongst the flowers. Keep an eye on the forest floor for the brown Seychelles skink, *Mabuya seychellensis*. Amongst the molluscs, the endemic Praslin snail, *Pachnodus praslinus*, with a twirled and pointed shell, and the large *Stylodonta studeriana* snail are usually found on the *coco de mer*. The white slug, *Vaginula seychellsis*, particularly favours the flowers on the catkin of the male *coco de mer*.

The enigmatic bird of Praslin is the black parrot. It is, in reality, a dark chocolate-brown and is closely related to the Vasa parrots of Madagascar. They tend to move about in small family parties, whistling and calling to each other as they search out their favourite ripe fruits. They are likely to be heard before they are seen. Also commonly seen in the forest are Seychelles blue pigeons and noisy Seychelles bulbuls. At the beginning of the walk into the palm forest are some *takamaka* trees; when these are flowering, it is easy to see the Seychelles sunbirds feeding off the sweet nectar.

The west coast: Grande Anse to Anse Kerlan via the airport
Grande Anse

Grande Anse has a lovely curved beach which, though often covered in washed-up seaweeds and seagrasses during the southeast trades, is popular. Looking out beyond the beach, the islands of Cousin and Cousine seem to float upon the ocean. A thriving settlement spreads out along the shore of the bay with hotels generally positioned along the beachfront and shops on the inland side of the road.

Palm Beach Hotel is one of the first in a series of accommodation establishments along this stretch of coastline. Approaching the village, popular **JBM Café** and take-away is located on the right-hand side of the road. It seems to be a favourite lunchtime place for the people who work in that part of Praslin and all the snacks are soon sold out. The

Jungle Nightclub (tel: 512683) is open on Fridays and Saturdays 22.00–04.00; admission SR50. The **Britannia Hotel and Restaurant** is a short way inland.

Beyond **Cable & Wireless** and the **petrol station**, open 06.00–20.00, a line of hotels starts with **Beach Villa** whose simple chalets are right on the beach. There are tempting views across to Cousin and Cousine islands. **Hotel Marechiaro** is perhaps the most sophisticated in Grande Anse, offering all amenities, including the **Capri Restaurant**, which is a member of the illustrious Chaînes des Rôtisseurs and specialises in home-made pasta and seafood. Bella Napoli Pizzeria and take-away, though set back from the road, is almost next door. Excursions over to the island reserve of Cousin can be arranged from the **Hotel Maison des Palmes**, which also has an art gallery. **Travel Services Seychelles** has an office across the road. The countryside flattens out beyond here and a few more beach villas and guesthouses are set in lovely gardens close to the beach.

Other practicalities

Seychelles Savings Bank, **MCB Seychelles** and **Barclays Bank** are represented in **Grande Anse**, and **Mason's Travel** has an office here. Among the shops, **Sergio's Super Store** sells groceries while **Praslin Trading Centre** offers fresh vegetables and meat. **Grand Bleu** car hire have their office in a modern building called House 2000 and there is a variety of other small shops including **Coco de Mer Boutique** and hairdressers on both sides of the road.

Amitié

Black Pearl of Seychelles is on the sea side of the road opposite the airport. It includes a small aquarium (open Mon–Fri 09.00–16.00; Sat 09.00–12.00. Admission SR25 adults, SR10 children) with giant clams and several species of reef fishes that can be viewed in shallow tanks. The rare black pearls are farmed off Praslin and Linneys of Australia crafts the pearls into fine jewellery, which can be purchased at the boutique (open Mon–Fri 10.00–16.00; Sat 10.00–12.00). **Creole Holidays** have their offices near the entrance to the airport.

The attractive **Ile de Palme Airport** is located about 4km from the Vallée de Mai road junction in the small village of Amitié, the agricultural centre of Praslin. Watch out for the traffic light warning of approaching aircraft where the road passes close to the end of the runway. **Helicopter Seychelles** and some tour operators have counters in the airport building – a bit hard to find between all the fountains and palm trees! **Touchdown Café** on the ground floor, near the check-in counter, is a good place for a snack or coffee while, upstairs, the **Touchdown Restaurant** incorporates a café, restaurant, bar and slot machines.

Part of the road past the airport has been washed away over the years and a sea wall has been constructed to protect the road as it continues in a northerly direction along Anse Kerlan.

Anse Kerlan

The Islander is a small guesthouse with the **Capricorn Restaurant** in the same premises. Close to the entrance of Lémuria, a small shopping centre houses the Praslin Boutique and a small general dealer. Exclusive **Lémuria**, a five-star hotel with a host of amenities pandering to every creature comfort, is the largest on Praslin and boasts the only 18-hole golf course in Seychelles. The gate is guarded and no-one is permitted to enter unless a prior arrangement has been made. If you feel like having a sundowner or dinner there, don't just drop in as you must make a reservation beforehand.

From this part of Praslin there are no roads over to the eastern side, only a series of tracks and paths, many of which are difficult to locate.

The south coast: Grande Anse past Pointe Consolation to Baie Ste Anne

From Grande Anse southwards the coastal road traverses some of the most stunning parts of Praslin. Beautiful and undeveloped, with tiny, wild beaches and clear water of the most unbelievable hues, this is what the Seychelles is all about. Anse Citron is followed by Anse Bateau and a clump of granite rocks known as Grosse Roche. In some places there are small parking bays where it is possible to park the car to admire the vistas with the islands of Cousin and Cousine sandwiched between the sky and the sea in the distance. Coral reefs fringe the shore, but the shallow waters are not particularly good for swimming.

Villa Flamboyant is close to the beach at Anse St Saveur and, further on, you will reach **Les Rochers Restaurant and Bungalow** on the picturesque beachfront. The road climbs a little towards the **Black Parrot Suites and Coco de Mer Hotel**, a fine establishment with welcoming staff, wonderful unspoilt vistas and real black parrots in the natural vegetation surrounding the hotel. At Anse Consolation, look out for the limestone reef in between the granite boulders as the road swings to the left and continues past the **Badamier** guesthouse at Anse Marie Louise. From its location at the top of the hill the luxurious **Château des Feuilles** has a commanding view of the ocean. **Chalets Côte Mer**, **Le Grand Bleu** and **Le Colibri**, three separate guesthouses, can be found down a very pot-holed and scruffy-looking road but do not be put off, they are there: high on the hillside of Pointe Cabris with great views. The steep road with several sharp, hairpin bends and stunning views of Baie Ste Anne, continues down to the jetty.

The east coast: Baie Ste Anne to Anse Lazio via Anse Volbert

Instead of taking the left turn towards Vallée de Mai in Baie Ste Anne village, follow the road along the curve of the bay where the land reclamation project is visible. In the village, Beatrice has a small general dealer shop and the **Coco Rouge Café** and take-away is always full of local people. **My Dream** guesthouse overlooks the bay and a little further on the **Cap Samy Art Gallery** (open Tue–Sat 10.00–16.00; tel: 232048) is along a short road away from the sea. Sheila Markham, artist and sculptor, exhibits here.

The eastern peninsula of Praslin reaches out to form a horseshoe providing shelter and protection to the beautiful natural harbour of Baie Ste Anne, now blemished by the land reclamation project. The very sheltered little bays of Anse Takamaka and Bonnet Carré can be found tucked in amongst the great granite boulders tinged with pink. Accessible only by boat, the **New Emerald Cove Hotel** at Anse la Farine is located on the tip of the eastern peninsula looking out over Baie Ste Anne.

Although the main road swings left to Anse Volbert one can continue towards Anse La Blague on a concrete road proceeding through wooded slopes with glimpses of the sea through the vegetation. **Iles Des Palmes** has bungalows along the beach at Anse Takamaka with views across to Baie Ste Anne. The narrow uneven road winds over to the other side of the peninsula and although it looks a bit rough, the smallest car can manage it. **La Vanille Restaurant and Bungalows** are beautifully situated close to the beach at Anse la Blague with views from the hillside overlooking Praslin's other Grande Anse. On a clear day you can see Les Soeurs, the two small sister islands, in the distance. A dive centre is located here and the snorkelling is reputed to be good. A small store and an art gallery are also in the vicinity. As the road goes no further, there is no option but to turn around, cross the peninsula again and return to the main road leading to Anse Volbert and Côte d'Or.

A small insignificant road on the right leads to **L'Archipel**, a hotel on the hillside overlooking the secluded beach of Anse Gouvernement with splendid views of rocky Ile St Pierre and Curieuse. A little further on, also on the right, is the grand-looking **Casino des Iles** (open 17.30–03.00, slots room open: 12.00–02.00). Free transport is offered to the casino (tel: 232500). The exclusive **Tante Mimi's Restaurant** is upstairs. In the same grounds as the casino, **Bernies Flowers and Gifts** can be found, and **George Camille** has a gallery selling his artworks in original, print and postcard format as well as other exclusive items like silken scarves.

Anse Volbert

This is a fine 2km-long stretch of beach along the Côte d'Or coastline with many accommodation options available and a good selection of small shops and restaurants. All the hotels and guesthouses will arrange excursions to other islands as well as snorkelling, scuba diving or fishing expeditions. The first accommodation is **Les Villas D'Or**, which was voted the best self-catering establishment of the Seychelles in 2003. **Acajou Hotel** is a little further on and then there is a stretch of

Above left Graceful fairy tern at Rémire (LM)

Above right A male frigatebird in the mangroves of the Aldabra lagoon (LM)

Right A red-tailed tropicbird nesting on Aldabra atoll (LM)

Below Portion of the dense sooty tern breeding colony on Bird island (LM)

Above Coco de mer palm with female flowers and maturing nuts (LM)

Right Pitcher plant *Nepenthes* on the summit of Mont Copolia, Mahé (LM)

Below Waterfall surrounded by endemic palms in Praslin National Park (LM)

woodland for the next kilometre or so before reaching the more touristy part of Praslin. **Côte D'Or Octopus Diving** offers scuba-diving trips. **Le Goulou** Creole restaurant is conveniently situated on the left and **L'Hirondelle** guesthouse is a little further on. At the fork in the road MCB will be able to attend to your banking needs; a small supermarket and a couple of telephones are nearby. Keeping to the beach side at the fork, the first stop is the **Gelateria de Luca** where the mango- or coconut-flavoured ice-creams for SR7 per cone are particularly good. Coffee and snacks are also available. For the late-night ravers, **Ma Belle Amie Disco and Night Club** is the place to go and on special occasions the disco is set up on the side of the road. Barracuda Boat Charter has a small setup nearby and **Nouvobanque** has an ATM outlet. **Verona's Boutique** sells a selection of colourful beachwear and is close to the **Computer Bureau Verimedia** internet café (open Mon–Sat 10.00–19.00; 30 minutes costs €5 and an hour €10; email: verimedi@email.sc), which incorporates a video shop. They also offer a service transferring digital pictures on to a CD, but they expect to be paid in euros or dollars and will take rupees under sufferance provided you produce the bank or hotel foreign-exchange receipt.

Set back from the road is **Laurier Guesthouse, Restaurant and Bar** offering a good value Creole buffet and across the road is **Rosemary's Guesthouse** which is practically right on the beach. Tantalising views of the tiny island of Chauve Souris can be glimpsed through the palm trees. The road ends at the **Berjaya Praslin Beach Hotel** which has all the amenities of a large hotel. On the beach side of the cul-de-sac is the Berjaya take-away and you can rent a bicycle here from the Côte d'Or bicycle hire.

Returning to the fork, the road then continues parallel to the beach but behind the resorts. The first small dirt road to the right goes down towards the beach and is lined with residential properties. The **Duc de Praslin Hotel** is set in a pretty garden filled with orchids and bright bougainvilleas and at the end of this road you will find the **Café des Artes**. This small bed and breakfast establishment is owned by Christine Harter, a local artist, who also exhibits her work in a gallery here. A watersports kiosk is located on the beach a short distance from Café des Artes.

Back on the main road, a steep paved road to the left climbs the hill passing several residential homes before reaching **Mango Lodge**, perched high on the hillside with the most stunning views on Praslin. On the sea side of the main road there is another large hotel, the **Paradise Sun**, which is beautifully situated on a lovely stretch of beach. **Sagittarius Watersports and Whitetip Divers** are also on the beach, just beyond the hotel. The road which has looped behind the hotels now reaches the coast at Anse Petite Cour where **La Réserve Hotel** is located. It boasts a remarkable restaurant built on stilts over the water.

From the rural and unspoilt coastline of Anse Possession one has great views of Curieuse, only a little way offshore. Anse Possesion has historical connections, as Marion Dufresne placed a Stone of Possession there in 1768, claiming Praslin for France. From Anse Takamaka and Anse Boudin, the road turns inland and near an unpretentious self-catering guesthouse, **Villa Manoir**, there is a secondary road leading off to the left to **Zimbabwe**. All the way up the hill, the views are stunning and, although public access ends at the closed gates, the road continues to the radio communication antennae at the summit. A sunset trip up here is fabulous with panoramic views of Mahé, Silhouette and North islands to the south and Curieuse, Aride, La Digue and many of the smaller islands to the north and east.

The road eventually descends to Anse Lazio, a breathtakingly beautiful, secluded beach with good snorkelling and swimming. It is often described as the most beautiful beach in the Seychelles with a long stretch of silvery sand framed by granite boulders. **Bonbon Plume**, a feet-in-the-sand restaurant, almost on the beach, is shaded by some remaining *takamaka* trees, coconut palms and umbrellas. A large thatched shelter is a haven in a sudden tropical downpour. Tasty Creole food is served and they can cater for large groups. **Le Chevalier Bay Bar and Restaurant** is on the other side of the parking area. Elna's Boutique (open 11.00–16.00 daily), adjoining the dining area, is crammed full of souvenirs of every description.

EXCURSIONS TO THE SATELLITE ISLANDS

Praslin is ideally situated as a springboard to the many surrounding islands. There are several options: trips that incorporate several islands in a day; one island per day; or else plan to spend a few days on La Digue, only 30 minutes away by ferry. All the hotels and guesthouses will be able to make arrangements for you or, if you prefer, go to one of the larger tour operators. Depending on the weather, landing on some of the islands can be tricky, as none of the small islands has a jetty. Many of the excursions include snorkelling and even though snorkel gear is promised, it is wise to check it thoroughly before you take off. Several of the neighbouring islands are nature reserves and most have no overnight accommodation except for La Digue. For more details, see *Chapter 8*.

Cousin Island Special Reserve

This bird sanctuary island is open to visitors on Tuesdays to Fridays, 09.30–12.00, and 14.00–16.00. Each visit lasts approximately 90 minutes. As the birds are completely unafraid of people and are breeding most of the year round, a strict behaviour code is in place for both visitors and management.

Aride

Aride is a bird reserve surrounded by a marine protected area. It takes about 90 minutes to get there from Praslin and the cost will depend on the number of people using the boat. It is only open to visitors on Sunday, Monday and Wednesday with special arrangements for Thursday. The landing fee is €30 or US$30 and will probably be included in the cost of the boat journey.

Curieuse

Curieuse can be easily visited on a day trip and any of the Praslin hotels will be able to arrange an excursion.

Ile St Pierre

This islet is no more than a clump of rocks with a few palm trees on top, but it is a very good snorkelling spot and is easily accessible by boat from Anse Volbert. It is often combined with a day excursion to Curieuse.

Les Soeurs and Ile Cocos

Grande Soeur has one of the most beautiful beaches in Seychelles and day trips can be arranged for a visit, frequently in combination with a snorkelling trip to Ile Cocos.

Many-spined pandanus

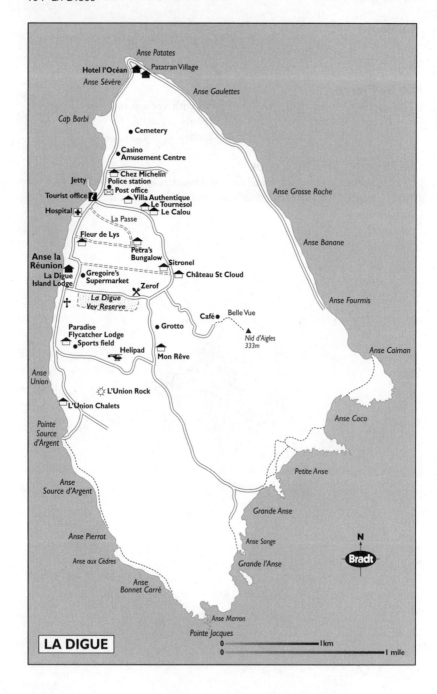

Anse Patates

Hotel l'Océan
Anse Sévère
Patatran Village
Anse Gaulettes

Cap Barbi

Cemetery

Casino
Amusement Centre

Chez Michelin
Jetty
Police station
Post office
Tourist office
Villa Authentique
Hospital
Le Tournesol
Le Calou
La Passe
Anse Grosse Roche

Fleur de Lys

Anse Banane

Petra's
Bungalow
Sitronel
Anse la
Réunion
La Digue
Island Lodge
Gregoire's
Supermarket
Château St Cloud
Zerof
La Digue
Vev Reserve
Anse Fourmis
Café
Belle Vue
Paradise
Flycatcher Lodge
Sports field
Grotto
Nid d'Aigles
333m
Anse Caiman
Helipad
Mon Rêve
Anse
Union
L'Union Rock
L'Union Chalets
Anse Coco
Pointe
Source
d'Argent
Anse
Source d'Argent
Petite Anse
Grande Anse
N
Anse Pierrot
Anse Songe
Bradt
Anse aux Cèdres
Grande l'Anse
Anse
Bonnet Carré
Anse Marron
Pointe Jacques
LA DIGUE
0   1 km
0   1 mile

La Digue

La Digue, with its dramatic, sculptured granite rocks and exquisite beaches, is a laid-back, inviting island in the sun. It lies 50km northeast of Mahé, 4km east of Praslin and is the fourth largest of the granitic islands. The 10km^2 island is almost completely encircled by coral reef and has no natural harbour. A jetty has been built at La Passe on the west coast and, recently, a breakwater has been constructed to provide more shelter, particularly during the northwest monsoons. The island is about 6km long, a little over 3km wide, and rises up to 333m at Nid d'Aigles, 'Eagles Nest', the highest peak.

Marion Dufresne, in his ship *La Digue*, made the first recorded discovery of this picturesque island in 1768, and the French took formal possession of it in 1771. Amid the lush vegetation, streams and swamps, the worst thing the early settlers had to contend with were the crocodiles, and they were soon eradicated along with the tortoises. The birdlife managed to cling on to a precarious existence, and the rare black paradise flycatcher is still present in low, but increasing numbers.

Coconut palms, magnificent white beaches, few shops, plenty of bicycles and a couple of ox carts all add up to a totally relaxed island-style way of life. At L'Union Estate copra is still processed in the old-fashioned way using an ox to turn the grinding wheel for extracting the coconut oil. Boats are built and repaired using traditional methods, and nobody is ever in a hurry. There are some lovely examples of Creole architecture nestling amongst the lush vegetation. Most of the 2,000 residents are involved in the tourism industry, others are fishermen and some are boat-builders. On La Digue you will find small, welcoming hotels, coconut and vanilla plantations, art studios and the most seductive beaches. Although the public telephones may not always work, the schooners and ferries do arrive and depart on time.

GETTING THERE AND AWAY
By sea
Inter-island schooners ply the seas between La Digue, Mahé and Praslin. The schooner takes about three hours from Mahé, and in rough weather the rolling motion may cause some *mal de mer*. A faster alternative from Mahé is to take *Cat Cocos* to Praslin, and then use the regular daily ferry service which operates between Praslin and La Digue. The crossing takes only about 30 minutes and a return ticket costs € 19 or US$19. For reservations, tel: 232329; fax: 232374.

Boats of various descriptions may also be chartered in Mahé in

FERRY SERVICE LA DIGUE–PRASLIN

Days	Depart La Digue	Arrive Praslin	Depart Praslin	Arrive La Digue
Daily	07.30	08.00	07.00	07.30
	09.30	10.00	09.00	09.30
	10.30	11.00	10.00	10.30
	12.00	12.30	11.15	11.45
Sundays only	14.00	14.30	12.00	12.30
	15.30	16.00	14.30	15.00
	16.30	17.00	16.00	16.30
Mon to Sat	17.45	18.15	17.15	17.45
Sundays only	18.15	18.45	17.45	18.15

order to make your own voyage of discovery to La Digue. Contact the Marine Charter Association in Victoria (tel: 322126; fax: 224679; email: mca@seychelles.net).

By air

Helicopter Seychelles (tel: 385858, fax: 373055) services La Digue. A minimum of two passengers is required and 72 hours' notice must be given. From Mahé to La Digue it costs €170 and from Praslin to La Digue, €85.

WHERE TO STAY

There is only one largish hotel on La Digue and it has 60 rooms. There is a variety of small hotels, self-catering and bed and breakfast establishments, many with a typically relaxed Creole atmosphere. Most of the small guesthouses will be able to arrange bicycle hire, snorkelling and diving trips as well as excursions to many of the nearby islands. All accommodation has to be paid for in foreign currency. Quoted prices are per person for two people sharing, bed and breakfast, unless otherwise stated.

Hotels and guesthouses

La Digue Island Lodge Anse la Réunion; tel: 234232; fax: 234132; email: reservation@ladigue.sc; www.ladigue.sc. The only largish hotel on the island, with gardens filled with exotic flowering shrubs, opening out on to the beach. There is a big swimming pool with a bar and delicious Creole food is served in the restaurant. A whole range of accommodation is available, including rustic A-frame chalets built of *takamaka* wood and thatched with latanier leaves, and the old, yellow Creole planter's house built in 1900 and now a National Heritage building. Free boat excursions are provided to the nearby islands of Ile Cocos, Grande Soeur, Marianne or even Félicité if there are no guests in residence. A landing fee of €10 is payable and guests are asked to provide their own snorkelling equipment. Sunset cruises are also available. Azzura Pro Dive will be able to arrange your diving expeditions; they can be found near the swimming pool or tel: 292535. €300 per double room per night, half board.

Accommodation at Félicité Private Lodge or L'Union Estate chalets can be arranged through La Digue Island Lodge.

Patatran Village Anse Patates; tel: 234333; fax: 234344; email: patatran@seychelles.net; www.the-seychelles.com/patatran. The hotel is set on the hillside overlooking the ocean with splendid views to Cocos, Les Soeurs and Félicité islands. A tiny, secluded beach between massive granite boulders is below the hotel. There are 18 rooms, 10 superior and 8 standard, some of which are ideal for families. €101–150 per double room per night, bed and breakfast.

Château St Cloud Anse la Réunion; tel: 234346; fax: 234345; email: stcloud@seychelles.net. The former vanilla plantation house is high on the hillside and is a 10-minute walk down to the beach. There are 10 rooms, €101–150 per double room, bed and breakfast.

L'Océan Hotel Anse Patates; 234180; fax: 234308; email: hocean@seychelles.net; www.hotelocean.info. This small hotel is located at the northern tip of La Digue close to Anse Severe and Anse Patates beaches. The 8 rooms are air conditioned and each has a private balcony. €200–260 per double room per night, bed and breakfast.

Le Calou Guesthouse La Passe; tel: 234083; fax: 234083; email: calou@seychelles.net; www.calou.de. Klaus is the owner of this simple but friendly establishment set back a little way from the beachfront. There are 5 rooms, each with fridge, fan and a veranda. Guests can use a small, shaded freshwater pool, hammocks and sunbeds and there is internet access. Meals are Creole style but the atmosphere is German and many guests return repeatedly. €123 for 2 people, dinner, bed and breakfast.

Chez Marston La Passe; tel: 234023; mobile: 514311; fax: 234023; email: mars@seychelles.net. A typical Seychellois establishment run by Marston Saint Ange and his family. It is close to the beach and the jetty, ideal for an informal holiday. €75–100 per double room per night, bed and breakfast.

Sitronel Guesthouse La Passe; tel: 234230; fax: 234230. About 1km from the jetty this relaxed guesthouse has 4 spacious rooms and Madame Guy provides a Creole dinner in the garden restaurant. €50–74 per double room per night, bed and breakfast.

Villa Authentique La Passe; tel: 234413; fax: 234413. Mrs Ah Kong runs this small guesthouse with 7 rooms in a garden setting. It is close to the jetty and beaches. €45 per person per night, €90 per double room per night, €75 per double room per night, bed and breakfast.

Le Tournesol Guesthouse and Restaurant La Passe; tel: 234155; fax: 234364; email: tournesol@seychelles.sc. Located conveniently close to beaches, this guesthouse has 3 spacious bungalows in the garden. The restaurant serves good Creole food. €75 per double room per night, bed and breakfast or €132 dinner, bed and breakfast for 2 people.

Villa Mon Rêve Anse la Réunion; tel: 234218; fax: 234218; email: vmonreve@hotmail.com. Located a little way from the sea, there are 5 rooms each with shower and ceiling fan. Creole food is the order of the day. Internet and a bar are for the use of guests only. €66 for a double room only, €82 for 2 people, bed and breakfast.

Pension Michel Anse la Réunion; tel: 234003; fax: 234003. This small guesthouse offers 7 well-equipped rooms close to the Veuve Reserve and beaches. €95 per double room per night, bed and breakfast.

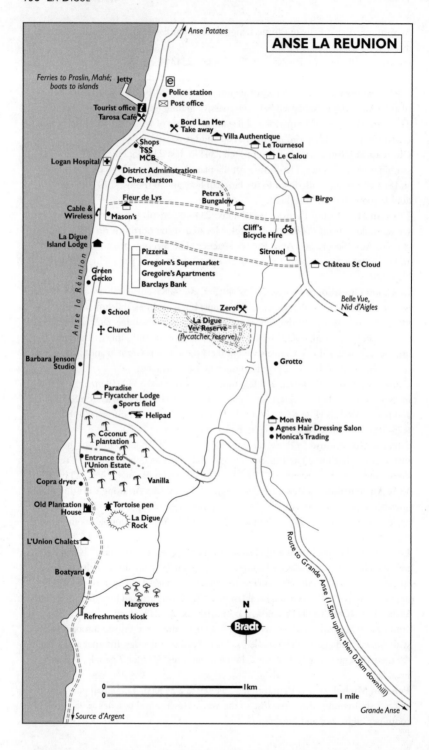

Anse Patates

ANSE LA REUNION

Ferries to Praslin, Mahé; **Jetty**
boats to islands

Police station
Post office

Tourist office
Tarosa Café

Bord Lan Mer
Take away
Villa Authentique
Le Tournesol

Shops
TSS
MCB
Le Calou

Logan Hospital

District Administration
Chez Marston

Fleur de Lys
Petra's
Bungalow
Birgo

Cable &
Wireless
Mason's

La Digue
Island Lodge
Cliff's
Bicycle Hire

Sitronel

Green
Gecko
Château St Cloud

Pizzeria
Gregoire's Supermarket
Gregoire's Apartments
Barclays Bank

Belle Vue,
Nid d'Aigles

School
Zerof

Church
La Digue
Vev Reserve
(flycatcher reserve)

Barbara Jenson
Studio
Grotto

Paradise
Flycatcher Lodge
Sports field
Mon Rêve

Helipad
Agnes Hair Dressing Salon
Monica's Trading

Coconut
plantation

Entrance to
l'Union Estate

Copra dryer
Vanilla

Old Plantation
House
Tortoise pen
La Digue
Rock

L'Union Chalets

Boatyard

Route to Grande Anse (1.5km uphill, then 0.5km downhill)

Mangroves

N

Refreshments kiosk

Bradt

0 ——————— 1 km
0 ——————— 1 mile

↓ *Source d'Argent*

Grande Anse

L'Orangerie La Passe. A small exclusive hotel owned by Creole Holidays and scheduled for opening sometime in 2005.

Self-catering
Fleur de Lys Anse la Réunion; tel: 234459; fax: 234304; email: fleurdelys@yahoo.com; www.fleurdelysey.com. All 4 attractive, spacious, colonial-style bungalows have well-equipped kitchens for self-catering. Mary and Ron Henry, your friendly hosts, will be able to arrange all your excursions. € 101–150 per double room per night, bed and breakfast.

Paradise Flycatcher Lodge Anse la Réunion; tel: 234423; fax: 234422; email: mcdurup@seychelles.net. The 4 spacious bungalows are 2 minutes' walk from the beach and offer self-catering options as well as a restaurant featuring Creole fare. € 148–191 per double room per night, bed and breakfast.

L'Union Estate Chalets L'Union; tel: 292525; fax: 234132; email: reservation@ladigue.sc; www.ladigue.sc. The chalets are set under the palms in the estate and close to Source d'Argent beach. Guests may use all the facilities at La Digue Island Lodge. The spacious chalets have well-equipped kitchenettes. € 500 for 4 people self catering.

Pension Residence La Passe; tel: 234304; fax: 234304; email: chezmich@seychelles.net; www.seychelles.net/chezmich. Guests have a choice of self-catering or bed and breakfast. There are 6 spacious bungalows close to the beach, each with a veranda. € 75–100 per double room per night, bed and breakfast, € 100 bungalow only.

Anse Sévère Bungalow Anse Sévère; tel: 247354; fax: 247354; email: clemco@seychelles.net. Located close to the beach it is ideal for a quiet Robinson Crusoe-style holiday. € 101 per double room per night, bed and breakfast.

WHERE TO EAT
Many of the smaller guesthouses have restaurants and will happily provide meals on request but it is necessary to book in advance as they are really simple, family-run establishments that serve traditional Creole meals generally featuring fresh fish.

La Digue Island Lodge Anse la Réunion; tel: 234232. A casual pool bar serves snacks and drinks throughout the day while Le Pêcheur restaurant with a high, thatched roof and feet-in-the-sand ambience offers a fine Creole buffet.

Patatran Restaurant at L'Océan Hotel, Anse Patates; tel: 234180. The restaurant has great views of the ocean and a good reputation for its spicy Creole fare. Guests can enjoy live music a few times a week. The dining tables are beach-life showcases with all manner of shells and seaweed on display.

Patatran Village Restaurant Anse Patates; tel: 234333. The restaurant has lovely views through the palms over the ocean. A snack menu is available for around € 15, starters are from € 12 and the main courses range between € 10–25. The highlight is the weekly Creole buffet with music and dancing. The restaurant has a good selection of South African wines.

Chez Marston Restaurant Anse la Réunion. A casual Creole restaurant, open 07.00–22.00 for breakfast, lunch and dinner.

La Bousir is an open-air stall selling welcome cool drinks and light meals along the path leading to the Source d'Argent beach.

DISCOVERING LA DIGUE

The nicest way to explore this small island is on foot. Cycling is also a great way to get around the island although, in hot weather, it can be a bit of a slog to get over to Grande Anse on the eastern side. At the jetty, and along the road, there are several bicycle-hire shops and all charge between SR40 and SR50 per day. Remember to check the tyres and brakes before you set off.

It is advisable to take plenty of water to drink, a hat and sunscreen when you head out on your travels. Maps and local information can be obtained from the tourist office at the jetty (tel: 234393; open 08.00–17.00). Ox carts are still available for transport around the island but are gradually being phased out and replaced by less rustic, open-sided lorries.

Start exploring the beautiful little island from the jetty. Several routes can be followed but, basically, they cover the coast to the north, the coast to the southwest, across the island to Grande Anse, and inland leading up the hill to Nid d'Aigles.

The north: La Passe to Anse Patates and Anse Grosse Roche

From La Passe jetty turn left, passing the **post office**, **police station** and courtroom. There are usually a couple of ox carts in the vicinity with the patient beasts waiting in the shade. There are lovely views of Praslin through the trees and, with pirogues (dugout canoes) lying on the beach, there are some good photographic opportunities. Look out for the white fairy terns roosting in the *takamaka* trees. **Logan Bicycle Hire** offers bicycles at SR50 per day or SR35 per day for three days. Safari Club Internet Bureau is open 10.00–12.30 and 13.30–17.00 and costs SR10 for 15 minutes.

A large building houses the only casino on La Digue. The old planter's house on the right is part of **Chez Michelin Pension**.

The road swings away from Cap Barbi, and on the right is the cemetery, complete with glistening white tombstones. The road curves round beautiful Anse Sévère to the northern point of La Digue. **Anse Sévère Bungalows**, a tiny self-catering establishment, has lovely views of the beach. Around the point, the gloriously situated **Patatran Restaurant** has stunning ocean views and serves delicious Creole-style food. It's open for lunch and dinner every day. The small **L'Océan Hotel** is associated with the restaurant. **Patatran Village Hotel**, set into the hillside, is only a little way down the road and the rooms, each named after a flower, have magnificent views from their balconies.

There is reasonable snorkelling off the beach but the area can be susceptible to large swells and strong currents especially during the northwest monsoon. The road continues along the northeast coast towards Anse Grosse Roche and beyond, but it becomes very sandy and difficult for bicycle riding.

The southwest: La Passe to Anse Source d'Argent

To explore the southwest of La Digue, turn right at the jetty. There are some small shops selling postcards and souvenirs as well as a branch of **MCB** with a convenient ATM. The Tarosa, a small cafeteria close to the jetty, sells icy drinks and light snacks. Service is slow, but why hurry? The road to the south is characterised by a tunnel of tall, shady *badamier* trees. On the left is a large wooden building flying the Seychelles flag which houses the district administration, the social centre and the library. The **Logan Hospital** is on the sea side of the road, and was named after Sir Marston Logan, governor of the Seychelles between 1942 and 1947. **Chez Marston Restaurant** is on the left and a little further on is Cabon de Laura, a small boutique. **Lionel's Bicycle Hire** is nearby (tel: 234026); he charges SR40 per day. Almost opposite Cable & Wireless is a small track, and a little way along it you will find **Fleur de Lys**, a charming self-catering establishment. **Petra's Bungalow** is about 200m further on. There are some really old, traditional Creole houses in this part of La Digue, their balconies and verandas overflowing with pot plants. The attractive Sunshine Guesthouse occupies one of these renovated Creole houses.

Back on the main road, **Mason's Travel** (tel: 234227) is located in a little house.

Anse la Réunion, a dazzling white beach, runs all the way from the jetty to L'Union Estate. On the rocks beyond the beach is the La Digue Cross, which was erected in 1931 by a Swedish priest to commemorate those who had perished while attempting to land on the island. Glimpses of Praslin through the trees over the turquoise sea are spectacular. Terns and waders are often seen on this part of the beach, especially from December to February.

The road swings to the left with the large (for La Digue!) **Gregoire's Supermarket** which stocks everything from stationery to delicious hot pastries. In the same building a pizzeria, open 10.30–22.30, offers pizza and pasta dishes and **Barclays Bank** has a branch, open 10.00–14.30, Mon–Fri. **La Digue Island Lodge** (see page 159) is on the right behind a fence, though you have to proceed past the hotel to La Réunion Road then double back for 50m to reach it. The Azzura Pro Dive Centre (tel: 292535) can be found close to the swimming pool in the hotel grounds. The Green Gecko art and craft boutique, selling silk paintings and clothes, is near the lodge.

Continuing southwards along the road to Source d'Argent, La Digue School and the Church of the Assumption are on the left. On August 15, Assumption Day, La Digue celebrates with a joyous festival commencing with a procession and mass followed by music and dancing, art exhibitions and stalls selling food and drink. Everything comes to a standstill as La Digue has a party and welcomes visitors from the other islands.

The **Barbara Jenson Studio**, featuring original work by the artist, is always worth a visit. As you approach L'Union Estate the road divides and the left fork heads inland and joins the road leading over to the east coast and Grande Anse. A short distance up this road there is a sports field and the **helipad**. The right fork leads to L'Union Estate with an entrance fee of €4 or

US$4. At this old coconut plantation, copra is still being produced using traditional methods. The old calorifier, or drying shed, is fuelled from the discarded husks and, after the thick white coconut meat has been dried, the patient old ox will turn the grinding wheel to extract the coconut oil. Try some sweet coconut water and taste as much fresh coconut as you like.

Moving on through the estate, there is the beautiful old plantation house built of the local hardwood and thatched with palm leaves. It has been restored to its former glory, and is used by the president as a holiday house. Behind the old house and bounded by spectacular chunks of granite is a pen with giant Aldabra tortoises. Along the path towards the beach there are vanilla vines supported on poles. The vanilla pods ripen around September when they are treated, cured and put out to dry in the sun. Beyond the vanilla is a marshy area with some mangroves next to a small river. Chinese bitterns can sometimes be seen skulking among the vegetation, and this area is known for *tortues-soupapes*, or terrapins.

Closer to the beach is the boat yard, with boats up on blocks being repaired and new ones being built. Located within the grounds of the estate, very close to the beach, are the **L'Union Estate Chalets** which offer self-catering accommodation. Along the small path leading from the estate to the beaches is a rustic stall, **La Bousir** (the same name as the nearby stream), selling cold drinks, snacks and souvenirs.

Wind your way through the palms, *badamier* trees and great granite boulders which characterise the dramatic landscape of the next few beaches. Note the enormous palm spiders with their incredibly strong webs spanned between the rocks.

There are no facilities on the beach, so do as the locals do and change behind a rock if you plan on swimming. Snorkelling is best at high tide though you have to swim out beyond the seagrass beds. Be careful of the currents as the tide recedes.

The first wonderful beach is Pointe Source d'Argent and, from here, there is a series of small beaches and enticing coves framed by enormous boulders: Anse Pierrot, Anse aux Cèdres and then Anse Bonnet Carré. Coconut palms bow over the white sands and the crystal-clear, turquoise water beckons. Several Hollywood movies have been filmed on these beautiful beaches. At very low tide you may be able to walk around the southern rocks of Pointe Jacques to Anse Marron. But remember that you have to return while the tide is still low, otherwise you might be stuck till the next low tide and have to spend a very uncomfortable time perched on the rocks.

Grande Anse: Anse la Réunion to Grande Anse via the flycatcher reserve

From the jetty take the route to the south but instead of turning towards La Digue Island Lodge, turn left, away from the sea and proceed along La Réunion Road. On the left side of the road there are some small shops, and on the right is the beginning of the flycatcher reserve.

A special reserve, **La Digue Vev Reserve** (*vev* is the Creole name for the black paradise flycatcher) has been established as a safe haven for these

VANILLA

Vanilla was used to flavour the *xocoatl*, the chocolate drink of the Aztecs. The Spanish conquistadors took it back to Spain, giving it the name *vainilla* from the diminutive of the word for pod – *vaina*. Although there is an indigenous variety of vanilla growing on some of the Seychelles islands, it is the orchid, *Vanilla planifolia,* native to Mexico, that is propagated to produce the flavourful pods.

Vanilla is a creeping vine with a fleshy stem no thicker than a thumb, and aerial roots that cling to the host tree. The leaves are thick and firm and the flowers are pale green. As there are no natural pollinators for vanilla on the Seychelles, each flower has to be pollinated by hand which is a very delicate job performed with a small stick. After successful pollination, the long, bean-shaped seed pods develop and can reach their full length of 20cm within four to six weeks, attaining maturity nine months later. When the bases of the thick, fleshy pods turn yellow, they are picked by hand and immediately plunged into a cauldron of boiling water. Thereafter the pods, now chocolate brown, are placed on drying racks in the Seychelles sunshine. It takes about four months for the curing process to be completed. The soft, pliable pods, filled with hundreds of pinprick-sized seeds, are then sorted according to length, and neatly tied into bundles with raffia strands.

On La Digue, pure vanilla essence is extracted from the pods and this is sold in the Victoria Market. The flavour and bouquet of the real thing is sublime and a gourmet's delight. In addition to the usual culinary uses of vanilla essence, there are many delightful uses for the pods themselves. Several pods placed in a jar of sugar will impart a wonderful vanilla flavour, as will a pod in the tea pot or in the coffee filter. A couple of pods soaking in a bottle of white rum adds a distinctive flavour and colour – add a measure of this to chocolate sauce for something memorable!

endemic birds. The Royal Society for Nature Conservation established the 15ha reserve in 1987 for the protection of this single species. The small resource centre at the entrance to the reserve provides information about these endangered birds. An educational initiative at the local school has taught the children to value these rare and beautiful birds, instead of shooting them with catapults. From the road, a short, flat path leads to the interior of the reserve. The forest consists mainly of *takamaka* and *badamier* trees. Listen for the whistling calls of the flycatchers as they flit amongst the trees, and see if you can spot a delicate nest of soft lichens and leaves bound together with spider webs gently swaying at the end of a branch. A walk through the reserve will take about 30 minutes but you may want to spend more time observing the fabulous flycatchers.

Continue up the road past the reserve. The **Zerof Bar and Restaurant** specialising in Creole food will be on your left and is open for lunch and dinner. At the T-junction, turn right into the road coming from Château St Cloud. The grotto, from where the Assumption procession begins, is on the left. A bit further down the road the **Villa Mon Rêve** is a little guesthouse with a bar and restaurant for guests only. They can arrange trips to nearby islands and cater for your wedding. Agnes Hair Dressing Salon (tel: 715656), is adjacent with Monica's Trading Store next door. Soon after, near Roche Bois, lies a road on the right going down to L'Union Estate and the southern end of Anse la Réunion. Continue on the Grande Anse road, which is a bit bumpy and fairly steep in parts, for about 2km. Most of this rural way is in deep shade among great boulders, streams and some small farms.

The dramatically beautiful beach of Grande Anse lies before you. It can be wild, rough and dangerous as the huge waves crash in from the Indian Ocean. Body surfing in the shore breakers can be exhilarating but, because of the dangerous currents, it is not recommended for genteel bathing. Take time to look around – you may well see white-tailed tropic birds flying about, as well as enormous, harmless fruit bats with furry faces, also known as flying foxes. A rustic beach restaurant operates irregularly at Grande Anse.

From Grande Anse there is a track leading westwards to Anse Songe and, if you can find it, another track behind the marshes leads to Petite Anse and Anse Cocos. It is possible to continue over the headland to Anse Caiman and, from there, a long walk will take you up the wild and remote east coast past Anse Fourmis and Anse Grosse Roche right up to Anse Patates.

The inland road

From the jetty at La Passe, a road leads directly away from the sea. This can best be described as the accommodation road as here you will find many little places to stay. Closest to the pier is **Villa Authentique**, a family guesthouse. The B&M Store is nearby, then fairly close together are **Le Tournesol**, rustic **Le Calou** and **Birgo** with Cliff's Bicycle Hire on the opposite side of the road. There are several other small establishments in this area that were not operating at the time of writing this guide. A little further on you get to **Château St Cloud**, an old planter's house, half of which has been renovated to provide accommodation. It even has a tiny museum with a collection of old household items. **Sitronel** is across the road. There are several small shops along the way, and this is the part of the island to see some typical old La Digue houses.

Continue along and the next road that leads off to the left is the start of the walk up to **Belle Vue** and Nid d'Aigles, the highest point on La Digue. The walk is steep but the phenomenal views of La Digue, Praslin and other islands, are superb. Follow the concrete road up the hill and when it forks, keep left. The Belle Vue Café, en route, sells the coldest Cokes on La Digue! The walk takes about two hours up and down.

Back at the Bell Vue junction, you could follow the road down to the Flycatcher Reserve and back to Anse la Réunion or continue on to the L'Union Estate or over to Grande Anse.

EXCURSIONS FROM LA DIGUE

If you are staying on La Digue it is easy to take the regular ferry across to Praslin for the day. Take a morning schooner over and there will be sufficient time to visit the Vallée de Mai and return on the 17.00 schooner.

La Digue is the ideal island from which to set off on a trip to the small neighbouring islands of Ile Cocos, Marianne and Les Soeurs. The waters surrounding these little islands are good for snorkelling, and the islands themselves are a retreat from sleepy La Digue! La Digue Island Lodge will be able to make all the necessary arrangements to visit the islands, including a snorkel on the way and a delicious beach barbecue for lunch. Remy Uranie of Jungle Tour (tel: 234281) offers to teach visitors about the vegetation, fruits and vegetables of La Digue. Lone Wolf Charters (tel: 570344), in Mason's Travel, offers trips to the nearby islands and can take you fishing.

Private boat owners on La Digue also take tourists on fishing expeditions. Enquire at the tourist office at La Passe jetty.

Sooty terns

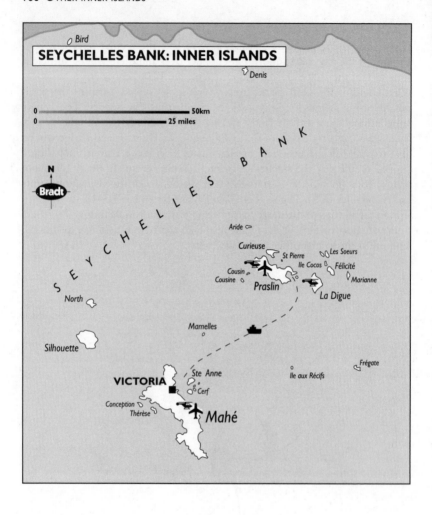

Other Inner Islands

The inner granitic islands of the Seychelles Bank encompass Mahé, Praslin, La Digue and a host of smaller satellite islands. Silhouette, North, Mamelles and Frégate islands, which are closest to Mahé, as well as Aride, Cousin, Cousine, Curieuse, Ile St Pierre, Félicité, Les Soeurs, Marianne and Ile Cocos, which are nearer to Praslin and La Digue, will be covered in this chapter. In addition, Bird and Denis islands, which are coralline in origin, and found on the northern edge of the Seychelles Bank, will be discussed. The status of the various islands differs, as some are set apart as nature reserves, some are privately owned with exclusive guest lodges, and others are a combination of both. A very encouraging aspect of the privately owned islands is the strong conservation ethic the owners foster.

SILHOUETTE

From Beau Vallon on Mahé, the familiar shape of this island is a silhouette against the sunset. The green and verdant island rises out of the encircling coral reef to Mont Dauban at a height of 740m. It is almost round, roughly 5km in diameter, and covers an area of 20km². Because of the protective nature of the surrounding reef, landing on Silhouette has never been easy, and this has guarded the island from over-development and exploitation. It is probably the most densely vegetated island in the Indian Ocean, and its higher slopes and summit are clad in largely undisturbed, pristine forest with a high level of endemic flora and fauna. The Anse Mondon Valley is exceptionally rich in its biodiversity with many rare Seychelles hardwood trees, shrubs and orchids. Silhouette has a population of a mere 120 inhabitants. The pace of life on Silhouette moves slowly: there are no motor cars, only one tractor, no roads, no police station and only one small shop selling essentials.

The Dauban family from Mauritius were the first settlers to arrive on Silhouette at the end of the 19th century. They gradually acquired the entire island and a thriving farming community developed. Coconut and cinnamon plantations were established on the fairly level plateau at about 500m, patchouli was grown for the perfume trade, fruit trees supplied the local market and, by the 1950s, the population had increased to around 1,000. After the crash in the world copra market most of the workers drifted back to Mahé. There is a small jetty at La Passe on the east coast, which is the site of the largest settlement, and both Silhouette Island Lodge and the Nature Protection Trust of Seychelles are located there.

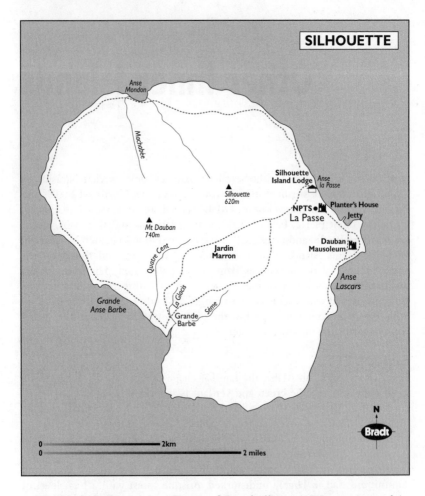

The **Nature Protection Trust of Seychelles** (NPTS) was started in 1996 by Ron and Gill Gerlach. Despite the great biological diversity and value of Silhouette, it has no legal environmental protection and NPTS is campaigning for reserve status. They aim to protect the natural habitats and to restore degraded areas to their original state. NPTS, a member of the World Conservation Union (IUCN), is a non-profit, non-governmental organisation registered in the Seychelles under the patronage of Sir David Attenborough. The initial phase of the Nature Protection Trust's management plan has been the establishment of an information centre and a small laboratory which tourists are welcome to visit. Their major projects include the conservation of the Seychelles tortoises and terrapins.

Getting there and away
The easiest way to make the 19km trip from Mahé to Silhouette is by using the services of **Helicopter Seychelles**, and all guests to Silhouette Island Lodge,

the only tourist accommodation on the island, are transported in this way. For day visits, boat trips, which are often combined with snorkelling and beach barbecues, can be arranged. The **Boat House** (tel: 247898; fax: 247955) at Beau Vallon uses two boats, *Blue Fin* and *Yellow Fin*, for excursions over to Silhouette. Both the Marine Charter Association and the tour operators in Victoria will be able to advise on alternative vessels to use to get across to Silhouette.

Where to stay

Silhouette Island Lodge Tel: 224003/224445; fax: 224897; email: sillodge@seychelles.net; www.silhouette-seychelles.com. This is the only hotel, and, at present, has 12 charming wooden bungalows shaded by coconut palms and *takamaka* trees. They are situated close to the beach with great snorkelling and dive sites nearby. The restaurant serves delicious Creole and Italian food. Snorkelling, diving and deep-sea fishing trips can be arranged through the lodge. Day visitors are not encouraged. There are plans to upgrade the hotel in the future so before you decide to stay in this lovely secluded spot, do check that it is operational. Tariff: €450–500 per double room per night with full board.

Things to see and do

As there are no roads or cars, the only way to explore the island is to walk. There are several well-marked paths as this is how the residents get from one side of the island to the other. The **NPTS Information Centre** is not far from La Passe Jetty and it is well worth a visit. Giant tortoises roam around in huge pens close to the information centre and, in time, once the breeding herd has been established, youngsters will be released into the wild. Ron and Gill Gerlach exude enthusiasm for their baby tortoises and terrapins, which they nurture from eggs to adults. They can also provide a wealth of information about the natural history of the Seychelles to anyone who is interested.

Silhouette is an island of importance for its natural history and an easy walking trail through a recently rehabilitated forest area is open to day visitors. The information centre will point you in the right direction.

Near the jetty, the old Planter's House, now in a sad state of repair, was built by August Dauban in the 1860s with rare Seychelles hardwood.

The path from the jetty over to the west splits into two but both tracks finish at Grande Barbe. You will need a whole day to enjoy the delights of the walk, which is steep and arduous in parts, but well worth the exertion as it passes through forests with sandalwood, ferns, orchids and pitcher plants. Look out, too, for the endemic stick insect, recently rediscovered by a team of Cambridge undergraduates. Once on the western side at Grande Barbe there is a church overlooking a glorious beach. The Séme River enters the sea at Grande Barbe. A path leads to Anse Mondon on the northern shore and continues along the coast back to La Passe. From La Passe you can also walk to Anse Lascars, passing Pointe Ramasse Tout and Anse Cimitère. The Dauban family **mausoleum** is located near Pointe Ramasse Tout. The classic old edifice is a copy of the Eglise de la Madeline in Paris and was created to resemble marble but the spreading rust reveals its true nature.

There are good snorkelling and diving spots around Silhouette and excursions can be arranged on Mahé with most of the tour companies. Between November and March, birdwatching can be exciting as many migrants stop over on the island and, from time to time, it may be possible to see crab plovers, whimbrels, greenshanks and Eurasian oystercatchers to name but a few.

NORTH ISLAND

North Island lies almost 5km north of Silhouette and 30km north of Mahé. It covers an area of 210ha and reaches a rocky height of 214m. It has four superb beaches, framed by massive granite slabs and palm trees.

North Island had been in the Beaufond family since it was first awarded to Madame Celerine Beaufond in 1826. Like most of the Seychelles islands, it had large colonies of breeding seabirds which contributed considerable guano that was mined and sold for fertiliser. The island later became a coconut plantation but, after the collapse of the copra industry, it was sold. It remained as a farm but, neglected, it became overgrown with many alien plants. Cattle, goats and pigs became feral and cats and rats proliferated decimating birds and other animals.

The potential for tourism and restoration of the island was recognised when Norisco (part of Wilderness Safaris) bought it in 1997. Their aim was to remove the alien plants and animals, restore the natural balance of the island and create a small, exclusive lodge in harmony with the environment. An extensive rat eradication programme was carried out to make North Island one of the few rat-free islands in Seychelles and an area of land was cleared for construction of the lodge. Impressive indigenous plant nurseries were established and over a hundred thousand plants of 73 species were grown from seed. At least half of these have been planted out already and reintroduction of some of the rare and endangered Seychelles bird species is planned.

A resident ecologist and a marine biologist work closely together, running conservation programmes on all aspects of the environment. Hawksbill and green turtles nest on the beaches and, now that vermin animals have been exterminated, the hatchlings stand a better chance of survival. A turtle monitoring and tagging programme is running in collaboration with others in Seychelles. Tropic birds are returning to nest, and kestrels and sunbirds have been sighted.

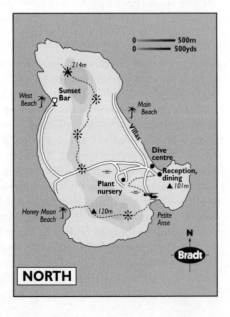

Getting there and away

The island is exclusively for lodge residents and no day visitors are permitted. Reservations may be made at info@north-island.com and for further information check the website: www.north-island.com. Transfers from Mahé are by helicopter and take 20 minutes; €659 per four passengers. It is also possible to transfer by boat which takes about an hour.

Where to stay

North Island Lodge was opened in July 2003 and all the buildings are on the eastern side of the island. The lodge was built using craftsmen from Africa, Zanzibar and Seychelles, creating a fusion of cultures and architectural styles to produce a 'Robinson Crusoe styled luxury paradise'. It takes barefoot luxury into another realm with stunning sensual designs and an aura of sophisticated, stylish calm created by the use of weathered wood, velvet cushions, glass, thatch and coral. The lounge, bar and dining room are open-air spaces under high thatch that flow on to a large deck and the beach. Ponds and waterfalls lend a tranquil ambience and an enormous rimflow swimming pool sweeps along the granite curve of the hillside, shaded by palms and forest vegetation.

Eleven secluded, self-contained villas face the sunrise and all have areas of over 400m². Each villa consists of two spacious bedrooms, a lounge and dining area under a thatch cover on a deck with a swirling plunge pool and sala (a thatch-covered daybed) leading down to the beach. The main bedroom has a huge bed, separate dressing area and bathroom complex more like a spa with an oversized bath, a daybed, massage bed, an indoor shower and an open-air shower (with water gushing down a hollowed-out log). The second bedroom has two single beds and its own bathroom. A separate well-equipped kitchen enables the chef to prepare and serve gourmet meals in your villa and each villa has a butler attending to all your needs.

On arrival, once the formalities are over, each guest is met by the executive chef who discusses the 'no menu' concept and plans the meals with each person. Food is prepared to the highest standards by five chefs and three pastry chefs. Guests may eat in the dining room, on the beach or in their villa. The majority of the vegetables are grown in organic gardens on the island (with the surplus exported to other islands), the fish could not be fresher, and many local plants are used in the preparation of the gourmet food. The executive chef is passionate about food and has the knack of knowing exactly how to mix different flavours and textures using unexpected ingredients. It could be called contemporary ethnic cuisine blending the flavours of the Indian Ocean using spices grown in the region. The *North Island Cookbook* by Geoffrey Murray and Dereck Nair was published in 2004 (for a sample recipe, see page 221).

Villas 1–9 cost €1,235 per person per night, Villa Royale costs €3,940 for two people and Villa North Island costs €4,500 for two people. Children under the age of three are free; €190 per child aged 3–12 and €635 per child aged 13–19. Included are all meals and drinks (except for premier drinks on the special reserve list), scuba diving, snorkelling, sea kayaking, fly-fishing, catamaran sailing, mountain bikes, use of the library and gymnasium and all the government taxes and service charges.

Things to see and do

North Island has an unhurried, tranquil atmosphere and the combination of seclusion, location, accommodation, services and facilities provides the epitome of sophisticated, yet simple, luxury. There is a wide range of activities for guests and many of these take advantage of the superb natural environment. Walks with the resident ecologist are to be recommended as he will enthusiastically tell you all about the island, the indigenous plant nursery and the management strategies in place to restore the environment. Participate in the various watersports on offer like sailing, scuba diving and snorkelling or take a boat to Silhouette for a picnic. Visit the health spa and indulge in one of their treatments. Take your buggy to the western side of the island to the Sunset Bar and enjoy a magnificent sunset while the barman creates a special cocktail to celebrate the day. Sit under the stars and see how many constellations you can find. Best of all, revel in the sheer beauty of the island and applaud the owners for their far-sighted dreams to create such a special sanctuary for guests and nature.

MAMELLES

Uninhabited Mamelles lies about 15km northeast of Victoria, Mahé, and about 30km southwest of Praslin. The lowish island reaches a height of 42m and there is a lighthouse on the summit. It is home to many breeding seabirds. The wreck of the tanker *Ennerdale*, which dates from 1970, lies in close proximity, and is a favoured dive site.

FREGATE

Frégate, 55km east of Mahé, is a privately owned island with an exclusive lodge. The island reaches a height of 125m and massive slabs of *glacis* dominate the plateau. Like so many islands of the Seychelles, Frégate also saw removal of endemic trees and plants to make way for coconut plantations. Nowadays, although the island is still dominated by coconut palms, large areas of woodland have been rehabilitated with a variety of indigenous trees including *takamakas*, *badamiers*, palms and screw pines. Sadly, many of the mighty sandragon trees have died as a result of a fatal wilt disease that has attacked the species throughout the Seychelles.

The efforts of the conservation team on Frégate are famous for the recovery of the endangered magpie robins. The smart black and white birds had declined to a critical number of only 24 but the total population now stands at around 100, with almost half on Frégate. When the numbers started increasing, some were relocated to Cousin, Cousine and Aride. It is also one of three islands supporting a population of the Seychelles fody, which are now so numerous they even come into the restaurant to share in the breakfast crumbs. Some of the rare Seychelles white-eyes have been relocated to Frégate and are thriving. Much of the success of the rehabilitation process has been due to the replanting of hundreds of indigenous trees and plants, the extensive rat eradication programme and the construction of an impressive rat-proof fence around the harbour area.

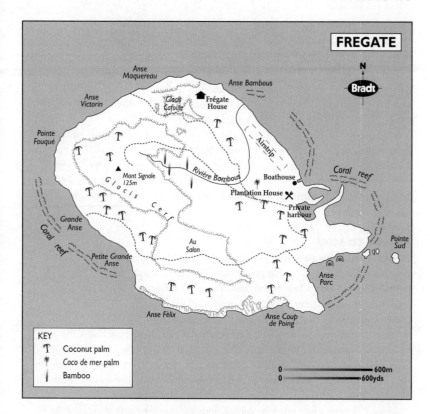

Remarkably, Frégate is the only known home of a strange insect, the 4cm-long giant tenebrionid beetle, *Pulposipes herculeanus*. This weird but harmless creature has long legs and rough bumpy wing cases but cannot fly. Small groups of these beetles can be seen on tree trunks around Frégate. A small herd of reintroduced Aldabra tortoises has an easy life on this beautiful little island. The juvenile tortoises are held in captivity until they are sufficiently mature to be released among the free herd.

Frégate is also famous for its stories of Arab sailors and pirate treasure which are fuelled by a few scattered ruins, some ancient graves, an old well and some interesting artefacts discovered on the island. Lazare Picault made the first recorded visit to the island in 1744 when he sailed from Mauritius via Chagos on his second exploratory expedition. He named the island Frégate, after the stately frigatebirds which occur in the area. Other early explorers noted the presence of giant tortoises, turtles and dugongs as well as the absence of crocodiles. Hawksbill and green turtles still haul up on to the beaches of Frégate to lay their eggs. Countless noddies and white terns breed on the island and large fruit bats can also be seen hanging in the trees.

A team of 14 people, under the resident conservation and ecology manager, is responsible for maintaining the island, protecting the habitat and nurturing the critically endangered species that have found refuge on Frégate.

Getting there and away

The island is for the exclusive use of the resident guests and day visitors are not permitted. Reservations can be made through Unique Experiences (Touristik GmbH, Egerlaender Strasse 47, D-63069 Offenbach, Germany; tel: +49 69 83 83 7635; fax: +49 69 83 83 7636; email: unique.experiences@debitel.net; www.fregate.com). There is also an office on Mahé (206 Aarti Chambers, Mont Fleuri Road, Victoria; tel: 323123, fax: 324169).

Transfers to the island can be organised, when you make your reservation, with Air Seychelles on a chartered Twin Otter (€750 each way for the 20-seater plane) or by helicopter with Helicopter Seychelles (€735 each way for four passengers). The flying time from Mahé to Frégate is approximately 20 minutes. The cost will vary according to the number of passengers flying.

Where to stay

Frégate Island Private is the epitome of a luxurious getaway with only 16 beautifully constructed, widely spaced villas giving the feeling of total seclusion and privacy. A central reception area, adorned with fresh flowers and Michael Adams paintings, houses the restaurants, bar, shop, gym, library and various offices. The architecture captures the essence of Indonesia using African hardwoods, marble flooring and Balinese alang-alang roof thatching. The freshwater swimming pool below the restaurant is surrounded by granite boulders and has lovely ocean views. The old Plantation House has been given a facelift and now houses a restaurant and museum with artefacts of historical interest as well as a shell collection. The new Rock Spa sited high on a hillside offers an exclusive range of health and beauty therapies.

Most of the 16 private villas are spread along the northern granite cliffs of the island commanding magnificent views of palms, turquoise ocean and distant islands. Tall glass doors open on to a deck surrounding the two large rooms that comprise each 200m² villa. The main bedroom has an en-suite bathroom with indoor and outdoor showers and a huge bath. The lounge is comfortably elegant with two wide Balinese daybeds, beautiful carved furniture, interesting artefacts, grey granite, polished mahogany and exquisite natural cottons, linen and silk that combine to create an ambience of simple but gracious luxury. Each villa has a jacuzzi and thatch-covered daybed. €1,900 per villa for two people sharing. Children are welcome: up to five years €100 per night, 6–11 years €200 per night, 12–18 years €300 per night. There is also a 15% tax and service charge.

Things to see and do

Take advantage of all the seclusion and relax with room service to your villa. If you venture out you could spend a few hours rejuvenating in the Rock Spa, take tea in the well-stocked library, workout in the gym or play a game of tennis. Fine meals are served in the casual Pirates bar, the Frégate House restaurant in the Pavilion and the Plantation House which is open three times a week for a speciality evening buffet.

It is a great experience to take a buggy to explore the island and discover the secluded beaches. Enjoy some of the spectacular lookout points and watching the sunset from Mont Signal is particularly spectacular. For the ultimate romantic experience flip the 'Private' sign at Anse Macquereau, walk down the steps to the stunning little beach, and you will be undisturbed – loungers and a daybed are there for your convenience.

A small harbour has facilities for transport vessels bringing in the necessary goods for the efficient running of the island. It is also the departure point for all the marine-based activities like the sunset cruises, fishing, kayaking, snorkelling and scuba diving.

You can also take an organised tour to get a broad overview of how the island operates, how Frégate produces its own water, electricity and food from the plantation gardens and hydroponics centre. The resident ecologist also leads walks and this is an excellent way to get an appreciation for the remarkable rehabilitation that has taken place on the island. For children 6–12 years of age, the Castaways Club has been designed to enhance their island experience with outdoor activities and nature conservation programmes.

ARIDE

Aride Island Nature Reserve (c/o GPO Grande Anse, Praslin; tel: 321600, email: aride@seychelles.net; www.arideisland.net), a special nature reserve, is the most northerly of the granitic islands, lying 10km north of Praslin and 50km northeast of Mahé. The only beach on Aride faces south, which makes landing here very tricky when the southeast trades are blowing, and this, in fact, protected the island from colonisation until 1851. Only 1,500m long and a little over 500m wide, Aride has majestic granite cliffs rising steeply from the shoreline to the highest point, Gros la Tête, 134m above sea level.

The Chenard family owned the island for over a century and during the copra production era a large amount of natural vegetation was cleared to make way for coconut palms. It was declared a private nature reserve in 1970 when copra production ceased. Christopher Cadbury then purchased the island in 1973 on behalf of the Royal Society for Nature Conservation (RSNC). In 1975 it was declared a Special Nature Reserve by the Seychelles government. In June 2004 the responsibility for Aride was transferred to the Island Conservation Society (ICS), a newly formed Seychelles organisation. The lease has been linked to conservation and management goals set out by RSNC and it is expected that the ICS will improve the management of the island. One of the most alarming problems facing Aride is poaching, with turtles and sooty tern eggs being targeted as well as illegal fishing in the marine reserve. It is hoped that, with a local organisation in control, poaching will diminish. Most of the coconut palms and fruit trees have been removed and the natural vegetation is rapidly regenerating. An island warden, his staff and research officers are the only people living on Aride, amounting to about ten people.

In the western Indian Ocean, Aride is second only to Aldabra in its importance as a seabird breeding colony. Ten species of seabirds, plus a variety of land birds, nest on the 68ha island. It is a haven for two endemic plant species, Wright's gardenia, found growing naturally in the wild only on Aride,

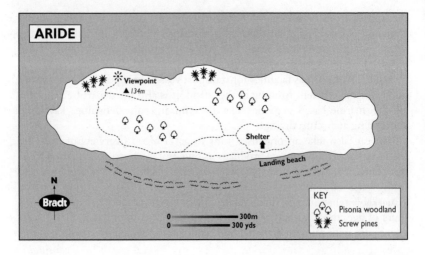

and the creeping Aride peponium. The island lies within a marine protected area and is partly surrounded by coral reef. Hawksbill turtles come ashore to lay their eggs from October to February, but it is possible to see them swimming around the island at any time.

Getting there and away

Boat departures are from Praslin and any of the tour operators or hotels and guesthouses on Praslin or Mahé can make the necessary arrangements to visit Aride. However, should you wish to make your own arrangements with a local boat owner all of the following can be recommended:

Kevin L'Esperance's boats Paradise Sun Hotel, Côte d'Or; tel: 521137 or 232234
Octopus Diving Anse Volbert; tel: 232602 or 513098
Louis Bedier's boats Côte d'Or; tel: 232192 or 232398
Basil Ferrari's boats Maison des Palmes, Grande Anse; tel: 233411

The boat trip takes about 90 minutes; on approaching Aride, look out for an outcrop of granite known as Booby Island, so named because of all the red-footed boobies that used to nest here. Getting closer to Aride you may notice a swirling mass of hundreds of thousands of sooty terns circling and displaying above the island. They start congregating in March prior to nesting there during June and July. Note that the huge, black creatures with broad wings flying around the island are not buzzards but giant fruit bats. Although the beach looks heavenly it is not always easy to land there, as there are sometimes sneaky little side swells to contend with. As there is no jetty, a rubber inflatable boat will usually transfer passengers from the larger boat to the beach. It is strongly advised to ensure that all cameras and valuables are safely secured inside a watertight bag.

A day tour could include a walk around the island with Aride Island staff followed by a beach barbecue and snorkelling. You could even bring your own picnic lunch and drinks. The landing fee is €30 or US$30 per person and it is often included with the cost of the boat transfer. Aride is open to visitors

Sunday, Monday and Wednesday from 10.00 to 15.00, and Thursday by special arrangement.

Things to see and do

On Aride there is no airstrip, road or accommodation for visitors. A shelter with tables and benches has been constructed on the beach and is perfect for a barbecue. There are a couple of toilets behind the shelter. A series of well-marked paths lead from there to the interior of the island, and Seychellois guides, informative and conversant in English, French and Creole, accompany the visitors. It is essential to keep to the paths, as shearwaters nest underground and, if you stand on the soft roof of a burrow, you are likely to squash eggs, a chick or a brooding adult, and possibly sprain your ankle. The guides will conduct the tour through the settlement area where some fruit trees and coconut palms still grow. Look out for Wright's gardenia, a small tree with creamy white, bell-shaped, fragrant flowers that produces a hard, green, shiny fruit resembling a lemon (hence the Creole name *bwa sitron*). While still on the flat coastal plateau, keep an eye out for the Seychelles warbler, one of the conservation success stories of the Seychelles, which was resurrected from the brink of extinction. The ground is literally covered with two species of skinks, the slender Seychelles skink and the larger, fatter Wright's skink. These harmless lizards devour birds' eggs with relish. Green and bronze geckos can often be seen in the vegetation, and further up the slopes there is an abundance of harmless, shiny giant millipedes which are black with orange legs.

The path to the summit veers away from the coast and, although mostly in the shade, it can be quite a slog. On the way, white-tailed tropicbirds will often be encountered nesting on the ground, and the speckled, downy chicks are trusting and fearless. A simple granite memorial plaque honouring the late Christopher Cadbury is located a little way up the hillside walk. Pause here for a moment to savour the unique features of this small granitic island. Breathtaking views from the top will be worth the uphill sweat. The crystal-clear, deep-blue sea melts into the horizon. To the north, Denis is a dot in the distance, while to the south, on a clear day, there is a superb panorama of all the granitic islands. Stately frigatebirds with long, tapering wings and deeply forked tails appear to hang effortlessly in mid-air above the lookout point. Sooty terns and noddies swirl around and may even perch in the surrounding Balfour's screw pines growing between the granite boulders.

Birds are prolific on Aride and the ten species of breeding seabirds include six species of terns with numbers fluctuating widely from year to year depending on food availability: up to 360,000 pairs of sooty terns; 16,000 pairs of brown noddies; 6,500 fairy terns; as well as bridled and roseate terns. An estimated 170,000 pairs of lesser noddies breed on Aride, choosing the *Pisonia grandis* trees in which to make their seaweed nests. The trees have very sticky seeds that sometimes get entangled in the bird's feathers, rendering them flightless and resulting in death.

There are approximately 32,000 Audubon's shearwaters and 18,000 wedgetail shearwaters breeding on the island, but they are seldom seen as the adult birds spend the daylight hours far out to sea, only returning at dusk or later. Shearwater burrows are difficult to locate as they are often concealed under rocks or tree roots. Both species of tropicbird, red-tailed and white-tailed, breed on Aride. Frigatebirds only breed on Aldabra but many, especially juveniles, spend the non-breeding season in the granitic islands, roosting on Aride. Numbers can reach over 3,000 in November.

The relocation of the highly endangered magpie robins on to Aride has not always been a success as many of the birds died in the early stages of the project. However, in 2005, with improved land-management techniques, the magpie robins are now thriving and there are at least 16 birds on the island in five distinct territories, and young are successfully being raised. Other land birds include the Seychelles warbler, moorhen, barred ground dove, blue pigeon and turtle doves. Aride is also a good spot for migrant birds. A wide variety, ranging from waders to unexpected species like the Jacobin cuckoo, Antarctic skua, Eleanora's falcon and even a hobby, have been recorded. Turnstones, common sandpipers and whimbrels frequent the shoreline and spotted flycatchers are seen among the trees from time to time. Early records show that before most of the natural vegetation was cleared to make way for coconuts, black parrots, the black paradise flycatcher and the Seychelles fody were all resident on Aride.

COUSIN

Located in a marine protected area, this small 27ha granitic island, encircled by a coral reef, is another conservation success story. Like the other granitic islands, it too had most of the natural vegetation cleared to make way for the production of copra and some cotton, thus almost eliminating the endemic birds and plants. Green and hawksbill turtles, captured by the thousand for their ornamental shells and meat, were almost wiped out, and sooty tern egg collecting totally obliterated the breeding colony of these birds.

In the early 1960s, when a bird count revealed only 29 Seychelles warblers left in the entire world, the World Wildlife Fund, with financial assistance from Christopher Cadbury, collected enough money to purchase Cousin for the Royal Society for Nature Conservation as a sanctuary for birds and other animals. The island was further protected when it was declared a Special Reserve by the Seychelles government in 1974. The island now falls under the management of Nature Seychelles. Much of the alien vegetation was gradually removed and the recovery of the natural vegetation has been remarkable. While it is still possible to see introduced plants like coffee and cotton, the mixed woodland of pisonia and tortoise trees (*Morinda citrifolia*), as well as beach crest plants, has regenerated with vigour. As the natural vegetation was restored, the numbers of Seychelles warblers increased dramatically. Birds have been relocated to Aride, Frégate and Cousine and there are now hundreds of warblers warbling away on all four islands. This species has now been removed from the red data list, a magnificent achievement for a group of dedicated people on a tiny island. Magpie robins have been relocated to Cousin from Frégate and they too are thriving with an annual increase in the population.

This island bird sanctuary is a popular tourist destination with about 600 visitors per week. It is also playing an important role in science, as local and international students are involved in studies on different aspects of botanical, ornithological and marine research.

Getting there and away

Boat trips generally depart from the beach at Maison des Palmes at Grande Anse, Praslin, for the 3km, half-hour journey across to Cousin, but they may also depart from Anse Volbert giving an added bonus of seeing another side of Praslin. Arrangements to visit the island can be made with any of the Praslin tour operators. As there is no jetty, passengers will be transferred from their boat to the island in a small rubber inflatable boat. Although it is generally a much more sedate landing than at Aride, ensure that all cameras and valuables are secure in a watertight bag. There is no overnight accommodation on Cousin. The island is open to visitors Tuesdays to Fridays 09.30–12.00 and 14.00–16.00. It is closed on public holidays. Landings take place 09.30–10.00 and 13.45–14.00. The management of Cousin welcomes visitors, reaches out to local people through awareness and educational programmes, undertakes to protect the rich biodiversity, and maintains the reserve as a heritage for all mankind. There is a strict tourism code of ethics for Cousin put in place to protect the apparently fearless bird populations as well as the visitors.

Things to see and do

An attractive shelter for visitors is located on the beach near the landing site. It contains information about the biodiversity of Cousin, and T-shirts and the Nature Seychelles newsletter *Zwazo* are on sale. The staff give visitors a short talk about the work being done on the island and explain the rules. Flash photography is forbidden, as is swimming, collecting shells and picnicking. The nesting birds appear completely fearless and, although it is easy to approach them, it is imperative that they are not disturbed – never try to touch them.

Knowledgeable and informative guides will accompany you around the island on the wide paths, pointing out important and interesting aspects of the island. The walk around the island takes about an hour and a half. It is mostly flat but there is a raised area of rocky granite in the centre which rises to a height of 53m above sea level. Nesting amongst these rocks are Audubon's and wedge-tailed shearwaters. With no rats or cats, ground-nesting birds flourish on Cousin. White-tailed tropicbirds and their unguarded, fat, speckled chicks are easily seen on the ground near the path, usually close to a tree trunk or rocky boulder. Lesser noddies nest in huge numbers – there are up to 100,000 pairs on Cousin. Brown noddies, fairy terns and bridled terns all use the little island for breeding and roosting purposes. Many waders feed on the sandy beaches of Praslin during the day but return to their overnight roosts on Cousin. Turnstones, though, spend their days on Cousin feeding under the

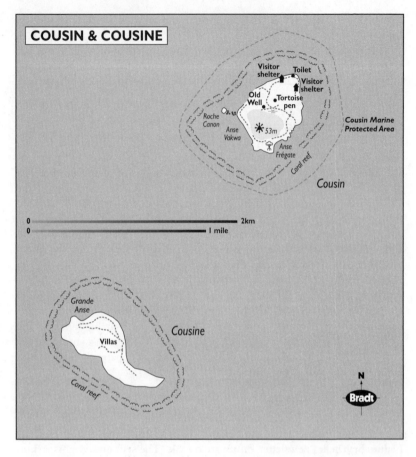

trees as well as on the beaches and rocky shores, and frequently go over to Booby Island for the night roost.

The most endangered of all Seychelles birds is the magpie robin. More than 30 are alive and well and rearing young on Cousin, and these handsome black- and-white birds are easily seen fossicking among the leaf litter for grubs. It remains to be seen whether they will have the same outstanding recovery success as the Seychelles warbler has had. The Seychelles fody, locally known as the *tok-tok*, is only found on Cousin, Cousine and Frégate. The Madagascar fody, bright red in breeding colours, is a common inhabitant of most of the Seychelles islands. The two species can thus be seen together on Cousin.

Cousin is not only an important bird sanctuary but the lovely sandy beaches are favoured and important nesting sites for the hawksbill turtle. They are vigorously protected and monitoring and tagging programmes continue. Several reintroduced Aldabra tortoises wander around freely on Cousin, seeking out the shade in the noonday sun. As on Aride, there is an abundance of skinks and geckos.

COUSINE

Cousine, a privately owned nature reserve, lies 6km off the west coast of Praslin and covers an area of 25ha. The sister island to Cousin, it has similar topography. A conservation team manages the island, and their mission is 'to promote and practice nature conservation and our aim is to share this philosophy with our guests'. Cousine is home to five species of endemic birds, and many thousands of seabirds breed on the island. It boasts the remarkable status of having no alien or introduced mammals.

Getting there and away

Guests use a helicopter for the transfer, from Mahé; it will cost €1,280 and from Praslin €65.

Where to stay

Cousine Island Resort Tel: 321107; mobile: 713420 or 713418; fax: 323805; email: cousine@seychelles.net; www.cousineisland.com. Four spacious villas built in the old, French colonial style are positioned to ensure maximum privacy and are only about 30m from the beach. The air-conditioned villas each have a private veranda, jacuzzi, kitchenette, with fridge, coffee maker and mini bar. IDD telephone, satellite TV, VCR and a mini sound system complete the range of amenities. The dining room, bar, lounge and well-stocked library are situated in a pavilion overlooking a freshwater swimming pool. Fine international cuisine is served with an emphasis on fresh seafood. There is a minimum stay of 3 nights but during the peak season from around 20 December to 10 January a minimum of 7 nights is required. Children under 15 years of age are not catered for. €1,000 per villa per night for 2 people sharing. This includes full board, soft drinks and mineral water, snorkelling and guided walks.

Things to see and do

There is no nightlife or organised entertainment, but the conservation officer is available to take guests around and explain the interesting aspects of the island. Magpie robins have been successfully relocated to Cousine and there are 12 individuals on the island. The Seychelles warbler is abundant and this is one of the three islands where the Seychelles fody can be found. Other endemic birds are the blue pigeon and the Seychelles sunbird. Breeding seabirds include fairy terns, tropicbirds, noddies and shearwaters. Both green and hawksbill turtles clamber on to the beach to lay their eggs, and with some luck they can be observed between September and January. It may also be possible to see the tiny hatchlings emerge and make their way down to the sea. An indigenous tree planting programme is in progress and guests may participate if they wish. The solitude, beautiful beaches and views over to Praslin, Cousin and Aride are to be savoured.

CURIEUSE

Curieuse, located only 1km from the northern tip of Praslin, is dominated by rugged sculpted granite. Curieuse Peak reaches a height of 172m. The island

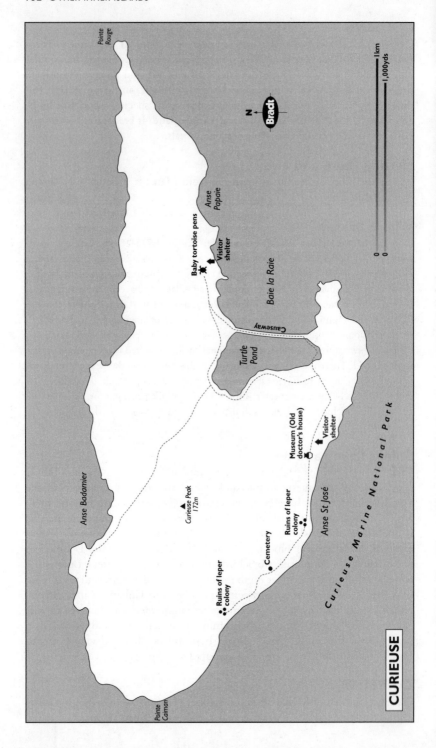

CURIEUSE

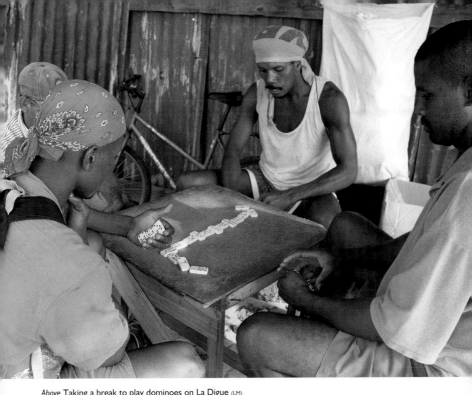

Above Taking a break to play dominoes on La Digue (LM)
Below left Little girls on their way to take part in Sports Day on La Digue (LM)
Below right A typical Creole house on La Digue (LM)

Above Twa Zwazo bicentennial monument in downtown Victoria, Mahé (LB)

Right The clocktower in Victoria with the law court in the background (LB)

Below A riot of colour at Fiennes Esplanade souvenir kiosk, Mahé (LM)

is about 3km long and about 2km wide. The marine park extends from the Anse Boudin shores of Praslin to surround Curieuse and the islet of St Pierre. The mangrove forests, sandy beaches, rocky shores and coral reefs form part of the marine park. Hawksbill turtles come ashore to nest during the northeast monsoons and are frequently seen while snorkelling.

Curieuse is the only other island, apart from Praslin, where a few *coco de mer* palms can be found growing in the wild. Many were destroyed in the successive fires that have plagued the island over the years, and bare patches of red earth can still be seen through the vegetation. Because of the red soil, Curieuse was originally known as Ile Rouge or Red Island until 1768 when Marion Dufresne renamed the island after his ship, *La Curieuse*. With careful management and tree-planting programmes, the island is recovering and looks green and lush in many places.

In 1833, a leper colony was established on Curieuse and the ruined remains of the village lend an eerie atmosphere to the southwest coast around Anse St José. Windows, doors and roofs have all gone and the remains of the stone buildings are covered in moss, creeping vines and other invading plants. Great *badamier* and *takamaka* trees cast dark shadows over the deserted colony that faces on to a most beautiful beach – at least the sufferers had wonderful vistas across to Praslin to help cheer them up! A large colonial villa that housed the doctor during his visits to the colony has been renovated and houses the resource centre and a museum. Downstairs, artefacts of a historical nature are on display, while upstairs the displays are related to environmental issues. There are sometimes art exhibitions, including children's art resulting from awareness campaigns in the schools on the main islands. A tiny shop sells local delicacies such as cassava and breadfruit crisps, 'nougat' from coconut and *badamier* kernels and coconut ice.

A herd of about 250 giant Aldabra tortoises was relocated on to Curieuse with the aim of having a breeding colony outside of Aldabra. However, many have been poached and numbers are down to about a hundred, though they are breeding well now. The hatchlings are kept in enclosures until they are five years old, when they are released into the wild and allowed to roam and forage freely. Black parrots can sometimes be heard whistling and calling, but they are not common and are difficult to spot.

Getting there and away

Day trips can be arranged from most of the hotels on Praslin, and boat departures are from Anse Volbert. Arrival on Curieuse is either at Anse St José or on the beautiful beach of Baie la Raie. A snorkelling visit to Ile St Pierre is often included in the day outing.

Things to see and do

On arriving at **Baie la Raie** you will clearly see a long causeway across the western inlet. This was constructed to serve as a turtle holding pen where captured turtles could be kept until they were transported to the market in Mahé. In places, the wall has crumbled and broken and access across it is not possible. The map of Curieuse still shows the path as it may well be repaired one day. Early in the morning, before it is too hot, visitors are often welcomed on to magnificent Baie la Raie by a couple of giant tortoises taking a walk on the beach. The smooth, gleaming white beach is bounded by some of the most spectacular grooved granite rocks in the Seychelles.

There is a substantial shelter for visitors that can accommodate a cruise ship full of people, and toilets are located nearby. The warden will show visitors around the tortoise nurseries in this part of the island, and there are always groups of adults to be found on the closely cropped grass in this area. Sometimes a coconut falls down and crashes on to an unsuspecting snoozing tortoise leaving a slightly cracked and dented carapace. They seem to survive this without any panel beating! March is tortoise mating season and their loud ringing groans echo around the island. The eggs hatch about two months later and the ever-vigilant staff collect many of the soft-shelled creatures to protect and rear until they are truly able to fend for themselves. There are usually a few specimens of *coco de mer* nuts to look at on a bench near the warden's office. Swimming and snorkelling are allowed off this beach. At low tide the bay is very shallow and hardly deep enough for swimming; the seabed is covered with seagrass which is not particularly exciting for snorkelling. When the tide comes in it is easy to swim out to the reef where the marine life is much more diverse.

The warden or his charming staff take visitors on a guided walk. Starting at the visitor shelter, the path leads to the causeway, often a great place to see some marine life close up. On occasions there are groups of squid near the surface, bonefish and blacktip reef sharks which cruise in the shallow waters, and the occasional sightings of hawksbill turtles are a treat. Batfish, scissortail sergeants and many other colourful reef fishes are easily seen in the clear waters on either side of the low causeway wall when the tide is relatively high. Mangroves line the shoreward edge of the turtle pond and, at low water, many of the mangrove dwellers and wading birds will be on the exposed mud amongst the root systems of the trees. From the causeway a path goes through the mangroves on the landward side of the turtle pond. It is a lovely walk, partly on a boardwalk through mangroves and partly on sand. Near the beginning of the walk is a collection of black granite rocks looking like foreboding Rodin creations with inland views over swampy ground. Further on, there is a bit of a climb on an easy path with a lookout point giving great views across Baie la Raie. While walking across the sandy patches, notice the large crab burrows and lookout for the beach hibiscus, a common tree in this area. The bright, golden-yellow flowers turn reddish-brown as they mature, and the nectar is much loved by Seychelles sunbirds. At the end of the turtle pond a large notice on the boardwalk lists the names of the main mangrove species present. Littered on the mud floor among the mangrove roots are the long, spiralled brown whelk shells, which make wonderful homes for hermit crabs when their owners die. From this point it takes about 20 minutes to walk over the low saddle to the old doctor's house and visitor's shelter at Anse St José.

Day trips will often begin at **Anse St José** near the doctor's house/museum. A path runs close to the beach in a northwesterly direction past a little staff house. Scattered ruins can be seen at intervals on either side of the cemetery. A barbecue generally takes place at Anse St José near the little museum where a thatched shelter, tables and benches make for a cheerful rustic dining area, perfect for eating the scrumptious, freshly grilled, Creole-style fish.

A clearly marked path from the shelter to Baie la Raie links up with the boardwalk that has already been discussed. It is an easy walk from here to see the tortoise sanctuary on the other side. Two hours will allow plenty of time for the return walk and a good look at the tortoises. Allow more time for swimming and snorkelling or arrange for the boatman to collect you from this side. When travelling by boat between Anse St José and Baie la Raie, look out for groups of *coco de mer* growing on the rocky hillside.

ILE ST PIERRE

'Miniature paradise' could be another name for this enchanting islet. Gloriously sculpted pink and grey granite arises from the clear, turquoise water and a perfect, tiny beach is exposed at low tide. The fairy-tale islet has a tiara of emerald-green palms. Regular boat trips are made to Ile St Pierre from Anse Volbert on Praslin and arrangements can be made through any of the hotels. Although there are a couple of palms, there is very little shade and no fresh water on the island. It is advisable to take plenty of sunscreen and water as well as snorkelling gear. Landing on the rocks at high tide can be a bit of a wobble, so ensure that all valuables are well protected in a watertight bag. Underwater, the dazzling colours of the teeming reef fishes complete the picture of a miniature island paradise.

FELICITE, LES SOEURS, ILE COCOS AND MARIANNE
Félicité
Félicité, a small, rocky, granite island, 227m high and 275ha in extent, lies 4km northeast of La Digue. There is a beach on the protected southwest side of the island where small boats can land.

Where to stay
Félicité Private Lodge Tel: 234232; fax: 234100; office, tel: 234233; fax: 234123; email: felicite@seychelles.net; www.ladigue.sc; c/o La Digue Island Lodge, Anse Réunion, La Digue. This private hideaway has 2 villas in the style of a colonial plantation house, and 4 A-frame chalets with accommodation for 16 guests. It is possible to add a few extra beds, slightly increasing the total number of guests. Once a group booking has been made no other guests will be accommodated, making it a totally private island. Day visitors are not allowed. Boat transfers from Praslin or La Digue are included in the price. A helicopter transfer may also be arranged. Tariff: € 1,000 per person per night. Children 6–12 years, € 400 per child per night. There is a minimum stay of 5 nights. Rates include full board with all alcoholic and non-alcoholic drinks.

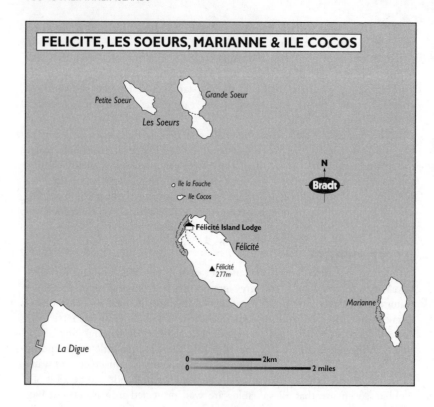

Things to see and do

On this very relaxing island guests can enjoy the freshwater pool, play tennis, swim at La Penice beach, walk the few island paths, and sail within a 15km radius of the island on a private yacht. Boat trips to nearby islands with snorkelling can be arranged and diving can be pursued with the Azzura Pro Dive Centre at La Digue Island Lodge.

Les Soeurs

These two little islands lie about 3km north of Félicité and offer relatively good diving and snorkelling.

The larger, eastern island, Grande Soeur, rises to a rocky height of 113m and covers an area of 100ha. It is only about 200m wide in the middle and there are several walks around the island. Much of the natural vegetation is interspersed with coconut palms but it is the massive grey granite boulders which dominate this island. Boats land on the western beach, which is also the best snorkelling side of the island. The silvery-white eastern beach, framed by sculpted granite rocks and fringed with palms, must be one of the most beautiful in all Seychelles. A small community lives here raising their chickens and ducks and living off fresh fish and coconuts. The island is for the exclusive use of guests from Château des Feuilles, Praslin, during the weekend but is open to visitors during the week. Excursions to this 'Robinson Crusoe' retreat, which often include a beach barbecue, can be arranged by most of the tour operators on Praslin and La Digue.

The western island, or Petite Soeur, attains a height of 105m and is separated from its big sister by a deep channel. It is a clump of granite rocks with sparse vegetation scattered around it.

Ile Cocos

This small island, located between Félicité and Les Soeurs, was closed to the public for about ten years as much of the coral had been damaged by tourists. It is now part of a marine protected area with a warden in charge, and it is open for day visitors. In spite of the heavily damaged coral, snorkelling can be rewarding with a fair selection of reef fishes to be seen.

Marianne

Marianne is about 4km east of Félicité and the granite rocks rise up to about 129m. A little beach on the southwest side allows access in calm weather only. Marine life around this island is particularly rich and diving and snorkelling are good.

DENIS

Denis, on the most northerly part of the shallow Seychelles Bank, lies about 95km north of Mahé. This privately owned island is only 2km long and, at most, 1.5km wide, and covers an area of 120ha. It is an emerald-green, flat coral island edged by white beaches with coral reefs protecting the southern side. Denis de Trobriand, master of the *Etoile*, was the first to discover the island in 1773; he claimed it for France and gave it his name. It suffered the same fate as many of the other islands as, firstly, guano mining was undertaken, followed

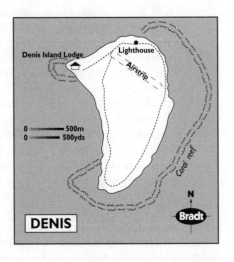

by the development of coconut plantations. Since then, a rat eradication programme has been successfully carried out and several species of endemic birds are slowly being reintroduced. A lighthouse was erected in 1910 to warn passing ships of the hazards of the shallow area close to the northern side of the island.

The present owner bought the island in 1976 as his own little piece of paradise. He proceeded to build chalets to accommodate guests, and the island now operates as the ultimate tropical getaway.

Getting there and away

The most convenient way to get there is by helicopter. The charter costs €1,269 for four people and takes about 30 minutes from Mahé.

Where to stay

Denis Island Lodge Tel: 321143; email: denisfo@seychelles.net; rlarue@masonstravel.com; office tel: 288963; fax: 288828. The 25 cottages are spacious, airy and attractively decorated and the restaurant serves excellent cuisine. €990 per cottage for 2 people sharing with full board.

Things to see and do

A lattice of paths criss-crosses the island and it is impossible to get lost. Watersports are a major feature of Denis, and it is a favoured spot for big game fishermen. The Seychelles Bank plummets steeply down to a depth of 2,000m near the island. World records for dog-tooth tuna have been set here and marlin, sailfish, tuna and barracuda are plentiful. The 50 island workers live in a tiny village earning their living working in the hotel or on the farm and small coconut plantation.

BIRD

Remote Bird Island, another privately owned sandy speck in the ocean, lies 105km northwest of Mahé on the edge of the Seychelles Bank. It is in fact the most northerly island in Seychelles being a mere fraction further north than Denis. It covers only 70ha of land, is 1,500m long and 750m wide. Very little is known of the early history of Bird but the first recorded visit was in 1771 when the master of *The Eagle* charted the island. In 1808, a French privateer, *Hirondelle*, with 180 people on board, was wrecked on the reef and the survivors remained on the island for three weeks while they constructed a raft, before sailing to Mahé. Bird was originally called Ile aux Vaches Marines ('Island of Sea Cows'), after all the dugongs that lazed around in the clear waters. They have become extinct but the island is still often referred to as Ile aux Vaches and it appears on many maps as such. In 1896 guano was already being mined on the island and 17,000 tonnes were removed between 1900 and 1905. At the end of that phase, coconuts were planted for the copra industry. The present owner bought the island in 1967, an airstrip was cleared, and a small tourist lodge was developed. The owner declared the island a wildlife sanctuary in 1986 and the lodge was upgraded. Over the years it has been enlarged and refurbished but it maintains its integrity as an unpretentious hotel with a blend of hospitality, relaxation and simplicity in a non-sophisticated natural environment.

Getting there and away

Any of the tour operators on Mahé will be able to arrange a visit to the island. Alternatively, the Bird Island office in Independence Avenue, Victoria, will make all the necessary arrangements. Air Seychelles flights, in small aircraft, depart from the domestic airport and take about 30 minutes. Guests are met on the grass runway and are taken to the reception area where the friendly

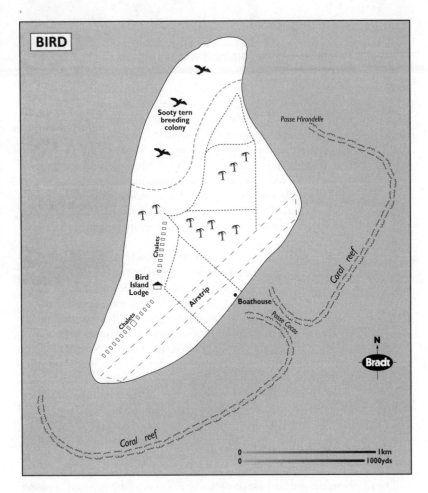

island managers give an informative talk about the island. They are passionate about the island and its inhabitants. A motor-boat trip from Mahé to Bird takes about eight hours.

Where to stay

Bird Island Lodge Tel: 224925; fax: 225074; office tel: 323322; fax: 323335; email: birdland@seychelles.net; www.birdseychelles.com. The spacious, comfortable bungalows close to the beach are a short walk away from the reception and dining areas. A relaxed and informal atmosphere prevails and the excellent food is usually served buffet style using fresh fish, and vegetables grown on the island. There are no bright lights at night that might interfere with the habits of the wildlife and there is no TV in the bungalows to detract from the natural sounds. The well-ventilated, airy rooms have ceiling fans but no air conditioning, and with such beautiful beaches, who needs a swimming pool? It is refreshing to find a down-to-earth hotel without the 5-star trappings. €430 per bungalow for 2 people, full board.

Things to see and do

Bird, as its name implies, is for the birds, and they are the main tourist attraction of the island. Paths traverse the island and visitors are free to wander anywhere.

About 800,000 pairs of sooty terns breed there during the southeasterly trade wind season. Their first 'wide awake' calls are heard as early as February when they gather prior to nesting. Great noisy masses of terns swirl over the island like a low, hazy cloud. The sooty tern colony is at the northern end of the island, reached by walking along the beach and following the sign inland. A small raised platform enables guests to have a good view over the nesting ground without disturbing the birds. As the Seychellois consider their eggs a great delicacy, they used to be gathered in vast quantities, thereby causing the sooty tern numbers to decline. Now with a conservation ethic on the island, and only a controlled number of eggs (around 3%) being harvested annually, the terns are no longer threatened and the Seychellois are delighted to have an annual supply of tern eggs.

Cats and rats have been eradicated from the island, but there is an infestation of 'crazy ants' plaguing the birds, especially the chicks. Efforts are under way to eliminate the ants during the non-breeding season. Large numbers of lesser and brown noddies are quite fearless and take no notice of the hotel guests. This is the best place to see these two easily confused species close up. Fairy terns are in abundance and many waders frequent the beautiful beaches. Madagascar fodies are also common, but interestingly enough there are no sunbirds. Besides the birds, 13 giant Aldabra tortoises live out a quiet life, roaming wherever they please. The largest tortoise in the world, Esmeralda, lives on the island and weighs in at 304kg! A yellow-and-black radiated tortoise from Madagascar, called Jeremy, can also be found wandering around. Both green and hawksbill turtles use the sandy beaches for their nests, which are closely monitored by staff, together with interested guests, under a programme initiated by Dr Jeanne Mortimer. As many as 13,000 turtle hatchlings can emerge in one season.

The northern tip of the island projects out to sea as a long exposed sand spit which is good for observing wading birds. The spit changes size and shape with the monsoons. Snorkelling inside the reef is not so good as it is covered with seagrass beds, and the currents are strong around Passe Cocos. The management will advise on the best snorkelling spots. Deep-sea fishing can be arranged at the hotel reception.

Outer Coralline Islands

The outer islands of the Seychelles, scattered across a vast area of the western Indian Ocean, are isolated groups of coral islands, hundreds of kilometres from anywhere. The Amirantes, a string of about ten islands, are the closest to Mahé; Alphonse consists of three islands; the Farquhar group is made up of two atolls; and Plat and Coëtivy are two far-flung islands, neither of them near to any other part of the Seychelles. Many of the outer islands are surrounded by coral reefs with shallow lagoons protecting some of the most fabulous beaches imaginable. The islands are not on regular shipping routes and, though many are uninhabited, others may have a small staff of contract workers on the still-active coconut plantations. Some of the islands are being developed as exclusive getaway tourist destinations.

After the colonisation and exploitation of the granitic islands of the Seychelles in the late 18th century, it did not take long for people to spread to the outer islands. The first concessions were granted around 1815, and work was usually done for the absentee landlords by slave labour, with a *commandeur* or overseer in charge. Rich guano deposits were mined, fish and turtles were exploited, and sooty tern eggs were collected by the thousand. Cotton and a little maize were grown before coconut palms were planted on the islands. The plantation system was created and it remains today as Seychellois island managers and contract workers live out a lonely existence far from the gregarious lifestyle of Mahé. Most of the islands are owned by the government, and are managed by the para-statal Islands Development Company.

Airstrips have been built on some of the islands, but for the others, the only contact with the outside world is the radio-telephone and the supply ship, which calls about every two months. The eagerly awaited ship delivers mail, fuel and provisions and brings new staff to the islands to relieve those whose contracts have expired. It is possible to visit these far-flung islands by yacht and permission has to be obtained from the Islands Development Company in Mahé. Should you arrive without permission it is unlikely that you will be permitted on to the islands. Note that the maps used in this text should not be used for navigation purposes.

THE AMIRANTES

The Amirantes Bank has ten islands, several shoals and many submerged reefs, which are strung out between 5° and 6° south. African Banks, in the north, is

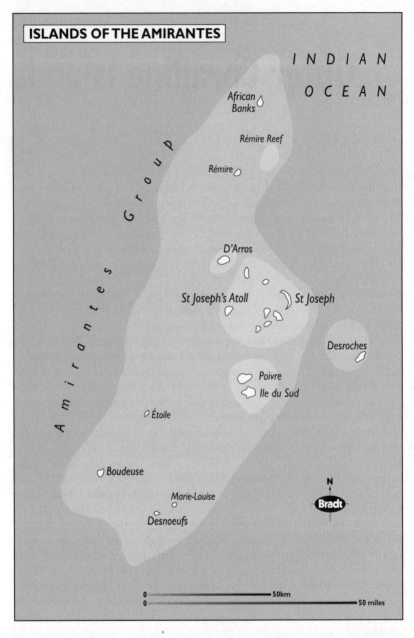

ISLANDS OF THE AMIRANTES

Amirantes Group

INDIAN OCEAN

African Banks

Rémire Reef

Rémire

D'Arros

St Joseph's Atoll

St Joseph

Desroches

Poivre

Ile du Sud

Étoile

Boudeuse

Marie-Louise

Desnoeufs

N

Bradt

0 ——— 50km
0 ——————— 50 miles

about 250km from Mahé, and Desnoeufs, the most southerly, is about 135km further south. The main islands in the group are Rémire, D'Arros, St Joseph's Atoll, Desroches, Poivre, Etoile, Boudeuse and Marie-Louise. This remote group of islands was discovered by the Portuguese navigator, Vasco da Gama, on his second voyage to India in 1502. They were subsequently known as *Ilhas do Almirantes* after the famous admiral. It is possible that 17th-century pirates used the quiet lagoons and sandy beaches for shelter after marauding sprees, but it is more likely that they came to grief on the treacherous reefs surrounding many of the islands. In fact, voyaging among the outer islands reveals many latter-day shipwrecks. Funnels and bulkheads loom out of the breakers crashing on to the coral reefs and sometimes, on still and calm days, they appear as mirages hovering on the ocean surface.

Desroches

Desroches, a sandy cay on the rim of a submerged nearly circular atoll, is a long, narrow, flat island, 5km long, 1km wide, covering an area of about 320ha. The island, covered in coconut palms and casuarina trees, is 230km south of Mahé and approximately 16km east of the main Amirantes Bank. Desroches was named after François Julien Desroches, governor of Mauritius from 1767 to 1772. The exclusive Desroches Island Resort is located on the western side of the island and there is an airstrip within easy walking distance of the lodge. A lighthouse, located at the northeastern end of the island, warns mariners of the dangers of the treacherous reefs. The northern part of the island is run as a coconut plantation and farm, and there is a settlement on the northern shore. The first coconut plantations were started in 1875 and copra is still processed on the island before being transported to Mahé. Fresh vegetables from the farm are sold to the lodge and pigs, chicken and sheep are also raised.

This is the ultimate get-away-from-it-all island. The only noise you are likely to hear above the ocean waves is the gentle cooing of the little barred ground doves. There are long stretches of dazzling white beaches with sheltered swimming on the northern shore. The southern shore, which is a favoured spot for fly-fishing, is guarded by a wide reef that almost dries at low tide. During the northwest monsoons, hawksbill turtles clamber on to the beaches to lay their eggs above the high tide mark, and it is possible to see them during the day. A few giant Aldabra tortoises roam freely around the island seeking out deep shade in the heat. As mosquitoes lurking in the undergrowth can be a nuisance, ensure that you have plenty of insect repellent. Seabirds are often seen feeding in the quiet waters of the lagoon, and turnstones, usually associated with the shore, frequent the grassy areas under the coconut palms.

Getting there and away

There are five flights per week and they will be arranged by IDC in conjunction with accommodation at the lodge. A return trip from Mahé costs €265 and the flight takes about 45 minutes. The baggage allowance is 15kg per person.

Where to stay

Desroches Island Resort Tel: 229003; fax: 229002; office tel: 322322; fax: 322744; email: desroches@seychelles.net; www.desroches-island.net; booking: reservation@mk-resorts.com; for more information: info@mk-resorts.com. There are 20 luxurious, air-conditioned junior suites decorated in a blend of island style and

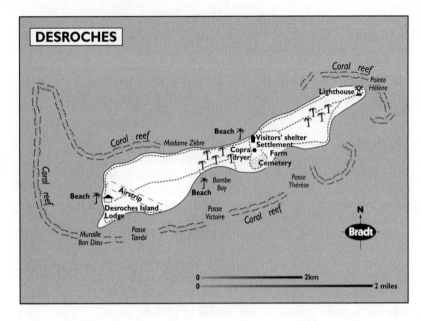

modern comfort with IDD telephone, cable TV and tea- and coffee-making facilities. Your own private patio is less than 4m from the beach. The main dining room serves fine international gourmet or innovative Creole-style cuisine with an emphasis on the freshest seafood. Lunches are served in the relaxed, feet-in-the-sand, beach restaurant. The resort has various special offers for couples on honeymoon. There is a minimum stay of 3 nights during the low season. €637 per suite per night for 2 people sharing on full board.

Things to see and do

Bicycles are available and it is possible to walk or cycle around most of the island on flat easy paths, visit the coconut plantation and look for the old cemetery, maybe even climb to the top of the lighthouse. Keen birdwatchers should bring binoculars as migrant birds often stop over on Desroches on passage migration. A floodlit tennis court is available as are canoes, windsurfers and pedalos. There is a library, a boutique and some indoor games. Desroches is well known for its good scuba diving on the reef drop-off known as the Desroches Drop and there is a well-equipped PADI dive centre. Snorkelling too, can be very rewarding. Desroches is well situated for big-game fishing and the resort boat, *Cookie Two*, is well equipped to take guests deep-sea fishing. Fly-fishing in the southern lagoon, particularly for bonefish, can provide hours of entertainment. For some though, the 14km of unspoilt beaches are the perfect getaway. Trips to Poivre and D'Arros can be arranged.

Poivre

Poivre, about 40km west of Desroches, consists of two sandy cays, a shallow lagoon and many reefs. It is close to the eastern end of the Amirantes Bank and about 270km southwest of Mahé. This uninhabited island, covered in coconuts and casuarinas, was named after Pierre Poivre, the quartermaster on Mauritius who was instrumental in setting up the spice industry in the Seychelles in the late 1770s. Excursions to Poivre can be arranged through Desroches Island Lodge.

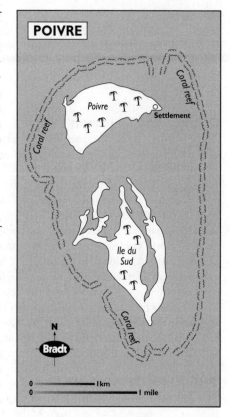

Etoile and Boudeuse

These two sandy cays, 30km apart, are located southwest of Poivre. Uninhabited, both are bird reserves with large numbers of sooty terns nesting on them.

Marie-Louise and Desnoeufs

Marie-Louise and Desnoeufs, about 10km apart, are the southernmost islets of the Amirantes group, roughly 325km from Mahé. Each island has a small settlement. Marie-Louise, no more than a sandy cay with a clump of casuarinas, covers an area of about 500m². It is encircled by a coral reef, and landing there is hazardous because of rough surf and hidden wrecks. Failing to live up to her name, the surveying ship *Alert* ran aground in 1882, and in 1905 a steamer sank in the anchorage. Desnoeufs covers an area of 35ha and is an extraordinary sooty tern colony. In the breeding season, May to early August, the sky above the island is a seething, hovering mass of hundreds of thousands of these black-and-white birds. The sound of them calling almost eclipses the roar of the surf. A large part of the colony has been set aside as a sanctuary, but the remainder is officially harvested and crates of the fragile eggs are transported back to the market on Mahé. It is a tricky manoeuvre to hoist the boxes of eggs on board the supply ship from the tiny boat, rocking and rolling in the heavy swells of the southeast trades.

African Banks

African Banks is made up of two small, very low islands joined by a sand spit and coral reef. It covers an area less than 1km². It has low beach crest bush, a couple of coconut palms, a derelict fishermen's hut and is uninhabited except for thousands of seabirds.

Rémire

Rémire, lying on a small reef, is a sandy, oval island of about 1km². It has a landing strip for light aircraft and is inhabited by the workers on the coconut plantation and vegetable gardens. Rémire was also known as Eagle Island. It was stripped of its guano before coconuts were planted.

D'Arros and St Joseph's Atoll

These islands, about 1km apart, are privately owned by Iranian royalty. D'Arros is an oval, sandy cay perched on a flat reef and was named after Baron d'Arros, marine commander on Mauritius in 1771. Although most of the island is covered in coconut palms, there is a significant portion of natural coastal forest with *Guettada*, *Morinda* and *Terminalia* species dominating. Birdlife is notable with about 480 Seychelles fodies and 260 Madagascar fodies. Interestingly, although it has a rat and cat population, both common and lesser noddies breed on the island. The enormous robber crab, *Birgus latro*, is widespread on the island but most abundant on the south coast.

St Joseph's Atoll consists of a ring of eight islets surrounded by submerged coral reefs with St Joseph's Island the largest and easternmost of the group. There is very little natural vegetation left, coconut palms being the dominant vegetation. A large population of approximately 19,000 breeding pairs of wedge-tailed shearwaters are nesting on one of the smaller islets. Grey herons as well as black-naped and crested terns are to be found on some of the islets.

THE ALPHONSE GROUP

The Alphonse group of islands lie on a separate bank south of the Amirantes Bank at 7° south and 400km from Mahé. They were named after the captain of a French ship that visited the island in 1730. Alphonse, a sand cay on the rim of a circular atoll which is exposed at low tide, is a small, flat, triangular-shaped island covered in coconut palms. There are paths and a road that weave through the lush coconut plantation and you can see the plantation manager's shabby old house. Two sides of the island extend to embrace the large, sheltered lagoon and it makes an ideal holiday escape. Alphonse frequently experiences less rain than the granitic islands, especially during the northwest monsoons. Small boats can enter the lagoon only at high tide through the southwestern channel. Shipwrecks lie on either side of the lagoon and bear testimony to the strong currents and shallow reefs hiding beneath the clear turquoise water. *Dot*, a French coal steamer, ran aground en route to Réunion in 1873, and on the other side is the wreck of the *Tamatave*, grounded in 1903.

Bijoutier and St François

These two tiny gems, both adorned by a topknot of coconut palms, are set in a coral reef separated from Alphonse by a deep channel. Bijoutier is only 5km south of Alphonse.

St François, a small atoll, 17ha in extent, is a further 7km south and is regarded as the best fly-fishing destination in the world. It is also an important bird area as hundreds of crab plovers gather there during the non-breeding season with over 1,200 recorded at one time. These small islands are uninhabited and will give you the feeling of being a castaway on a deserted island.

Getting there and away
The one-hour IDC flight to Alphonse will be arranged in conjunction with the resort, and there are five flights per week. The return fare from Mahé is €275 and the luggage allowance is 15kg.

Where to stay
Alphonse Island Resort Tel: 229030 or 322322; fax: 229034 or 322744; email: alphonse@seychelles.net; for reservations: reservation@mk-resorts.com. This is the only accommodation in the Amirantes. There are 25 standard, air-conditioned, thatched A-frame chalets and 5 executive villas. Each one has a jacuzzi as well as an outdoor shower. The restaurant offers delicious, inventive, Creole cuisine with plenty of fresh fish. €470 for the standard chalet for 2 people per night.

Things to see and do
Besides relaxing by the pool and soaking up the sun there is a surprising amount of things to

ALPHONSE GROUP

do on Alphonse. Birdwatching can be interesting as many migrating birds visit the island and Amur falcons, Oriental pratincole, Madagascar lesser cuckoo and white and grey wagtails have been seen. Walking along the shore of the lagoon can also be fascinating with all sorts of wonderful creatures to be seen in the intertidal zone, particularly at ebb tide. Look out for the large crabs! Take a bicycle and cycle around the island under the shade of tall coconut palms or play a game of tennis. Pedalos and Hobie-cats are available to enjoy in the lagoon. It is possible to arrange to visit Bijoutier for the day and have a picnic there; wear sunhats and use plenty of sunscreen. The excellent dive centre is run by Brigitte Mayer-Jumeau, who will take you to some very special spots. The coral appears to be recovering well from the coral bleaching in 1998.

Another big attraction is the fly-fishing in the lagoon around St François and over 40 fish species can be caught on fly. Frontiers Travel UK and USA (email: alphonse@shackletoninternational.com; www.frontierstrvl.com) can arrange the package tours of six days and seven nights. The concession allows limited rods only and the fishing season is mid-May to mid-September. Deep-sea fishing is another big attraction and this can also be arranged through Frontiers Travel. Using conventional big-game tackle, all the fishing is carried out on a catch and release basis, except for a small amount that supplies the hotel. Blue-water fly-fishing can be an exciting experience and the fish targeted include wahoo, tuna and sail fish.

THE FARQUHAR GROUP

Providence and Farquhar are two atolls 60km apart lying on the Farquhar Ridge at 10° south. Exquisite and remote, each island is surrounded by sandy cays, sheltered lagoons, shallow coral reefs and clear, deep turquoise water. Although there are plans afoot, no tourist facilities currently exist on either of these islands but both have settlements and active coconut plantations run by the Islands Development Company. Once the copra is dried, it is bagged and transported to Mahé aboard the supply ship which calls every two months. Agriculture plays a minor role with only a few cows and pigs being reared for local use. Fishing is an important feature of these outer islands, with several vessels working in the area.

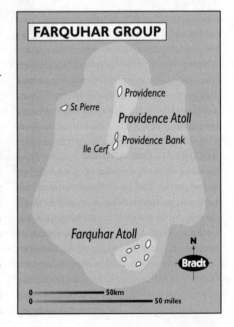

Farquhar Atoll

Farquhar is the most important of the eleven islands that make up the Farquhar Atoll. The atoll is ear-shaped with most of the islands on the eastern rim of the atoll. It has one of the most beautiful and sheltered lagoons in the Seychelles. Sparkling clear water, wide coral reefs and shimmering, silvery beaches make Farquhar a tantalising island. There is an airstrip with a heart-shaped sign that says 'Welcome to Farquhar'. A small guesthouse, reserved for visiting scientists and officials, may be let out to tourists

Above Inter-island schooners at La Digue island (LM)

Left Parrot fish (LM)

Below Small fishing harbour at Bel Ombre, Mahé (LM)

Right Giant Aldabra
tortoise (LM))

Below A huge
coconut crab on
Aldabra atoll (LM)

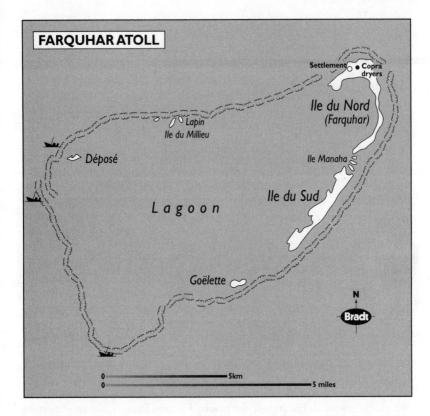

if it is not in official use. There are no tourist facilities, just a simple house with a couple of bedrooms and a lovely spacious veranda. Contact the IDC in Mahé for availability and cost (tel: 224640; fax 224467; Farquhar tel: 229029). The picturesque settlement and copra-drying sheds are surrounded by coconut palms, casuarinas and *badamier* trees. Many of the surrounding islets and reefs are littered with shipwrecks, and there are great hulks of rusting metal visible, especially when the tide is low. Snorkelling and scuba diving are good, particularly in November and April. A large number of sooty terns breed on the small island of Goëlette.

Providence
Providence atoll is about 710km from Mahé and comprises Providence Island in the north and some banks at the southern extremity of the atoll. Landing on Providence is a hazardous procedure because of the surrounding shallow reef and heavy surf. Over the years there have been many ships wrecked in the vicinity. A handful of contract workers run the coconut plantation.

St Pierre
St Pierre, 30km to the west of Providence, is a circular raised atoll 1,200m in diameter with rocky coastal cliffs characterised by caves and blowholes,

reaching a height of 10m above sea level. It is bare except for a clump of casuarinas, and is a seabird breeding colony with thousands of pairs of sooty terns nesting there during June and July.

Getting there and away

Tourists can visit these islands by sea, on their own yachts or by chartering vessels from Marine Charter Association in Mahé. It is important to obtain permission from the Islands Development Company in Mahé if you wish to go ashore. There are no tourist facilities. During the period when the southeast trades blow in May to September, the sea is often extremely rough. If you are considering staying at the guesthouse, it is possible to charter a flight through IDC.

PLAT

This tiny platform island, surrounded by coral reef with a sheltered lagoon, is located 140km south of Mahé and about 200km east of Desroches. There is a small settlement of contract workers looking after the coconut plantation. There are no tourist facilities.

COETIVY

Coëtivy is situated about 290km southeast of Mahé and 170km from Plat. It is 10km long and about 1km wide with a long, unbroken shoreline. It has a productive agricultural settlement run by the Seychelles Marketing Board. Copra, vegetables and pork are produced. Recently, prawn aquaculture began on Coëtivy and this venture already satisfies the entire domestic demand with the excess exported. Fishing off the nearby Fortune Bank is also an important source of fish for the Mahé market. Although there is an airstrip, there are no tourist facilities on the island.

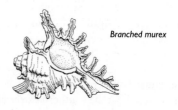

Branched murex

The Aldabra Group

The Aldabra group is made up of Aldabra, Assumption, Astove and Cosmoledo. The group is roughly 460km from the northern tip of Madagascar, 600km from the East African coast and over 1,000km from Mahé. The remote atolls were once covered in thick vegetation, home to hundreds of thousands of tortoises, nesting place for millions of breeding seabirds, and each year vast numbers of marine turtles laid their eggs in the soft sand on the seashore. This idyllic state lasted until the late 1800s when the islands suffered the same exploitation as that which occurred on all the other Seychelles islands. Concessions were granted to private individuals who cleared much of the natural vegetation on Assumption, Astove and Cosmoledo to make way for cotton, sisal, guano mining and, later, coconut plantations. Because of the harsh terrain of Aldabra, only small areas were cleared and planted with coconuts, but turtles and tortoises were heavily exploited there as well as on the other three islands.

Naturalists undertook many collections during the 19th and early 20th centuries, but it was only after 1960 that the first comprehensive scientific surveys of the Aldabra group were undertaken. Aldabra nearly became an airforce base in 1967 and, subsequently, the Royal Geographic Society and other institutions became involved in studying the natural history of the Aldabra group. Aldabra was declared a World Heritage Site in 1982 and the islands, the lagoon and the surrounding reefs are now protected areas.

There are no tourist facilities on any of the islands, and they are not on the general tourist route except for the occasional expedition-type cruise ship or live-aboard dive boat that may call at these out-of-the-way islands. They are visited regularly by the supply ship from Mahé, which calls at the outlying islands about every two months, delivering food, fuel and mail. Scientists are able to use the supply ship to get to these remote areas. Note that maps used in this text should not be used for navigation purposes.

ASSUMPTION

Assumption is surrounded by a narrow, fringing reef and covers an area of 11km² with a series of sand dunes on the southeastern shores attaining a height of 30m. There is a gap in the reef on the northwestern side of the island with a beautiful, long crescent of beach lining the bay. A dilapidated concrete pier stretches into the sea opposite the small settlement at the southern end of the

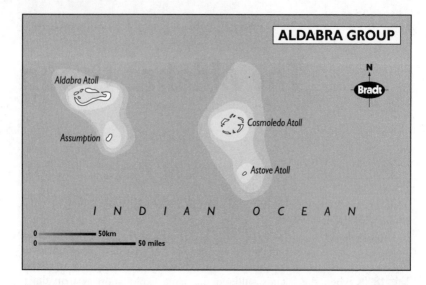

bay. There are a few houses and a string of little huts under the coconut palms surrounded by colourful flowers and lime trees growing in profusion. At the edge of the sea a few graves, some of which are crumbling into the ocean, are shaded by casuarinas.

Assumption has the only landing strip in the Aldabra group and it is mainly used as a connection to Aldabra for visiting scientists and staff changes (the 27km journey across to Aldabra has to be made by boat). Only about half-a-dozen people live on the island and they maintain the runway and the communications station. There is no tourist accommodation. The interior of the island is rough, coral limestone covered in low, scrubby bushes. In the past the main activity was guano mining, and when that came to an end in 1948, coconut plantations were set up to produce copra. With the denudation of the natural vegetation came the demise of the birdlife. Abbott's booby, once breeding on Assumption, is now confined to Christmas Island, further east in the Indian Ocean. Today, introduced Mozambique serins mix cheerfully with the noisy Mauritian red-whiskered bulbul, and the ubiquitous crows. Abbott's sunbird is also resident. During the years of exploitation, green and hawksbill turtles were hunted and now very few come to the island to lay their eggs. The slow, lumbering giant tortoises have also been wiped off the island.

ASTOVE

Located at 10° south, Astove is the most southerly of the Seychelles islands. It is a small, uninhabited atoll of 6km² embracing a shallow lagoon with only one opening to the sea. A reef with deep, spectacular drop-offs surrounds the island. This is an excellent diving and snorkelling spot with caves and overhangs creating amazing underwater scenery teeming with colourful reef fishes and turtles. History books tell tales of many shipwrecks on the treacherous reef. In 1760, a Portuguese ship, *Dom Royal*, laden with treasures and slaves, ran aground. The captain and crew tried to reach the East African coast on a raft and were never seen again, while the slaves were left to their own devices on the atoll. Several ships from Mauritius went to try to capture the slaves but were beaten off by the fierce and wild castaways. It was not until 1796 that a ship from Mahé finally captured some of the slaves, but it, too, was wrecked, with all on board ending up in a watery grave.

Like Assumption, Astove was exploited for its guano, followed by copra production. Tumbled-down ruins of a few houses, copra-drying sheds and stagnant water tanks are all that remain of the thriving little establishment that in 1968 was run by about 40 people.

The vegetation is impenetrable and the overgrown path from the old settlement to the lagoon is sometimes impossible to locate. Large, black-and-white, bird-wing butterflies are common, and the mosquitoes are a terrible menace. They will descend upon you in droves, so, if you ever land on Astove, take gallons of repellent and wear long-sleeved shirts and long trousers. Abbott's sunbirds, white eyes and the Madagascar cisticolas feast on these insects.

COSMOLEDO

Mysterious, wild and uninhabited, Cosmoledo's buildings are in ruins and overgrown plantations of coconuts and sisal are reminders of the past exploitation of this remote atoll. Cosmoledo comprises a dozen small islands encircling a huge, shallow lagoon that almost dries at low tide. The largest island is crescent-shaped Menai at 2.5 km^2, where there are several disintegrating buildings, a cemetery and the remains of a once productive coconut plantation. The other islands, some still unsurveyed, are Grande Ile (also known as Wizard Island), Ile du Nord, Ile Nord Est, Ile du Trou, Goëlettes, Grande Polyte, Pagode, Ile Sud Ouest, Ile Moustiques, Ile Baleine and Ile Chauve Souris.

The largest breeding colony of sooty terns in the Seychelles can be found on Cosmoledo, with over a million pairs nesting on the sandy islands. Three species of boobies – red-footed, brown and masked – also nest on the islands and small flocks of crab plovers can be seen feeding on the exposed coral flats at low tide at certain times of the year. Grey herons, a variety of terns and some remarkable passerines make their home on the islands. There is an endemic, resident population of Abbott's sunbird and their shining, jewelled, prismatic plumage provides flashes of colour as they dart among the vegetation. Taxonomic research is currently being carried out on the sunbirds and Madagascar white-eyes. Madagascar cisticolas are also common in the scrubby vegetation and can be seen flying between the tiny, vegetated clumps of *champignon* in the lagoon.

At high tide it is possible to ride in a flat-bottomed boat through parts of the lagoon, but there are many uncharted rocks and it is only in the two principal channels that there is any depth of water. Many fishes become trapped as the

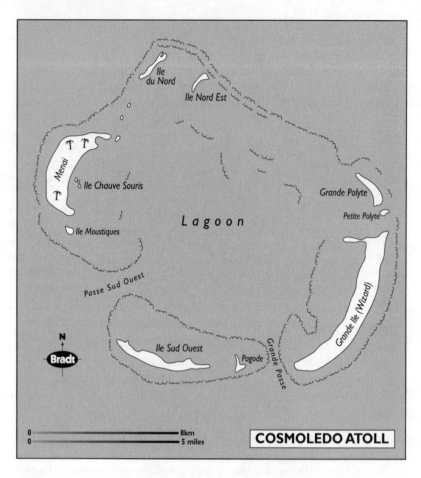

Ile
du Nord

Ile Nord Est

Menai

Ile Chauve Souris

Ile Moustiques

L a g o o n

Grande Polyte

Petite Polyte

Grande Ile (Wizard)

Passe Sud Ouest

N

Bradt

Ile Sud Ouest

Pagode

Grande passe

0 ————————— 8km
0 ————————— 5 miles

COSMOLEDO ATOLL

tide recedes, and it is easy to see eels and parrotfishes quietly waiting in the shallow pools for the tide to rise. Excellent snorkelling and diving are to be found off some of the reefs, particularly off Menai Island.

ALDABRA

Rugged, rough, remote and arid, this World Heritage Site wilderness atoll has survived the ravages of man over the centuries because of these very characteristics. The harsh nature of the atoll, with its sharp, jagged, limestone terrain and thick, impenetrable vegetation, prevented the full-scale exploitation that beset most of the other islands. Although it is not, and never has been, on any regular shipping routes, it was first recorded on early Portuguese charts in 1509, and it is highly likely that discovery by Arab seafarers preceded this date. The evocative name Aldabra probably stems from the Arabic word *Al-Khadra* meaning green, which could be a reference to the green-based cloud that can sometimes be seen hanging over the atoll, reflecting the colour of the vast interior lagoon.

The elliptically shaped atoll is approximately 34km long and about 14km across, which makes it the largest raised coral atoll in the world. The rim of the atoll is broken by four channels which link the massive, shallow lagoon to the ocean. The four islands thus formed are Grande Terre or Main Island, which is by far the largest, Picard, hosting the settlement, Polymnie, the smallest, and Malabar, which runs straight along the northern edge of the atoll. The islands of Aldabra make up an area of 154km², which accounts for almost one-third of all the Seychelles land territory. The lagoon inside the ring of islands is 11km across and 27km long, big enough so that one cannot see over from one side to the other. The entire island of Mahé could easily fit inside the lagoon. The lagoon contains several small islands, namely Ile aux Cèdres, Ile Michel, Ile Esprit and Ile Moustiques.

Fringing platform reef encircles almost the entire atoll. The jagged, fossilised limestone cliffs undercut by constant wave action, and the desolate sand dunes rising up to 15m above sea level, form the barrier between sea and land. The sharp, pitted and strangely shaped limestone is known as *champignon* from the French word for mushroom. Many of the islets inside the lagoon are *champignon* with a flat, tabular surface and a slender stalk. Some are barren while others are covered in a variety of flowering plants including orchids and mangroves.

The largest channel is Grande Passe, or Main Channel, that separates Picard and Polymnie, and at least 60% of the lagoon water flows in and out through this gap, running at up to seven knots at spring tides. There are about eight islets and many small *champignon* lying across the entrance to West Channel, and a ragged series of *champignon* protects the entrance of Gionnet Channel. Passe Hoaureau in the northeast separates Grande Terre from Malabar.

The fascinating geological past of Aldabra reveals alternating marine and terrestrial periods caused by changes in sea level when the polar oceans froze during the various ice ages and melted during periods of warming. Fossilised remains of giant clams and corals, as well as bones of birds and reptiles, can be seen embedded in the substrate around the settlement and on the more inaccessible parts of the atoll. Aldabra's oceanic isolation, combined with its links to Africa and close proximity to Madagascar, has resulted in a unique flora and fauna with many endemic species – quite astonishing for so small an area of land. However, Aldabra is very large for an atoll, and as it is a raised atoll, inland habitats have evolved in addition to the coastal ones.

Aldabra, like the other islands in the group, was leased out to various entrepreneurs who gathered fish, turtles and tortoises there to sell in Mahé. The turtles were taken in vast numbers to satisfy the market as turtle soup and meat was all the rage in international cuisine; it was also very fashionable to have 'tortoiseshell' ornaments, hair clips and combs. The 'tortoiseshell' was derived from the beautiful, hard shell of the hawksbill turtle and not the tortoise.

History

In 1878, Admiral W J L Wharton carried out the first hydrographic survey of the Aldabra group and it was ten years later that the first settlement was established for commercial exploitation of the natural resources. Over the

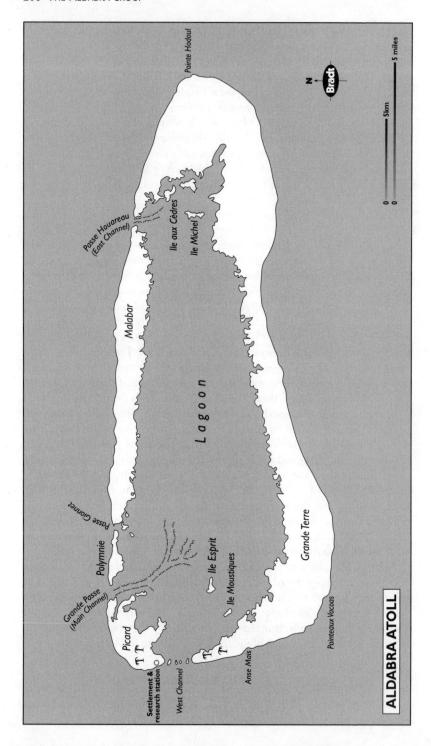

ALDABRA ATOLL

Pointe Hodoul

Passe Houareau
(East Channel)

Ile aux Cèdres

Ile Michel

Malabar

Lagoon

Passe Gionnet

Polymnie

Grande Passe
(Main Channel)

Ile Esprit

Ile Moustiques

Grande Terre

Picard

Settlement &
research station

West Channel

Anse Mais

Pointeaux Vacoas

5Km
0

5 miles
0

N

Bradt

years, although the lessees changed, the settlement remained on the west-facing sandy shore of Picard. A plantation house and office were built under the shade of huge *badamier* trees and a tiny wood and iron chapel was constructed which is still in use today. The remains of the two-roomed jail can be seen. It was generally used to allow offenders to cool off for a day or two after tempers had flared, usually over a woman or because of too much toddy (the potent alcoholic beverage made from fermented palm juice).

Because of the lack of water on the atoll, enormous, rectangular water tanks were built adjacent to each building. Near the settlement on Picard towards the West Channel lie the remains of an old turtle-bone crushing mill. Turtle bones were brought from the other islands to be processed on Aldabra. At a later time, coconuts, sisal and cotton were planted, but because of water shortages none of these agricultural ventures was very successful. The remnants of the coconut plantations both near the settlement and on the northwestern edge of Grande Terre, are all that are left. But thank goodness for the coconuts; they are the only little bit of fresh food available for the resident staff of Aldabra.

After World War II, commercial exploitation was temporarily halted but the lease recommenced in 1955 with some restrictions. Aldabra was declared a nature reserve with no human settlement allowed on Grande Terre and no more than 200 people allowed on the atoll at any one time. All animal life was protected and no introduced plants or animals were permitted. In the mid-1960s, the Royal Society of London conducted a series of expeditions to Aldabra to study the marine and terrestrial ecosystems.

The effects of the Cold War were felt even in such isolated places as Aldabra. The British created a new political entity known as the British Indian Ocean Territory with the queen signing the annexure documents on November 8 1965. Included with Aldabra were the Farquhar group, Desroches and the Chagos archipelago. The rationale for this was to establish an Anglo-American airforce base in the Indian Ocean. After much military research, it was decided to undertake this ambitious project on Aldabra, and construction of the long runways would have involved clearing much of the natural vegetation and getting rid of the nesting frigates and boobies. However, it was around this time that the ecological importance of Aldabra was being fully realised, and the battle was on between the military and the conservationists. Science won the day – the airforce base was subsequently built at Diego Garcia and Aldabra survived. The Royal Society bought the lease in 1970, stopped all exploitation, and built a research station. In 1980, the station was handed over to the Seychelles Island Foundation, which continues to administer the atoll as a conservation and research area under the patronage of the president of the Seychelles. Aldabra was declared a Special Reserve in 1981 and proclaimed a UNESCO World Heritage Site on November 19 1982. The brass plaque commemorating this momentous occasion bears the words 'Aldabra, wonder of nature, given to humanity by the people of the Republic of Seychelles'. A truly fitting accolade for the most majestic and ecologically intact, raised coral atoll on the planet.

The settlement

The World Heritage Site of Aldabra is uninhabited except for a handful of dedicated people who maintain the research station and continue the scientific programmes. There are generally between six and twelve people living at the settlement on Picard. A warden is in charge of the atoll, the staff, the researchers and ongoing monitoring. Mechanics, boatmen, rangers and field workers handle the chores associated with running the station and carry out the daily monitoring required for the scientific programmes. From time to time, visiting scientists from various universities and research institutes may stay on Aldabra for extended periods of time, completing scientific surveys and research. The current areas of monitoring include demographics of turtles, tortoises and white-throated rails, while observation programmes are being carried out on the seabirds that nest on the atoll.

There is an office block with a small laboratory and a library, a communal lounge with a large, covered veranda and a small accommodation block for visiting scientists. Island staff live in an assortment of houses around the research station. Workshops, a fuel depot and generators keep the station running smoothly. There is no shop as such but sometimes there is a small selection of books and Aldabra T-shirts for sale to visitors.

Getting there and away

The inaccessibility of Aldabra enhances its desirability. There is no airstrip, helipad or landing jetty. The supply boat from Mahé visits Aldabra every two months and live-aboard dive boats, cruise ships and yachts visit periodically. Aldabra has no tourist facilities. Small cruise ships visiting the atoll will anchor on the seaward side of the reef near the settlement. Those passengers lucky enough to go ashore will be accompanied by their expedition leader and transported to the beach adjacent to the station in their ship's inflatable boats.

Things to see and do

Aldabra is awesome in its wild, untamed and natural beauty. The warden and expedition leader will plan any excursions, taking into account the state of the tide. From the settlement you can walk to La Gigi, a small promontory at Passe Femme on the West Channel where you can see the World Heritage Site plaque resting on a coral cairn. At low tide it is possible to venture a little way up the edge of the lagoon and see four species of mangroves and typical *champignon*, some upright and others collapsed into the shallow water. The breathtaking views across the near-empty channel touch the soul, and the timeless beauty of the vast lagoon merging with the sky will be a lasting memory. Birds feed on the exposed coral reef, and frigates, boobies and fairy terns wheel overhead as they have done for centuries. The only sounds are the distant thunder of the surf crashing on the reef and the friendly twangs of the fairy terns as they curiously inspect the visitors.

Another interesting walk from the settlement takes one in a northerly direction along the coast to see the remains of the old settlement with the

MANGROVES

Mangrove is the collective name given to those trees that are capable of surviving in salt water and inundated mud. They generally grow around the shores of quiet estuaries or sheltered lagoons, with the roots of the trees exposed and submerged during the tidal cycle.

Mangrove trees are from several different families of flowering plants and they have thick, leathery leaves to prevent excess water loss. To enable the trees to grow in soft mud, an intricate root system has developed, and some species have strong prop-roots, which do just as the name implies, while others have sturdy buttress roots. Breathing roots or pneumatophores have developed in most species. These may look like pencils or fingers poking up out of the mud, or they may be gnarled, woody bumps. They are generally exposed to the air at low tide, and essentially their job is to supply the trees with oxygen. In non-mangrove plants this takes place in the soil, but as mangrove roots are submerged in water-logged mud, this special respiration mechanism is required.

Mangrove forests are important ecosystems as, besides providing coastal protection, the tangled root systems slow down currents allowing sediment and decaying plant matter to accumulate, thereby providing a sheltered, nutrient-rich habitat. Many species of fishes and crustaceans use mangroves as nursery areas for juveniles. Fiddler and marsh crabs (with their enlarged nippers) and several molluscs also frequent mangroves. Another characteristic species is the mud skipper, *Periopthalmus*, a small fish which is capable of spending considerable time out of the water. The trees provide an evergreen canopy, an ideal nesting site for birds.

On Aldabra there are seven species of mangroves, of which four are common. Fringing the mudflats is the white mangrove, *Avicennia marina*, which can attain 12m. The leaves are grey-green, the bark is smooth and whitish-grey, the seeds are ovoid and can float, and the spreading cable roots have pencil-like pneumatophores (Creole – *mangliye blan*). The black mangrove, *Bruguiera gymnorrhiza*, is a cone-shaped tree reaching 18m (Creole – *mangliye lat*). The aerial roots are knobbly, knee-like bumps, and the bark is rough and reddish-brown. A slender seed up to 25cm long is produced. It germinates on the parent tree before dropping into the mud, whereupon it rapidly develops roots. The Indian mangrove, *Ceriops tagal*, reaches 7m and has a buttressed trunk, prop roots and elbow-like pneumatophores (Creole – *mangliye zonn*). A 25cm-long seed pod will drop into the mud after germination has started. The bark is smooth and grey. The tallest tree in the mangrove forest is the red mangrove, *Rhizophora mucronata* (Creole – *mangliye rouz*), which reaches 20m. It is characterised by long prop or stilt roots which form a tangled mass around the tree base. The large, shiny leaves have a spiked tip, fragrant white flowers are present throughout the year, the 30cm-long seed pod is smooth and green, and the fissured bark is dark brown in colour.

little chapel under the shady *badamier* trees. A little further on, in a coconut grove, there is the old cemetery with the graves of Chinese sea cucumber harvesters. Turtle nesting pits can be seen along the crest of the beach. It is also possible to walk inland along some of the scientific transects but, at all times, it is essential to be aware of the fragility of the environment. The paths are not always easy to follow, and you don't want to get lost on Aldabra. It is very easy to get disorientated as there are no hills or buildings to give an indication of direction and, at first glance, all the vegetation and *champignon* look the same.

Depending on time and tide, it may be possible to visit one of the frigatebird colonies near Passe Gionnet inside the lagoon by boat. However, be aware that if the boats approach too close, the noise of the boat engines causes the most incredible disturbance to the courting or nesting birds. While inside the turquoise-green lagoon it might also be possible to stop on Polymnie or Malabar to look for the white-throated rails. They are curious little birds and will often come to investigate the arrival of strangers.

Diving and snorkelling at Aldabra are fabulous, particularly near the entrances to the channels. However, tidal currents are strong, so take advice from the warden and his staff. There are lots of big groupers, blacktip reef sharks and stingrays, and the vertical reef drop-off is marvellous.

Natural history

The inhospitable, and sometimes desolate interior of Aldabra, is home to thousands of giant tortoises, and turtles haul themselves out on to the beaches to lay their eggs. Aldabra is the last outpost of the small white-throated rail, the only flightless bird left in the Indian Ocean. The great colonies of frigatebirds and red-footed boobies nesting in the tall mangrove trees in the lagoon are remarkable. The rich botanical diversity is notable for its endemic species and is of great interest to botanists.

Turtles

Hunted to extinction on so many islands, green and hawksbill turtles find a last refuge on Aldabra, which is one of the few conserved nesting grounds in the Indian Ocean. Almost every night during the southeast trades, female green turtles come ashore on to the sandy beaches to lay their eggs in the soft sand above the high tide mark. First, using her front flippers, a great body pit is dug. Then, using her rear flippers, she will excavate a nest chamber into which she deposits up to 120 soft-shelled, round eggs. Two to three months later the tiny turtle hatchlings will clamber out of the soft sand and make the hazardous journey down to the water. Pied crows, sacred ibis, hermit and ghost crabs make a quick snack of the little critters as they run the gauntlet to the water. When the survivors eventually reach the sea, they then encounter the ever-present sharks and other fish predators. Natural mortality is thus high, and only a very small percentage actually survive to adulthood.

Hawksbill turtles nest on the protected sandy shores of the inner lagoon and will come up during the day from October to January to lay their eggs. The young hawksbill turtles spend a lot of time in the quiet protected areas around the mangrove stands as there is plenty of food and they are safe from predation (see *Marine turtles* in *Chapter 3*).

Tortoises

There are only two places in the world where giant tortoises still occur naturally: the Galápagos Islands in the Pacific and Aldabra. The Aldabra population of about 100,000 is much greater than that of Galápagos. These great, lumbering herbivores are easily seen around the Picard settlement grazing on the short turf. The tortoises are generally shy and on being approached will hiss and retreat into their shells, except, that is, for one very large and friendly tortoise near the settlement that loves having his neck stroked! In the noonday sun, they will hide under the

Aldabra giant tortoise

buildings and in the dense vegetation around the settlement. If they do not reach shade in time they stand the very real danger of quietly baking in their shells. The bleached, white carapaces seen in the more remote areas are testimony to those that succumbed in this way (for more details see *Chapter 3*).

Birds

Three of the four endemic species of land birds can easily be seen on Aldabra. The white-throated rail is the last of the flightless birds left in the Indian Ocean – the dodos and solitaires all met a sorry end in the hunter's pot. The rail can be seen on Picard, Polymnie and Malabar, and the other two endemic species, the Aldabra drongo and the Aldabra fody, can be seen around the settlement. The Aldabra brush warbler was last seen in 1983 and its status is thus uncertain. Other birds like Madagascar kestrels, sacred ibis, sunbirds, white-eyes, Comoro blue pigeons and Madagascar coucals can be seen on Picard.

The great colonies of nesting frigatebirds and red-footed boobies are spectacular. An estimated 10,000 pairs of greater and lesser frigatebirds nest in the canopy of the mangroves lining the shores of the inner lagoon. The acrobatic frigates, with their long, angular wings and deeply forked tails, are true masters of the air and, besides scooping their food from the surface of the water, they will harass any unsuspecting bird, chiefly the boobies. It is mainly the female greater frigatebirds that chase the boobies until in sheer desperation they regurgitate their last meals, which the agile frigates catch – classic kleptoparasitism! The frigate nests are squashed, cheek by jowl, among those of the red-footed boobies who tolerate them with dumb acceptance (which probably explains how they got their name). During the breeding season, October to January, the male frigates go courting with their inflated scarlet pouches dangling under their chins.

Dimorphic egrets, grey herons and green-backed herons feed on the exposed reef at low tide. A variety of terns breed on the small islands in the lagoon – common noddies as well as crested, black-naped, Caspian and fairy terns. A recently described race of Audubon's shearwater breeds on the little rocky *îlots* alongside the tropicbirds.

During the austral summer, many migrant waders visit Aldabra's shores including sandplovers, whimbrels, sandpipers and godwits. It is possible to see flocks of several hundred crab plovers – those enigmatic, elegant, Indian Ocean endemics. Some, particularly the juveniles, will spend a whole season on Aldabra before returning to the sandy shores of Oman to breed.

Plants

The vegetation of Aldabra can be broadly divided into six categories: mangroves, pemphis scrub, mixed scrub, tortoise turf, coconuts and casuarinas, and beach pioneer plants. Almost 90% of the lagoon is fringed with a variety of mangrove trees (see *Chapter 3* and box, page 209).

Pemphis acidula, commonly known as pemphis, is a small tree that forms dense impenetrable stands of woody vegetation. In the mixed scrub woodland there is a variety of trees including *Grewia*, *Sideroxylon*, *Acalypha*, *Ficus*, *Ochna* and *Jasminium elegans* with its fragrantly perfumed, white flowers. The splendid Aldabra lily, a member of the aloe family, which has orange-red flowers, is one of the more spectacular endemic plants found all over the atoll; it flowers at the end of the rainy season. There is also the endemic screw pine, *Pandanus aldabrensis*, which is only found in a few places around the atoll. A subspecies of the tropicbird orchid with sprays of white, waxy flowers, grows on some of the *îlots*.

Of the 22 species of short grasses identified from the tortoise turf (which consitutes the basic diet of the tortoises), eight are endemic and 12 are genetically dwarfed. There are endemic mosses, lichens, algae and ferns, many of which require further study. Casuarina trees can reach a height of 15m and their wispy, needle-like leaves provide gentle fringing shade along the shoreline. No-one seems sure if they were introduced by man or if they found their own way on to Aldabra by their seeds drifting over the ocean waves. The pioneer plants, *Scaveola* and *Tournefortia*, line the sandy shoreline.

Mammals

The only naturally occurring mammals on Aldabra are bats. The large fruit bats roost in the shady *badamier* trees around the old settlement and can be seen in the early evenings as they fly across the atoll in search of fruits. Differing slightly from the species found on the granitic islands, the Aldabra race is smaller and paler. Three other species of small insectivorous bats are also found on the atoll, though very little is known about them.

From August to October, humpback whales can be seen around Aldabra as they migrate from their feeding grounds in the cold Southern Ocean to calve in warm tropical waters. Huge pods of spinner dolphins regularly frolic in the surging waves just off the reef. It is a spectacular sight as they leap clear out of the water and perform acrobatic aerial twists.

Introduced rats, cats and goats have the potential for causing huge problems. Rats are common all over the atoll but especially around the camps and the settlement. Trapping programmes continue but often coconut crabs get into the traps and have to be extricated (with great care!). Feral cats are to be found on the western shores of Grande Terre and their footprints can be found each morning on the sand. There are goats on the eastern and northern parts of Grande Terre where they compete with the tortoises and destroy the trees so desperately needed for shade. Eradication programmes have been carried out from time to time, but with such harsh, jagged terrain and impenetrable vegetation it is a very difficult task.

Shore animals

The enormous, spectacular robber or coconut crabs are seldom seen by tourists as they spend most of the day hiding in their burrows around tree roots. Adults can grow up to 60cm in overall length, weigh up to 4kg and the colour varies from red to blueish black. At night, they forage and will eat vegetable matter, baby turtles or even dead tortoises. The mighty crustaceans attack dried coconuts with their massive pincers and use the torn-up fibres to line their burrows. They have to return to the sea to spawn and, when the larvae metamorphose, the tiny crabs seek out gastropod shells for protection (like hermit crabs). After their first moult they abandon their shell refuges and take up a terrestrial existence. Ghost crabs are very abundant along the sandy shores of the atoll.

Lagoon and reefs

The vast lagoon and flat reef platform are rich in marine life. As Aldabra and the surrounding ocean are all part of the World Heritage Site, all the creatures are protected and no shell collecting or fishing is allowed within one mile of the shore.

It is common to see spotted eagle rays and honeycomb stingrays wafting through the lagoon with quiet dignity, though manta rays are more commonly seen offshore. There is a large population of blacktip reef sharks that frequents the shallows. The diverse corals are in good condition and do not appear to have been as badly affected by the recent coral bleaching event as those reefs on the shallow Seychelles Bank. Many of the reef fish species are enormous, which is probably due to the protection from fishing afforded these slow-growing species. Diving and snorkelling are spectacular, both in the channels and along the reef drop-off.

Latter-day explorers lucky enough to visit Aldabra treat this amazing natural laboratory with the utmost respect. It can be cruel and harsh but, at the same time, it is extremely fragile. However, for those who never get there, just knowing that this protected, pristine place still exists on the planet should cheer the soul.

Black paradise flycatchers

Appendix 1

CREOLE LANGUAGE
Useful words and phrases

Hello	*Bonzour*
Goodbye	*Orevwar*
How are you?	*Konman sava?*
I am well	*Byen*
Thank you	*Mersi*
Thank you very much	*Mersi bokou*
Yes	*Wi*
No	*Non*
Please	*Sivouple*
Excuse me	*Ekskiz*
I am hungry	*Mon fain*
I am thirsty	*Mon swaf*
Only a little	*Zis en pe*
How much?	*Konbyen?*
Please stop here	*Aret ici sivouple*
I don't understand	*Mon pa konpran*
I have to get change	*Mon fodre ganny larzen sanze*
I like it here	*Mon kontan avek Sesel*
Where do you come from?	*Kote ou sorti?*
I come from …	*Mon sorti …*
Can you speak Creole?	*Ou kabab koz Kreol?*
Good luck	*Bonn sans*

airport	*erport*	island	*zil*
baggage	*bagaz*	market	*bazar*
bank	*labank*	police	*gard*
beach	*lanse*	post office	*lapos*
beer	*labyer*	today	*ozordi*
bus terminus	*stayson bis*	toilet	*kabinnen*
church	*leglize*	tomorrow	*demen*
ferry quay	*terminal bato*		
food	*manz*		
hospital	*lopital*		
hotel	*lotel*		

Numbers

1	*enn*	8	*wit*
2	*de*	9	*nef*
3	*trwa*	10	*sis*
4	*kat*	20	*cen*
5	*senk*	50	*senkant*
6	*sis*	100	*san*
7	*set*		

Appendix 2

ACCOMMODATION

The following is an at-a-glance summary of the various places to stay detailed in this guide, put together as an aid to planning your holiday. The type of accommodation indicated here is of necessity simplistic; for details of each venue, see the page number given.

Name	Location	Type	No of rooms/units	Page
Acajou	Praslin	hotel	28	138
Allamanda	Mahé	hotel	10	97
Alphonse Island Resort	Alphonse	hotel	30	197
Anonyme Resort	Mahé	hotel	6	98
Anse Sévère Bungalow	La Digue	guesthouse		159
Anse Soleil Beachcomber	Mahé	hotel	10	97
Anse Soleil Resort	Mahé	self-catering	4	97
Augerine	Mahé	guesthouse	4	95
Beau Vallon Bungalows	Mahé	guesthouse/ self-catering	12	95
Berjaya Beau Vallon Bay	Mahé	hotel	232	93
Berjaya Mahé Beach	Mahé	hotel	173	96
Berjaya Praslin Beach	Praslin	hotel	79	137
Bird Island Lodge	Bird	hotel	189	
Café des Artes	Praslin	hotel	5	139
Casuarina Beach	Mahé	hotel	20	97
Cerf Island	Mahé	hotel	12	98
Château des Feuilles	Praslin	hotel	9	138
Château St Cloud	La Digue	hotel	10	157
Chez Marston	La Digue	guesthouse	157	
Coco d'Or	Mahé	hotel	94	
Coco de Mer	Praslin	hotel	52	137
Coral Strand	Mahé	hotel	94	
Cousine Island Resort	Cousine	hotel	4	181
Daniella's Bungalows	Mahé	guesthouse	12	95
Denis Island Lodge	Denis	hotel	25	188
Desroches Island Resort	Desroches	hotel	20	193
Félicité Private Lodge	Félicité	hotel	6	185

Name	Location	Type	No of rooms/units	Page
Fleur de Lys	La Digue	self-catering	4	159
Frégate Island Private	Frégate	hotel	16	174
Georgina's Cottage Beach	Mahé	guesthouse	5	95
Hilltop	Mahé	guesthouse	8	93
Indian Ocean Lodge	Praslin	hotel	32	138
L'Archipel	Praslin	hotel		138
L'Habitation des Cerfs	Mahé	hotel	10	98
L'Hirondelle	Praslin	self-catering	4	139
L'Océan	La Digue	hotel	8	157
L'Orangerie	La Digue	hotel		159
L'Union Estate Chalets	La Digue	self-catering		159
La Digue Island Lodge	La Digue	hotel		156
La Réserve	Praslin	hotel	30	137
La Vanille	Praslin	hotel	10	139
Le Calou	La Digue	guesthouse	5	157
Le Colibri	Praslin	guesthouse	13	139
Le Duc de Praslin	Praslin	hotel	15	139
Le Méridien Barbarons	Mahé	hotel		96
Le Méridien Fisherman's Cove	Mahé	hotel	70	93
Le Northolme	Mahé	hotel		94
Le Petit Village	Mahé	self-catering	10	94
Le Relax	Mahé	hotel	9	97
Le Sans Souci	Mahé	guesthouse	3	93
Le Tournesol	La Digue	guesthouse	3	157
Lémuria Resort	Praslin	hotel	104	137
Les Rochers Bungalow	Praslin	guesthouse	2	140
Les Villas d'Or	Praslin	guesthouse	8	139
Mango Lodge	Praslin	guesthouse	11	140
Marechiaro	Praslin	hotel	11	138
My Dream	Praslin	guesthouse	2	140
New Emerald Cove	Praslin	hotel	49	137
North Island Lodge	North Island	hotel	11	171
Palm Beach	Praslin	hotel	16	139
Panorama Relais des Iles	Mahé	hotel	10	95
Paradise Flycatcher Lodge	La Digue	self-catering	4	159
Paradise Sun	Praslin	hotel	80	137
Patatran Village	La Digue	hotel	18	157
Pension Michel	La Digue	guesthouse	7	157
Pension Residence	La Digue	guesthouse/ self-catering	6	159
Plantation Club	Mahé	hotel	200	96
Pti Payot	Mahé	self-catering	3	95
Romance Bungalows	Mahé	guesthouse	6	95

Name	Location	Type	No of rooms/units	Page
Rose Garden	Mahé	guesthouse	5	93
Sainte Anne Resort	Mahé	hotel	79	98
Seaview	Praslin	guesthouse	2	140
Silhouette Island Lodge	Silhouette	hotel	12	169
Sitronel	La Digue	guesthouse	4	157
Sunrise	Mahé	hotel/ self-catering	16	93
Sunset Beach	Mahé	hotel	29	94
Takamaka Residence	Mahé	hotel	10	98
Banyan Tree	Mahé	hotel	36	95
Val Mer Resort	Mahé	guesthouse	14	97
Villa Authentique	La Digue	guesthouse	7	157
Villa de Roses	Mahé	guesthouse/ self-catering	8	95
Villa Manoir	Praslin	self-catering	2	140
Villa Mon Rêve	La Digue	guesthouse	5	157
Wharf	Mahé	hotel	16	93
Xanadu	Mahé	guesthouse	8	98

Appendix

FURTHER READING
General

Alexander, D *Holiday in Seychelles* Purnell, Cape Town, 1972. 105pp. Though dated, this anecdotal account includes much information about history, fauna and flora, and life of the Seychellois people.

Burridge, G *Voices from a Corner of Eden* Savy Publishers, Seychelles, 1998. 313pp. Personal account of life on St Joseph's Atoll in the Amirantes. Full of anecdotes, descriptions and astonishing tales of both real events and fantasies.

Lionnet, G *The Seychelles* David & Charles, Newton Abbott, 1972. 200pp. Factual coverage of geology, geography, flora, fauna and history of the Seychelles.

Lionnet, G *The Romance of a Palm – Coco de mer* L'île aux images editions, Mauritius, 1986. 95pp. Small book with every possible detail about the unique *coco de mer* palm.

Mancham, J R *Paradise Raped*, Methuen, London, 1983. 256pp. Personal account by the first president of independent Seychelles.

Pavard, C *Seychelles from One Island to Another*, GMR Group, Seychelles, 1983. 175pp. Marvellous annotated photographs of human activities and wildlife in the Seychelles. Covers inner islands as well as more distant islands of Amirantes, Farquhar, Coëtivy, Aldabra, Cosmoledo and Assumption.

Thomas, A *Forgotten Eden* Longman Group, London, 1973. 185pp. Anecdotal account of life in the Seychelles in the 1960s.

Vine, P *Seychelles* Immel Publishing, London, 1989. 208pp. Colourful book which focuses on the history, natural history, people and traditions of the Seychelles. Includes a section depicting art of Seychellois artists.

History

Bulpin, T V *Islands in a Forgotten Sea* Howard Timmins, Cape Town, 1958. 435pp. Classic text about the history of human exploits in the western Indian Ocean. Great tales of Arab sailors, pirates, colonial powers and the islands in the Sea of Zanj. Includes detailed list of early historical literature about the western Indian Ocean.

Farmer, H V *Seychelles Postage Stamps and Postal History* Robson Lowe Ltd, London, 1955. 123pp. Detailed descriptions of the stamps and postal history of the Seychelles for serious philatelists.

Lee, C *Political Castaways* Elmtree Books, London, 1976. 169pp. Revealing account of political exiles banished to remote Seychelles.

SWEET CHILLI GRILLED PRAWNS, WATERMELON AND CUCUMBER SALAD

Sweet chilli prawns

20 large prawns, peeled, de-veined
1tbl (15ml) garlic, chopped
1tbl (15ml) ginger, peeled, grated
$^1/_3$ cup (80ml) Thai sweet chilli sauce
4 coriander root, cleaned, finely chopped
2tbl (30ml) fish sauce (or salt to taste)
Method: Combine all ingredients and leave to marinate. Grill over medium high heat, quickly, for about 45 seconds each side, or until pink. Remove and toss in a bowl with $^1/_4$ cup (60ml) of dressing.

Dressing

$^1/_4$ cup (60ml) lime juice
2 large cloves garlic
1 medium size chilli, seeds removed, or to taste
$^1/_4$ cup (60ml) fish sauce
$^1/_4$ cup (60ml) raw sugar
$^2/_3$ cup (160ml) water
Method: Blend chilli, garlic and sugar until fine. Add remaining ingredients and blend to combine.

Salad

2 cups (500ml) watermelon, cubed (as deseeded as possible)
1 cup (250ml) cucumber, peeled, seeded, julienne
1 small red onion, peeled, slivered
2 green onions, slivered
$^1/_4$ cup (60ml) mint leaves
$^1/_4$ cup (60ml) coriander leaves
$^1/_4$ cup (60ml) holy basil leaves
1 large bunch watercress, thick stem discarded
1 small red bell pepper, seeded, thinly julienne
2 medium tomatoes, julienne
Method: Gently toss all ingredients with $^3/_4$ cup (175ml) of dressing. Divide between four plates; arrange five cooked prawns on each plate; garnish with lime slices.

From 'North Island Cookbook' by Geoffrey Murray and Dereck Nair (see page 171)

Travel guides

Heady, S *Visitor's Guide – Seychelles* Moorland Publishing, Derbyshire, 1995. 208pp.
Insightful guide to Mahé and some of the other granitic islands. Many colourful photographs augment the text.

Skerrett, A & Skerrett, J *Spectrum Guide to Seychelles* Camerapix Publishers International, Nairobi, 1993. 352pp. A comprehensive guide with many colour photographs of what to see when visiting the Seychelles.

Environment

Gabriel, M, Marshall, S & Jennings, S 'Seychelles' in *Seas at the Millennium: An environmental evaluation*, volume 2. Sheppard, C R C (ed). Elsevier Science, Amsterdam, 2000, pp232–42. Up-to-date marine environment status report for the Seychelles highlighting the importance of the reefs and the effects of recent coral bleaching and human activities.

Hill, M J (ed) *Biodiversity Surveys and Conservation Potential of Inner Seychelles Islands*. Atoll Research Bulletin No 495, Smithsonian Institution, USA, 2002, 272pp. Latest scientific surveys of plants, invertebrates, reptiles, amphibians and birds of the inner Seychelles. Conservation status of terrestrial fauna and flora of each island is assessed.

Jennings, S M, Marshall, P & Naim, O 'The Seychelles' in *Coral Reefs of the Western Indian Ocean: Their Ecology and Conservation* McClanahan, T R & Sheppard, C R C (eds). Oxford University Press, New York, 2000, pp 399–432. A summary of the state of knowledge on Seychelles reefs and associated human impacts including fishing, tourism and pollution. Useful tables documenting the history of scientific research and marine conservation as well as lists of relevant conservation organisations.

Seychelles Fishing Authority *Seychelles Fishing Authority Annual Report 2002*. 58pp. Annual report on the Seychelles fishing industry and associated scientific research.

Stoddart, D R (ed) *Biogeography and Ecology of the Seychelles Islands* W Junk Publishers, The Hague, 1984, 691pp. The definitive scientific work about the Seychelles consisting of a collation of chapters written by various authorities. Includes a history of scientific exploration in the Seychelles as well as accounts of the geology, climate, human population and the impact of man. Most of the chapters cover the fauna of the islands and include coral reefs, echinoderms, crabs, shrimps, fishes, terrestrial molluscs, insects, butterflies, ticks, frogs, tortoises, lizards, snakes, turtles, birds and mammals. The vegetation of both the granitic and coralline islands is also covered.

Wells, S (ed) 'Seychelles' in *Coral Reefs of the World. Volume 2: Indian Ocean, Red Sea and Gulf* UNEP & IUCN, Cambridge, 1988, pp291–305. Concise summary of information on Seychelles coral reefs as well as details of the various marine protected areas in the Seychelles.

Marine-life guides

Branch, G M, Griffiths, C L, Branch, M L & Beckley, L E *Two Oceans – A Guide to Marine Life of Southern Africa* David Philip Publishers, Cape Town, 1994, 360pp. This authoritative guidebook to the diversity of marine life in southern Africa is profusely illustrated with colour photographs of over 1,000 species of marine plants and animals, many of which occur in Seychelles waters.

Debelius, H *Indian Ocean Reef Guide* Ikan-Unterwasserarchiv, Frankfurt, 1999, 321pp. Profusely illustrated with underwater photographs, this guidebook covers much of the marine life occurring in Seychelles waters. Excellent fish pictures.

Jarrett, A G *Marine Shells of the Seychelles* Carole Green Publishers, 2000, 149pp. New guide to the wonderful array of marine molluscs found in Seychelles waters.

King, D *Reef Fishes & Corals – East Coast of Southern Africa* Struik Publishers, Cape Town, 1996, 128pp. A small guidebook with underwater photographs of many of the fishes and corals encountered in the southwestern Indian Ocean.

Lieske, E & Myers, R *Coral Reef Fishes: Indo-Pacific & Caribbean* HarperCollins, London, 1994, 400pp. Concise illustrated pocket guide that includes many of the fishes found on the reefs of the Seychelles.

Richmond, M D (ed) *A Guide to the Seashores of Eastern Africa and the Western Indian Ocean Islands* Sida/SAREC, Stockholm, 1997. 448pp. The most comprehensive guide to marine biodiversity of the western Indian Ocean. Covers everything from seaweeds to whales with concise information and colour illustrations. Also has good introductory section dealing with environment, people, human activities and conservation. Available in UK through Tylers Books (tylers@tylers-books.co.uk).

Smith, J L B & Smith, M M *The Fishes of Seychelles* Rhodes University, Grahamstown, 1963, 215pp. Detailed early account of fishes collected during one of the legendary 'JLB' scientific expeditions. Wonderful colour paintings by Margaret Smith.

Veron, J E N *Corals of Australia and the Indo-Pacific* Angus & Robertson Publishers, London, 1986, 644pp. The definitive illustrated scientific work on corals of the Indo-Pacific region. Distribution maps indicate which species are found in Seychelles waters.

Bird guides

Harrison, P *Seabirds – An Identification Guide* Christopher Helm Publishers, London, 1996, 448pp. The authoritative text on seabirds of the world. All species occurring in Seychelles waters are covered and illustrated in this classic work.

Sinclair, I & Langrand, O *Birds of the Indian Ocean Islands* Struik, Cape Town, 1998, 185pp. Excellent field guide to the identification of the birds, both land and sea, occurring on the Seychelles and other Indian Ocean islands. Well illustrated, concise and a handy size.

Skerrett, A *Beautiful Birds of Seychelles* Camerapix Publishers International, Nairobi, 1994, 128pp. Small book with colour photographs of most of the birds breeding in the Seychelles and a short text on each.

Skerrett, A & Bullock, I *A Birdwatchers' Guide to Seychelles* Prion Ltd, Cambridge, 1992, 71pp. Useful guide for the serious birdwatcher who wants to get the most out of a visit to the Seychelles. Includes information on various birdwatching sites as well as a comprehensive checklist of birds to be seen around the islands.

Skerrett, A, Bullock, I & Disley, T *Field Guide to the Birds of the Seychelles* Christopher Helm and Princeton University Press, 2001, 320pp, 53 colour plates. Contains a wealth of information about all the birds in Seychelles as well as many that may occur here on migration.

Navigation and diving

Hydrographic Department *South Indian Ocean Pilot* British Navy, Somerset, 1971, 333pp. This pilot book amplifies details on Admiralty charts and is a mine of information about Seychelles islands. Particularly useful for those voyaging in Seychelles waters, it provides extensive information on reefs, shoals, anchorages, currents and weather.

Rondeau, A *Nautical Pilot of the Seychelles* Praxys Marine, Paris, 1997, 252pp. An excellent guide to cruising in Seychelles waters. Text is bilingual (French and English) and accompanied by numerous small charts of anchorages.

Salm, R *A Guide to Snorkelling and Diving in the Seychelles* Octavian Books, London, 1997, 60pp. Useful information for divers and includes details of the dive sites around the granitic islands and Amirantes.

Venter, A J *Under the Indian Ocean* Purnell, Cape Town, 1973, 219pp. Anecdotal accounts of diving adventures at various Indian Ocean localities. Contains information on shipwrecks on Seychelles islands as well as dive sites on Mahé.

Wood, L *Diving and Snorkeling Guide to the Seychelles* Pisces Books, USA, 1997, 89pp. A well-illustrated guide with information on most of the well-known dive sites of Mahé, Praslin and La Digue as well as notes on marine life of the Seychelles.

Aldabra

Amin, M, Willetts, D & Skerrett, A *Aldabra World Heritage Site* Camerapix Publishers International, Nairobi, 1995, 192pp. A wonderful, large-format book filled with the excellent photographs of Mohamed Amin and Duncan Willets. Chapters by various authorities showcase the magnificent biodiversity of the atoll which was proclaimed a World Heritage Site in 1982.

Beamish, T *Aldabra Alone* Allen & Unwin, London, 1970, 222pp. Interesting account of how efforts to establish an Anglo-American airforce base on Aldabra were thwarted, and subsequent conservation of the atoll as a World Heritage Site.

Seaton, A J, Beaver, K & Afif, M (eds) *A Focus on Aldabra* Seychelles Island Foundation, Victoria, 1991, 178pp. This book synthesises much of the scientific research done on the atoll and presents it in a more user-friendly fashion. It covers studies on the geology, marine and terrestrial environments as well as current management of the atoll.

WEBSITES

There are several websites which provide useful information for travellers visiting the Seychelles, although not all of them are updated that frequently.

www.sey.net This site offers a wide range of topics about the Seychelles including accommodation, activities, weather and commerce. Appears to be updated frequently.

www.seychelles.uk.com A good site run by the UK Seychelles Tourist Office. Lots of tempting photographs.

www.seychelles-travel.co.uk This site lists most of the hotels and provides detailed information and photographs of the establishments. A price list can be downloaded.

www.airseychelles.net Air Seychelles offices worldwide are listed with full contact details. Plenty of photographs and maps.

www.airseychelles-guide.com Potentially a useful site though some sections are still under construction.

www.travelmole.com/item/26925/101 This site gives up-to date information on the latest developments in the hotel industry.

www.seychelles-online.com.sc Carries the front page of the Seychelles daily newspaper *The Nation*, together with other useful information for travellers.

WIN £100 CASH!

READER QUESTIONNAIRE

Send in your completed questionnaire for the chance to win £100 cash in our regular draw

All respondents may order a Bradt guide at half the UK retail price – please complete the order form overleaf.

(Entries may be posted or faxed to us, or scanned and emailed.)

We are interested in getting feedback from our readers to help us plan future Bradt guides. Please complete this quick questionnaire and return it to us to enter into our draw.

Have you used any other Bradt guides? If so, which titles? . . . .
. . . .

What other publishers' travel guides do you use regularly? . . . .
. . . .

Where did you buy this guidebook? . . . .

What was the main purpose of your trip to the Seychelles (or for what other reason did you read our guide)? eg: holiday/business/charity etc. . . . .
. . . .

What other destinations would you like to see covered by a Bradt guide?
. . . .

Would you like to receive our catalogue/newsletters?

YES / NO (If yes, please complete details on reverse)

If yes – by post or email? . . . .

Age (circle relevant category) 16–25   26–45   46–60   60+

Male/Female (delete as appropriate)

Home country . . . .

Please send us any comments about our guide to the Seychelles or other Bradt Travel Guides. . . . .
. . . .
. . . .
. . . .

Bradt Travel Guides

23 High Street, Chalfont St Peter, Bucks SL9 9QE, UK
Telephone: +44 (0)1753 893444 Fax: +44 (0)1753 892333
Email: info@bradtguides.com
www.bradtguides.com

CLAIM YOUR HALF-PRICE BRADT GUIDE!

Order Form

To order your half-price copy of a Bradt guide, and to enter our prize draw to win £100 (see overleaf), please fill in the order form below, complete the questionnaire overleaf, and send it to Bradt Travel Guides by post, fax or email.

Please send me one copy of the following guide at half the UK retail price

Title	*Retail price*	*Half price*
. . . .	. . . .	. . . .

Please send the following additional guides at full UK retail price

No	*Title*	*Retail price*	*Total*
. . .	. . . .	. . . .	. . . .
. . .	. . . .	. . . .	. . . .
. . .	. . . .	. . . .	. . . .

Sub total . . . .
Post & packing . . . .
(£1 per book UK; £2 per book Europe; £3 per book rest of world)
Total . . . .

Name . . . .

Address . . . .

Tel . . . .   Email . . . .

☐ I enclose a cheque for £ . . . . made payable to Bradt Travel Guides Ltd

☐ I would like to pay by credit card. Number: . . . .

  Expiry date: . . . / . . .   3-digit security code (on reverse of card) . . . . .

☐ Please add my name to your catalogue mailing list.

Send your order on this form, with the completed questionnaire, to:

Bradt Travel Guides/SEY
23 High Street, Chalfont St Peter, Bucks SL9 9QE
Tel: +44 (0)1753 893444 Fax: +44 (0)1753 892333
Email: info@bradtguides.com
www.bradtguides.com

Bradt Travel Guides

Africa Overland	£15.99
Albania	£13.95
Amazon	£14.95
Antarctica: A Guide to the Wildlife	£14.95
The Arctic: A Guide to Coastal	
Wildlife	£14.95
Armenia with Nagorno Karabagh	£13.95
Azores	£12.95
Baghdad City Guide	£9.95
Baltic Capitals: Tallinn, Riga,	
Vilnius, Kaliningrad	£11.95
Bosnia & Herzegovina	£13.95
Botswana: Okavango Delta,	
Chobe, Northern Kalahari	£14.95
British Isles: Wildlife of Coastal	
Waters	£14.95
Budapest City Guide	£7.95
Cambodia	£11.95
Cameroon	£13.95
Canada: North – Yukon, Northwest Territories	
£13.95	
Canary Islands	£13.95
Cape Verde Islands	£12.95
Cayman Islands	£12.95
Chile	£16.95
Chile & Argentina: Trekking	
Guide	£12.95
China: Yunnan Province	£13.95
Cork City Guide	£6.95
Costa Rica	£13.99
Croatia	£12.95
Dubrovnik City Guide	£6.95
East & Southern Africa:	
Backpacker's Manual	£14.95
Eccentric America	£13.95
Eccentric Britain	£13.99
Eccentric California	£13.99
Eccentric Edinburgh	£5.95
Eccentric France	£12.95
Eccentric London	£12.95
Eccentric Oxford	£5.95
Ecuador, Peru & Bolivia:	
Backpacker's Manual	£13.95
Ecuador: Climbing & Hiking	£13.95
Eritrea	£12.95
Estonia	£12.95
Ethiopia	£13.95
Falkland Islands	£13.95
Faroe Islands	£13.95
Gabon, São Tomé & Príncipe	£13.95
Galápagos Wildlife	£15.99
Gambia, The	£12.95
Georgia with Armenia	£13.95
Ghana	£13.95
Iran	£14.99
Iraq	£14.95
Kabul Mini Guide	£9.95

Kenya	£14.95
Kiev City Guide	£7.95
Latvia	£13.99
Lille City Guide	£6.99
Lithuania	£13.99
Ljubljana City Guide	£6.99
London: In the Footsteps of	
the Famous	£10.95
Macedonia	£13.95
Madagascar	£14.95
Madagascar Wildlife	£14.95
Malawi	£12.95
Maldives	£13.99
Mali	£13.95
Mauritius	£12.95
Mongolia	£14.95
Montenegro	£13.99
Mozambique	£12.95
Namibia	£14.95
Nigeria	£15.99
North Cyprus	£12.95
North Korea	£13.95
Palestine with Jerusalem	£12.95
Panama	£13.95
Paris, Lille & Brussels: Eurostar Cities	£11.95
Peru & Bolivia: Backpacking &	
Trekking	£12.95
Riga City Guide	£6.95
River Thames: In the	
Footsteps of the Famous	£10.95
Rwanda	£13.95
St Helena, Ascension,	
Tristan da Cunha	£14.95
Serbia	£13.99
Seychelles	£13.99
Singapore	£11.95
Slovenia	£12.99
South Africa: Budget Travel Guide	£11.95
Southern African Wildlife	£18.95
Spitsbergen	£14.99
Sri Lanka	£12.95
Sudan	£13.95
Switzerland: Rail, Road, Lake	£12.99
Tallinn City Guide	£6.95
Tanzania	£14.95
Tasmania	£12.95
Turkmenistan	£14.99
Tibet	£12.95
Uganda	£13.95
Ukraine	£14.95
USA by Rail	£13.99
Venezuela	£14.95
Vilnius City Guide	£6.99
Your Child Abroad: A Travel	
Health Guide	£9.95
Zambia	£15.95
Zanzibar	£12.95

Index

Page numbers in bold indicate major entries;
those in italics indicate maps